ASSESSMENT FOR READING INSTRUCTION

SOLVING PROBLEMS IN THE TEACHING OF LITERACY
Cathy Collins Block, Series Editor

Recent Volumes

Bringing Words to Life: Robust Vocabulary Instruction
Isabel L. Beck, Margaret G. McKeown, and Linda Kucan

Help for Struggling Readers: Strategies for Grades 3–8
Michael C. McKenna

Reading to Learn: Lessons from Exemplary Fourth-Grade Classrooms
Richard L. Allington and Peter H. Johnston

A Sound Start: Phonemic Awareness Lessons for Reading Success
Christine E. McCormick, Rebecca N. Throneburg, and Jean M. Smitley

Organizing and Managing the Language Arts Block: A Professional Development Guide
Lesley Mandel Morrow

Teaching Strategic Processes in Reading
Janice F. Almasi

Exploring the Literature of Fact: Children's Nonfiction Trade Books in the Elementary Classroom
Barbara Moss

Literacy and Young Children: Research-Based Practices
Edited by Diane M. Barone and Lesley Mandel Morrow

Concept-Oriented Reading Instruction: Engaging Classrooms, Lifelong Learners
Emily Anderson Swan

Struggling Readers: Assessment and Instruction in Grades K–6
Ernest Balajthy and Sally Lipa-Wade

Explaining Reading: A Resource for Teaching Concepts, Skills, and Strategies
Gerald G. Duffy

Rethinking Reading Comprehension
Edited by Anne P. Sweet and Catherine E. Snow

Exemplary Literacy Teachers: Promoting Success for All Children in Grades K–5
Cathy Collins Block and John N. Mangieri

Assessment for Reading Instruction
Michael C. McKenna and Steven A. Stahl

ASSESSMENT
FOR
READING INSTRUCTION

Michael C. McKenna
Steven A. Stahl

THE GUILFORD PRESS
New York   London

© 2003 The Guilford Press
A Division of Guilford Publications, Inc.
72 Spring St., New York, NY 10012
www.guilford.com

Printed in the United States of America

This book is prined on acid-free paper.

Last digit is print number: 9 8 7 6 5 4

Library of Congress Cataloging-in-Publication Data

McKenna, Michael C.
   Assessment for reading instruction / Michael C. McKenna, Steven A. Stahl.
     p. cm. — (Solving problems in the teaching of literacy)
   ISBN 1-57230-867-2 (paper)
   1. Reading—Ability testing. 2. Reading. I. Stahl, Steven A. II. Title. III. Series.
LB1050.46.M35 2003
372.48—dc21

                                  2002151199

For our wives, Beverly and Kay

About the Authors

Michael C. McKenna, PhD, is Professor of Reading at Georgia Southern University in Savannah, where he teaches graduate courses and conducts research. He has authored or coauthored nine books and more than 70 articles, chapters, and technical reports on a range of literacy topics. His research has been sponsored by the National Reading Research Center (NRRC) and the Center for the Improvement of Early Reading Achievement (CIERA). He serves on the editorial boards of *Reading Research Quarterly*, the *Journal of Literacy Research*, and *Scientific Studies in Reading*. His articles have appeared in each of these journals as well as the *Journal of Educational Psychology*, *Educational Researcher*, *The Reading Teacher*, and others. His research interests include comprehension in content settings, reading attitudes, technology applications, and beginning reading.

Steven A. Stahl, EdD, is Professor of Reading at the University of Illinois at Urbana–Champaign, where he teaches graduate courses in reading. His nationally prominent research into beginning reading, phonics, fluency, and vocabulary instruction has contributed greatly to our understanding of these areas. He has served as a principal investigator with the Center for the Study of Reading and the National Reading Research Center. He codirected the Center for the Improvement of Early Reading Achievement (CIERA). His articles have appeared in every major reading journal, and he has a special interest in synthesizing research for teachers. His belief that classroom practice must be founded on validated instructional methods has led to his continuing advocacy for evidence-based approaches.

Contents

1

Introduction to Reading Assessment

THREE STRUGGLING READERS: A PREFACE

Consider these three children:

Josh is a third grader reading approximately at the mid-first-grade level. He struggles to pronounce unfamiliar words, sometimes by making guesses from their first letter and sometimes attempting to sound them out, from left to right. He does, however, know a fair number of words by sight, and whenever he encounters one of them, he can pronounce it immediately.

Latrelle, a fourth grader reading at a second-grade level, has acquired a good store of words that she recognizes at sight, and she can successfully pronounce almost any familiar word she encounters while reading. Her pace is slow, however, and her oral reading is expressionless. She does not group words into meaningful phrases as she reads, and she tends to ignore punctuation.

Sean, another fourth grader, is a proficient oral reader who can read aloud just about anything he is given, but he often has problems comprehending new material. This difficulty is especially evident when he is asked to read nonfiction, and when he is expected to draw conclusions about what he reads. He is a fair student when new content is explained by his teacher, but he has problems whenever he must learn it on his own from print.

The term *struggling reader* has become popular precisely because it lacks precision. When students leave the primary grades with significant problems, they present grave challenges to their teachers. They struggle, regardless of the cause, until they either catch up or give up. The children cited above are composites of real cases and represent important patterns that teachers must be prepared to identify and address. Much of this book focuses on the assessment of younger children, but we would like to begin by considering where declining trajectories can lead.

MODELS OF READING ASSESSMENT

All reading assessment is based on a model. This model can be explicitly laid out, as we intend to do here, or haphazardly formulated. Without a model, a reading specialist has no way of making sense of the observations derived from the reading assessment battery. The model helps the reading specialist recognize patterns in the data, determine the course of instruction, identify the child's strengths, and identify which aspects of reading knowledge are obstructing the child with reading problems.

A model should provide a roadmap, a set of directions to help the reading specialist navigate the assessment procedure and provide guidelines for interpretation. Not every child needs to receive every assessment. An effective model helps you determine which measures may best inform you about the child's needs.

The Deficit Model

The term *diagnosis*, as you might suspect, has a medical origin. Its use is based on the assumption that reading difficulties are much like physiological disorders. This conventional view, sometimes called the "medical model," assumes that the difficulty, or deficiency, resides within the student, and that the teacher, like a physician, must identify it and respond appropriately with instructional techniques designed to have a medicinal or therapeutic effect. This thinking has led, predictably, to terms such as *remediation* and *remedial reader*.

Very few in the field of reading still explicitly defend this model. There is little evidence that most children's reading problems are due to a single remediable cause. Even though research in the field of neuropsychology continues to identify possible neurological causes for reading problems (Pugh et al., 2001; Riccio & Hynd, 1996; Shaywitz, 1996), this work has not produced definitive results, nor does it show promise of "remediating" children with reading problems in the near future.

The Contextual Model

An alternative view of reading assessment does not deny that reading difficulties often reflect deficits within students, but it broadens the perspective to include two other possibilities as well. One is the notion that there may be a mismatch between the type of instruction provided and the manner in which a given child learns. The second possibility is that contextual factors beyond the scope of the school (such as a disadvantaged or emotionally troubled home life) may impair reading development. The contextual model suggests that reading difficulties can be traced to an interaction between the student, the methods or materials used with the student, and the broader context in which the student functions.

This model is quite different from a "learning style" model, which suggests that children have individual "learning styles" that can be diagnosed and matched to appropriate instruction (e.g., Carbo, Dunn, & Dunn, 1986). In the learning style model, children are classified as either visual or auditory learners and matched with either more holistic or more phonics-oriented instruction. This model has been tested repeatedly and not found to be valid (Stahl, 1999b). The contextual model,in contrast, views individual students as well as instructional methods as more complex than the learning model conception, with students having individual needs which are, or are not, met by the instruction they receive. Student needs may be attitudinal, motivational, or cognitive in nature, and instruction may or may not meet any of those needs.

Stage Models

Stages of Reading Development

The first of the stage models that may be used in assessing children was formulated by Chall (1996), who characterized reading development as progressing through six stages as the child moves from emergent literacy, or the beginning period of becoming aware of print, to advanced literacy activity, such as that needed to assimilate material in a graduate course. An overview of Chall's model is presented in Table 1.1, in which we have slightly adapted her terminology.

Although Chall's model provides a blueprint for overall reading development, it was not developed specifically for analysis of reading difficulties. For that purpose, we prefer the model of Spear-Swerling and Sternberg (1996), who combined Chall's model of overall reading stages with Ehri's (1998) discussion of the development of word recognition and their own observations of struggling readers to suggest a roadmap of reading achievement that pinpoints areas where children get "off track" from the normal course of development. This model is shown in Figure 1.1.

Growth of Word Recognition

The first four stages of Spear-Swerling and Sternberg's model rely on Ehri's (1998) model of the growth of word recognition. Ehri describes the growth of children's knowledge of words as progressing through four qualitatively different phases. At first, children recognize words through distinctive visual features, such as the "tail" in *monkey* or the two "eyes" in *look*. Ehri has called this stage *visual cue reading*. In one study (Gough, Juel, & Griffith, 1992), a group of prereaders learned words presented on a series of flashcards, one of which had a thumbprint in the corner. When shown the cards again, this time with the thumbprint on a different card, they tended to misread the thumbprinted card as the word in the first set, suggesting that they were attending to the thumbprint rather than the letters.

TABLE 1.1. Jeanne Chall's Model of the Stages of Reading Development

Stage	Name	What child is learning	Typical activities	Materials
Stage 0 Birth to grade 1	Emergent literacy	Functions of written language, alphabet, phonemic awareness	Story reading, "pseudoreading," alphabet activities, rhyming, nursery rhymes, invented spelling	Books (including predictable stories), letters, writing materials, *Sesame Street*
Stage 1 Beginning grade 1	Decoding	Letter–sound correspondences	Teacher-directed reading instruction, phonics instruction	Preprimers and primers, phonics materials, writing materials, trade books
Stage 2 End of grade 1 to end of grade 3	Confirmation and fluency	Automatic word recognition, use of context	Reading narratives, generally about known topics	Basal readers, trade books, workbooks
Stage 3 Grades 4 to 8	Learning the new (single viewpoint)	How to learn from text, vocabulary knowledge, strategies	Reading and studying content area materials, use of encyclopedias, strategy instruction	Basal readers, novels, encyclopedias, textbooks in content areas
Stage 4 High school and early college	Multiple viewpoints	Reconciling different views	Critical reading, discourse synthesis, report writing	Texts containing multiple views, encyclopedias and other reference materials, magazines and journals, nonfiction books, etc.
Stage 5 Late college and graduate school	A world view	Developing a well-rounded view of the world	Learning what not to read as well as what to read	Professional materials

As children learn more and more words, a purely visual system of identification, such as the one these children were using, becomes unwieldy. As children develop rudimentary phonemic awareness, they begin to use individual letters, usually the first but sometimes the last, to identify words. This stage is called *phonemic cue reading* or *partial alphabetic coding* To get to this stage, the child needs to have an "alphabetic insight," or the realization that letters correspond to sounds in words. This requires both rudimentary phonological awareness as well as some letter–sound knowledge.

As children's written vocabulary increases, they need to further analyze words, examining more parts of an unfamiliar word to identify it. This leads to "full alphabetic coding," in which the child examines each letter in the word. This ability may come as the result of receiving instruction in decoding, or children can develop it on their own. This letter-by-letter decoding gives way, with practice, to "consolidated word recognition," in which a reader uses groups of letters, either as chunks or through analogies, to recognize words automatically, as proficient readers do (Chall, 1996; LaBerge & Samuels, 1974).

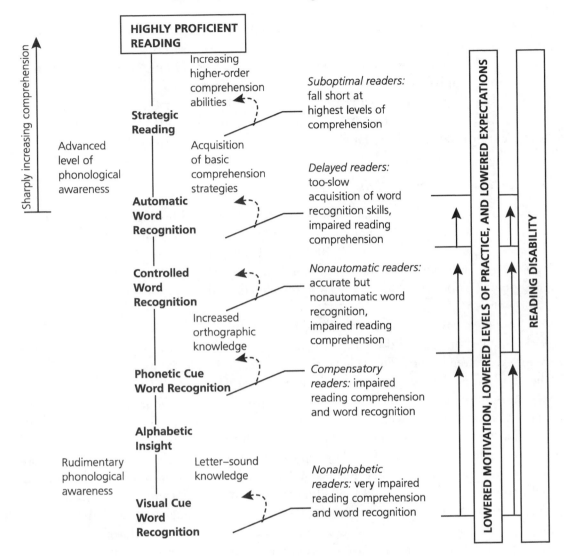

FIGURE 1.1. Spear-Swerling and Sternberg's stage model. From Spear-Swerling and Steinberg (1996). Copyright 1996 by Westview Press, a member of Perseus Books Group. Reprinted by permission.

This development of word recognition does not occur in a vacuum but in conjunction with growth in phonemic awareness and exposure to different types of text. Phonemic awareness is a part of phonological awareness, which "refers to a broad class of skills that involve attending to, thinking about, and intentionally manipulating the phonological aspects of spoken language" (Scarborough & Brady, 2001, p. 25). Phonemic awareness is that part of phonological awareness that processes phonemes rather than syllables or onsets and rimes. We (Stahl & McKenna, 2001; Stahl & Murray, 1998) suggest that phonological awareness develops first from an awareness of syllables, onsets, and rimes, to an awareness of initial phonemes, final phonemes, and, lastly, vowels. We also have found a parallel development in spelling (see also Bear, Invernizzi, Templeton, & Johnston, 2000).

Although phonemic awareness is related to reading, especially the decoding aspects of reading, the relationship does not seem to be strictly causal. Instead the relationship appears to be reciprocal, with simple phonemic awareness being necessary (although probably not sufficient) for children to develop rudimentary word recognition skills. After that point, growth in word recognition seems to enable further analysis of spoken words, which in turn enables further ability to decode more complex words (Beach, 1992; Perfetti, Beck, Bell, & Hughes, 1987).

The Development of Spelling

Children pass through a similar set of stages with respect to how they invent spellings for words. A number of different scales has attempted to capture this development (e.g., Bear et al., 2000; Gillet & Temple, 1990; Zutell & Rasinski, 1989). Many of these concentrate on early emergent spellings. Bear et al. suggest a 15-point scale, ranging from prealphabetic spellings to sophisticated knowledge of the morphemic structure of derived words.

Initially a child may spell a word by drawing a picture or scribbling something that looks like writing. As children learn that words need letters, they may use random letters to represent a word. This stage could be called *prephonemic spelling*. At this point, the children themselves are the only ones who can read what they have written.

As children begin to think about sounds in words, their spelling may represent only one sound in a word, usually an initial sound, and occasionally a final sound. This stage is called *early letter name spelling*. Sometimes children represent a word with a single letter, or pair of letters, but often they represent a word with the correct initial letter followed by some random letters. For example, one child in our reading clinic wrote *fish* with an initial *f* and continued by adding an additional six letters, stating that "words that begin with *f* have a lot of letters in them." As children analyze words further, they may use the names of letters to represent sounds. At this stage, children represent at least all of the consonants in a word, often not using vowels. For example, they might spell *girl* as GRL or *ten* as TN. As Treiman (1993) points out, children use some letter names to represent syllables, while not using others. This stage seems to represent a beginning of the analysis of words into phonemes, usually consonants.

As children learn more about how words are spelled, they use vowels, and the words they write resemble the actual word, like DRAGUN for *dragon*. Children usually master short vowels first, then long vowel patterns. This may reflect instruction, or it may reflect the simplicity of short vowel codings. Bear et al. (2000) call the stage in which children are including vowels, although not always correctly, *letter-name spelling*. At this point, children realize that all words need vowels, although they still have not mastered correct spelling of short vowels. When they can spell short vowels consistently, but not yet long vowels, Bear et al. (2000) term their spelling *within-word pattern spelling*. Their scale continues, but this is the appropriate range to discuss struggling readers, because this is the range of their spelling abilities. Table 1.2 summarizes these first four stages.

TABLE 1.2. Early Stages of Spelling Development

Spelling stage	Characteristics	Example
Prephonemic spelling	Child uses random letters, without regard to the sounds they may represent.	JNVW for *hat*
Early letter-name spelling	Child begins this stage by representing only one sound in a word, usually the first, but eventually represents all consonant sounds.	Early: FDZWD for *fish* Late: GRL for *girl*
Letter-name spelling	Child uses vowels but often does so incorrectly.	DRAGUN for *dragon*
Within-word pattern spelling	Child can consistently spell words with short vowels but not words with long vowels.	HOT for *hot* METE for *meet*

(A caveat before we leave the topic of spelling: It is our experience that children's spelling difficulties linger long after their reading problems have disappeared. We see college students who have a history of reading problems and who have compensated for, or even overcome, these problems, but are still dreadful spellers.)

Although Spear-Swerling and Sternberg (1996) describe reading development throughout the grades, most of their discussion is focused on word recognition and the early stages of reading. We find that this model serves as a good lens through which to view children with reading problems, but it is limited, and we feel the need to complement the model with a more fine-tuned cognitive view of reading. We use the stage model to roughly identify the stage of the child's reading and to determine where the child went "off track" (and how we can bring him or her back on track), but we use the cognitive model to guide more specific assessments.

Josh, Latrelle, and Sean Revisited

Returning to the three struggling readers described at the beginning of this chapter, the Spear-Swerling and Sternberg model can help us understand some of their needs. We suggest that before proceeding, you go back to the beginning of the chapter and try to place each of these children at the appropriate stage.

Josh seems to be in the beginning stages of acquiring alphabetic insight, in spite of his 3 years in school. In general, he seems to be a compensatory reader who uses his sight-word knowledge to compensate for his rudimentary decoding ability. We would want to know more about his specific abilities in decoding, and we might want to know more about his ability to comprehend. Latrelle would be classified as a nonautomatic reader, since she can read accurately but extremely slowly and without expression. Sean is a word-caller, who does not comprehend what he is reading, in spite of quick and accurate word reading.

The stage model is useful for giving us a general idea about these children, but it does not tell us specifically about what we need to teach them. The cognitive model, discussed below, provides a more accurate roadmap.

A Cognitive Model

A fourth model suggests that reading is composed of three separate components. Reading comprehension, the purpose of reading, is dependent on (1) automatic recognition of the words in the text, (2) comprehension of the language in the text, and (3) the ability to use the strategies needed to achieve one's purpose in reading the text. A child will have difficulties with comprehension if he or she has difficulty with any of these three components. If a child's word recognition is not automatic or sufficiently accurate, then comprehension will suffer. If the child does not understand the vocabulary, lacks appropriate background knowledge, or lacks knowledge of text structure or genre, comprehension will suffer. Children read different texts for different purposes. Sometimes these purposes are general, such as enjoyment or literal comprehension. But sometimes the purposes are specific, such as studying for a test or learning facts to include in a report. If the child can read the text but does not achieve the purpose of reading, then comprehension also will suffer.

This model, shown in Figure 1.2, is discussed in the sections that follow. We use this model to ask ourselves a series of questions, generated from the model, such as, "Does the child have difficulty with automatic word recognition?" or "Is the child's vocabulary knowledge an impediment to comprehension?" The answers to these questions suggest areas of strengths and weaknesses in the child with whom we are working.

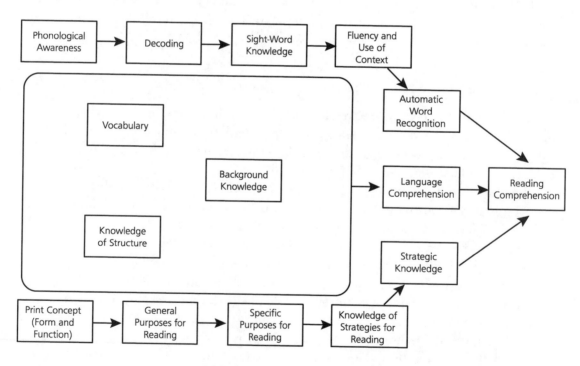

FIGURE 1.2. Cognitive model.

The first question to ask is whether or not the child has a reading problem. Often, teachers or reading specialists are told (by parents or other teachers) that a child has a reading problem when, in fact, the child does not. Sometimes a child does poorly on a standardized test, even when he or she is able to read grade-level material in the classroom without difficulty. Remember that a standardized test is one observation, for 1 or 2 days. Sometimes children simply have a hard time with testing or have difficulties on the day of that test. Children who come to school without breakfast or after witnessing an argument, or with some other problem, may not do as well on a standardized test as they might have. As we note in our chapter on standardized tests, such tests should not be the only source of information about a child's reading (or math, for that matter). Instead, a compilation of multiple sources of information is needed to understand whether the child's reading performance is part of a consistent pattern. This compilation involves not only standardized test results, but also at how the child reads the book used in the classroom, informal reading inventory results, and other information.

To answer this question, one must keep in mind that the purpose of reading is comprehension. If a child can comprehend texts at a level appropriate for his or her grade, then it may not matter whether the child can demonstrate mastery of other reading skills. Often, a child may do relatively poorly on a measure of phonics or decoding but still be able to comprehend acceptably. This discrepancy may reflect a problem with the assessment rather than a deficit in the child's skills. Observe the child closely to see whether he or she can use the skills in connected text, even though he or she may have difficulties applying them in isolation or with stating a rule.

So, Step 1 in the assessment process is to look at the reason for referral.

- If you have seen the child struggle with books in the classroom, then check the child's standardized test scores.
- If the child scored poorly on standardized tests, then closely observe the child in class.
- If further observation suggests that the child has difficulties both on standardized measures and in reading classroom texts, then give an informal reading inventory.

If a child has a significant problem with comprehension of age-appropriate texts, then the teacher should further examine the child's reading. Following our model, the teacher needs to ask the following questions about the child:

- Is the child able to read texts at his or her grade placement level, using automatic word recognition and adequate expression?
- Is the child able to comprehend the language of the text?
- Does the child have adequate knowledge of the purposes for reading?
- Does the child have strategies available to achieve those purposes?

These questions will be explored in the remainder of the chapter.

AUTOMATIC WORD RECOGNITION

If a child struggles with word recognition, comprehension will invariably suffer (LaBerge & Samuels, 1974). Word recognition needs to be automatic, so that the child does not have to devote conscious attention to the words in the text and can devote all of his or her cognitive effort to understanding what is read. When a child stumbles over words or s-s-s-sounds out many words, the child's understanding typically suffers.

To answer the first question about automatic word recognition—Is the child able to read texts at his or her grade placement level using automatic word recognition and adequate expression?—you must listen to the child read material intended for his or her grade level. This can be done by pulling the child aside and listening to a reading from a selected text, or it can be done through an informal reading inventory, as described in Chapter 3. If the child's reading is expressive and he or she can read at an instructional level appropriate to the grade placement, then you can reasonably conclude that the child's problem lies elsewhere. However, our clinical experience suggests that as many as 90% of the children we see have difficulties in this area. Sometimes the problems lie exclusively in this area; at other times the child will have difficulties with language comprehension and strategic knowledge as well. But word recognition difficulties underlie the vast majority of reading problems, so we spend a lot of time assessing them.

If a child is deemed to have difficulties in automatic word recognition, then the questions that follow are:

♦ Does the child make use of context to monitor his or her reading?
♦ Is the child fluent?

Context

Some educators (e.g., Goodman, 1993) suggest that children use context as a means of predicting words in a passage. According to these theorists, readers use information from context to minimize the use of letter–sound information to recognize words. For example, for the sentence

The boy pulled the red _____.

A reader may predict the word *wagon* before recognizing the word. If the first letter is *w*, then the reader may move on, without sounding out the word or using other word recognition skills. Other educators (e.g., Clay, 1993a) suggest that children use three types of cues to recognize words—graphophonemic, syntactic (part-of-speech), and semantic (meaning) information—and that effective word recognition involves the use of these three cueing systems. In the above example, a reader would predict the word to be a noun, because nouns always follow *the* and adjectives such as *red*. The reader would predict *wagon*, since wagons are pulled, typically by young children, and they are often red. If, instead of a *w*, the initial letter were a *c*, the reader might mentally search for words that begin with *c* and satisfy those semantic (meaning) constraints and come up with *cart*. A substitution like *wagging* would violate both syntactic and semantic constraints and might indicate that the child was paying more attention to sounding out the word than to the context.

This model is intuitively appealing, but research does not support it as a model of reading behavior. Effective readers would recognize the word *wagon* more quickly and reliably than they would be able to predict the word through the use of syntactic and semantic information (Stanovich, 1991). Research using a number of different approaches has found that good readers do not predict words but, instead, use their automatic word recognition processes to propel reading (Adams, 1990, 1998).

Although we do not feel that research supports this model (see Adams, 1998), we have found that good readers do use context in two principal ways. First, they use context to monitor their reading. A reader who produces *wagging* for *wagon* in the target sentence would realize that the word does not make sense and would go back and self-correct. Thus a good reader's miscues tend to make sense in context because of active monitoring, not predicting. Because of the importance of monitoring, we still support the examination of children's oral reading errors, or miscue analysis, as suggested by Goodman and Goodman (1977), and we provide a procedure for it in Chapter 3.

Good readers also use context to rapidly select the intended meaning of multiple-meaning words. Consider this sentence:

The rancher hired a new hand.

The word *hand* has several meanings, but proficient readers have no trouble discerning the correct one. They do so after the word is located in memory, not before. That is to say, the good reader does not use context to predict the word but to select the appropriate meaning once the word has been located.

Our experience is that all children, even struggling readers, tend to use context quite well. Stanovich (1980) suggests that struggling readers make greater use of context than good readers, because they have less word recognition skill and need to rely on context more. When we evaluate children in our clinic, usually 80% or more of their miscues are syntactically acceptable (the same part of speech as the text word), and 70% or more are semantically acceptable (make sense in the context of the sentence, even if their meaning is not the same as the word in the text). When children do not use context effectively, either the text is extremely difficult for them and they make random guesses, or they are not focused on context.

When children do not view connected text as meaningful, they do not consider context. Sometimes, if children are taught to overrely on words (which especially occurs in radical phonics programs), then they may lose sight of the importance of textual meaning and reading becomes nothing more than a rote exercise. This extreme position is rare, but occasionally we do see children who have been taught to focus in this manner. These children also tend to be significantly better at calling words than comprehending text. If the text is within the child's instructional level, and the child is not making contextually acceptable miscues, then the child's attention needs to be redirected to the meaning of the text, and he or she needs to be taught that texts are meaningful.

If a child is poor at using context, we would look at the child's interview data to see how he or she perceives reading, and we would evaluate the child's comprehension of texts read orally, to see whether he or she is focusing on comprehension during reading.

Fluency

Many children with reading problems can read accurately but cannot read quickly enough to make sense of what they are reading. If reading is not fluent, then comprehension usually suffers. We learn about the child's degree of fluency through observation of oral reading. Usually this observation is done through an informal reading inventory, but it also can be done by observing the child read a tradebook, or by using Benchmark texts for running records. In Chapter 3, we include a rubric or scoring guide that might be used to decide whether reading is fluent or not. Generally, however, the criteria can be stated simply as whether or not the child's reading sounds like language:

- Is the child halting or smooth in his or her reading?
- Does the child stop to sound out words excessively?
- Does the child have to repeat phrases excessively or self-correct excessively?

If a child engages in halting reading, with excessive sounding out, repetition, or self-correction, then the child may need work in fluency.

If the child is not fluent or accurate at reading texts written at the his or her grade placement level, then we need to ask two questions about the child's word recognition:

- Does the child have adequate sight-word knowledge?
- Does the child have adequate knowledge of decoding strategies?

Sight Words

The term *sight words* can be defined in two principal ways. Ehri (1998) uses the phrase *sight words* to refer to all the words that a child recognizes "at sight," or automatically. Under this definition, both common words, such as *the* and *what*, and uncommon words, such as *wolf* and *rescue*, might all be sight words for a given individual. Although we see the utility for an inclusive definition such as Ehri's, in this book we reserve the term *sight words* for the most frequently used words in the English language. Adams (1990) points out that the 105 most common words account for about 50% of running text. This is as true for adult text as it is for children's text. Further, these words are often irregular or use rare sound–symbol correspondences and need to be memorized so that they can use retrieved quickly and automatically.

There are several lists of the most frequently used words in English, notably the lists developed by Dolch (1936) and Fry (cited in Fry, Fountoukidis, & Polk, 1985). As one might expect, there is considerable overlap among lists. In addition, the words on any of these lists are worth assessing and teaching. Therefore, we do not recommend any particular list. We do include the Fry Instant Word List of 300 high-frequency words in Chapter 6.

In assessing children's sight-word knowledge, it is important to note both their accurate recognition of the words and their automaticity. Because so many textual words are sight words, slow recognition entails slow text reading in general. Sounding out a word like *with*, even if the child arrived at the correct pronunciation, would still impair comprehension, as would a halting pronunciation after a long pause. Therefore, one should note both the accuracy and speed of recognition. Each sight word on a list should be recognized in roughly half a second—that is, without hesitation.

In addition, one should observe children's recognition of sight words in context. Since sight words account for such a large percent of words in text, an informal reading inventory also gives ample opportunity to observe children's sight-word recognition skills in context. Again, sight words should be recognized *automatically*, without hesitation or sounding out.

Decoding

We are also interested in whether a child has the ability to decode unknown words. The ability to decode requires both a knowledge of the processes involved in decoding as well as knowledge of specific letter–sound relationships. We need to assess both.

Assessing the Process of Decoding

As suggested by Ehri's model, the process of decoding involves three successive understandings: acquisition of the alphabetic principle, the ability to blend letters into sounds, and the ability to use both phonograms and analogies. Children's acquisition of the alphabetic principle—the principle that letters can be used to represent sounds—is revealed by their use of letters as cues for words in both word recognition and spelling. Spelling may be a better assessment for a child's knowledge of the alphabetic principle, since children may use the first letter as a visual rather than phonemic cue.

Letter-by-letter decoding —the ability to blend letters together to make words—is the hallmark of Ehri's "full alphabetic coding" stage and Spear-Swerling and Sternberg's "controlled word recognition" stage. Although this phase is fairly short-lived, it is critical: Children need to appreciate individual letter–sound correspondences in order to move toward automatic word recognition. This ability can be evaluated by measures that tap children's knowledge of individual letter sounds as well as their decoding of short-vowel words. Since short vowels are usually taught first in most phonics curricula, we use short vowels as the test of children's blending ability.

The last stage involves being able to use both phonograms, or chunks of letters (such as *ick*, *ill*, *and*, and so on), and analogies (decoding *strike* by comparing it with *like*). Proficient readers decode words using these strategies. Studies have found that children need to be able to understand letter-by-letter decoding before they are able to benefit from analogy or phonogram instruction, but children need to use phonograms in order to read proficiently (e.g., Ehri & Robbins, 1985). Children are first able to use phonograms and analogies to decode monosyllabic words; later, they can use them to decode polysyllabic words.

Assessing the Content of Decoding

Even if a child has knowledge of a process such as letter-by-letter decoding, he or she still needs to learn certain linguistic facts. For letter-by-letter decoding, these facts would be:

- Consonant sounds (<u>s</u>un, <u>f</u>an, <u>t</u>oy, <u>d</u>og)
- Consonant digraphs (<u>th</u>at, <u>th</u>an, <u>sh</u>eep, <u>ch</u>ick, <u>wh</u>o, <u>ph</u>one)
- Consonant blends (<u>bl</u>ue, <u>st</u>ar, <u>sl</u>eep, <u>dr</u>ink, <u>str</u>ipe)
- Short vowels in consonant–vowel–consonant (CVC) words (c<u>a</u>t, p<u>e</u>t, p<u>i</u>n, d<u>u</u>ck, l<u>o</u>g)
- Vowel digraphs (b<u>oa</u>t, gr<u>ee</u>n, w<u>ai</u>t, p<u>ea</u>)
- Rule of silent *e* (r<u>a</u>c<u>e</u>, h<u>o</u>s<u>e</u>, b<u>i</u>k<u>e</u>)
- Vowel diphthongs (j<u>oi</u>n, c<u>ow</u>, b<u>oy</u>, p<u>aw</u>)
- *R*-controlled vowels (st<u>ar</u>, b<u>ir</u>d, w<u>or</u>ld, h<u>er</u>)
- *L*-controlled *a* (b<u>all</u>, p<u>al</u>, c<u>all</u>)
- Other variant vowels (l<u>igh</u>t, t<u>ough</u>, c<u>augh</u>t, th<u>ough</u>)

This list does not mean that children need to learn rules. The "rules" often do not apply to enough words to render them clear-cut. For example, the rule "when two vowels go walking, the first one does the talking" works only about 45% of the time (Adams, 1990). It works for *boat* but not for *bread* or *join* or *does*. And the "rule" of silent *e* only applies about 60% of the time. It works in *home* but not in *come*, in *drove* but not in *dove* or *love*, in *save* but not in *have*. Instead, children need to know *patterns* to help them identify individual words. Rather than presenting a rule, present lists of words that adhere to the pattern, so that children can internalize the pattern and do not have to think about the rule. As Cunningham (2001) has observed, the brain is more comfortable recognizing patterns than applying rules.

As for phonograms, there are hundreds of phonograms, or rimes, in the English language. Wylie and Durrell (1970) found 286 phonograms in their examination of primary-grade text, 272 of which are pronounced the same way in every word in which they appear, and they found 37 rimes that account for nearly 500 words. These rimes were used as a basis for the Z-test presented in Chapter 6. Clearly, these phonograms could be the start of a phonogram-based program, but they should be seen as only a start. One cannot teach all 272 phonograms, but one might expand beyond the initial set.

If a child has difficulties in decoding, then the next question we ask is:

- Does the child have adequate phonological awareness?

Phonological Awareness

Phonological awareness—or the awareness of sounds in spoken words—is a prerequisite for children to learn to decode. It is not uncommon for young children, kindergarteners, and even some first graders to be unable to think of words as a collection of sounds and, for example, to be unable to provide the first sound of *dog* or *fish*. Stanovich (1986), among many, suggests that early difficulties in phonological awareness underlie later reading problems. Children who do not think of the first sound of *mouse* as an /m/ will be unable to use the letter *m* to help recognize the word.

One child in our clinic, Heather, is a wonderful (and cute) example of this problem. Heather was a first grader when we saw her, the daughter of a dentist and a stay-at-home mother, living in a small Midwestern town. Her mother reported that Heather had difficulties in learning phonics, although she had no problems reading easy preprimer text by memorizing the words. From discussions with her mother, we suspected that she had difficulties with phonological awareness. When asked to say *meat* without the /m/, Heather thought for a while, then said, "Chicken." Although nonplussed, we went on, asking her to say *coat* without the /k/. After some thought, she said, "Jacket."

Heather's difficulties came about because she tended to view words as semantic units, as we might, in order to understand them in speech and reading. However, to learn to use an alphabetic language, to reach that vital alphabetic insight, the child needs to recognize that words are both meaningful *and* a collections of sounds. Because Heather did not have that alphabetic insight, she could not move forward. She was easy to teach, figured out the relations between letters and sounds, and went on to be a good reader. But she did need initial help to make sense of word recognition.

We have traced word recognition back to its roots, from fluent and automatic word recognition, to use of context, to knowledge of sight words and decoding, to phonological awareness. This cognitive view complements the stage view of Spear-Swerling and Sternberg. Put together, one can see how a reader can fall behind, and how a teacher can target instruction to put the reader back on the road to proficiency.

LANGUAGE COMPREHENSION

Even if a reader is a proficient word-caller, the child also must be able to comprehend what is read. We encounter children who are able to read fluently but cannot understand what they read. Often, this is just a matter of not attending to meaning. When children are given intensive phonics instruction, without being asked to attend to meaning, they may not focus on the meaning. This situation is rare and easily fixed.

Most of the other children who have comprehension problems have difficulties understanding the language of the text, even if they can read the words of which it is comprised. Although language comprehension involves a great number of elements, we find that the problems we see in the clinic occur largely in three areas. Put as questions, we ask ourselves:

♦ Does the child have an adequate *vocabulary* for his or her age and grade?
♦ Does the child have the *background knowledge* necessary to understand the particular passage that he or she is reading?
♦ Is the child able to use common *text structures* to aid in comprehension?

Vocabulary

Children's knowledge of word meanings is the best predictor of their comprehension, both of passages containing those words and of passages, in general (Stahl, 1999b). This factor may be predictive because knowledge of words enables children to comprehend passages, or because vocabulary knowledge is a measure of children's general knowledge or their general intelligence. Either way, children with reading problems tend to have problems with word meanings.

These problems also tend to worsen as children progress through school. Stanovich (1986) attributes this decline to what he calls *Matthew effects*, based on the notion from the Bible that the "rich will get richer and the poor will get poorer" (Matthew, 25:29). The notion of Matthew effects stems from Stanovich's observation that the gap between proficient and struggling readers widens over time (see Figure 1.3).

Stanovich suggests that many of the problems struggling readers encounter are not due to underlying causes but to these children's increasing lack of reading experience. In the case of vocabulary, children who have reading problems both read less text and read less challenging texts. Because they read increasingly less challenging material, they are exposed to fewer words of increasing difficulty. Because most words are

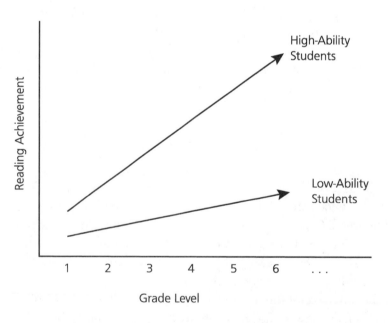

FIGURE 1.3. An example of the Matthew effect.

learned from exposure in context, children with reading problems learn fewer words. Because they know fewer words, they are less able to read challenging texts and therefore encounter fewer difficult words—thus engaging a downward cycle that exacerbates the differences between proficient and struggling readers.

Because vocabulary knowledge constitutes an important component of intelligence tests, we find that children with reading problems produce intelligence test scores that decline over time. This finding does not mean that they have less native intelligence, just that they have a relatively smaller vocabulary than their peers. But the decline in intelligence test scores can mean that these children lose a legal categorization, such as "learning disability," that is determined by intelligent test scores.

Over the school years, children learn an impressive number of word meanings. Estimates are that children typically enter first grade knowing between 3,000 and 6,000 words and learn between 1,000 and 3,000 new words per year, knowing as many as 45,000 words by the end of 12th grade (Nagy, 1988). This large number of words cannot be tested directly. Instead, tests are based on samples of words. We suggest a number of standardized tests that assess vocabulary, but we do not provide one in this book, because of the difficulties of accurately sampling such a large number of words.

Background Knowledge

Much has been written about the contribution of background knowledge to children's reading comprehension (e.g., Anderson & Pearson, 1984). Since the purpose of this book is to talk about assessment, we limit our discussion of background knowledge to its effects on assessment.

Children obviously differ in terms of background knowledge, and these differences affect their performance on reading tasks. Standardized measures deal with the issue of background knowledge by utilizing many short passages. If a child has strong knowledge of one topic and weak knowledge of another, the effects of background knowledge should average out over a number of passages.

On informal reading inventories, each level can be assessed in a single passage. On the Qualitative Reading Inventory 3 (Leslie & Caldwell, 2001), selections at the fifth-grade level include passages on Martin Luther King, Jr., and Andrew Carnegie. Since knowledge of Dr. King is taught each year, whereas Andrew Carnegie is generally taught only in high school history, the passage on Dr. King is more familiar to most students. Children may answer questions correctly based on their prior knowledge, rather than on what they just read. Often, children's answers seem plainly based on previous knowledge rather than on what was read. Teachers need to be cautious in interpreting the scores from passages about whose topic students can be assumed to be knowledgeable.

Some informal reading inventories provide a pretest for prior knowledge; others do not. If possible, we recommend that teachers administer passages on familiar as well as unfamiliar topics to compare children's responses under both conditions.

Text Structure

We also see children in the clinic who differ in terms of their knowledge of text structure. By *text structure*, we mean structural patterns in text that are common to particular genres. For example, one can identify the following elements for narratives:

- Setting, including
  - Time
  - Place
  - Major characters
  - Minor characters
- Problem that major character encounters
- Goal that major character is trying to achieve
- Events
  - Event 1
  - Event 2 . . .
- Resolution

Research has found that children tend to include these elements in their recall of narratives (e.g., Yussen & Ozcan, 1996). Narratives also can be thought of as comprising chains of events, with one event causing the next. These causal chains form the plot of the narrative.

Other genres have different elements. Most expository genres are structured around main ideas and supporting information. Sometimes the main idea is a cause-and-effect relationship or the presentation of a problem and solution, whereas other times the main idea is the topic around which the passage provides supporting and descriptive information.

We find that children who have reading problems also have difficulties perceiving text structures. This difficulty could be due to labored decoding that renders them unable to integrate information into a coherent whole, or because they do not understand how to discern the overall structure of a text. Either way, such children can benefit from instruction on text structure.

We assess children's knowledge of text structure through free recall. As discussed in Chapter 7, this recall involves having a child "tell you back" what he or she has read. Ordinarily, we expect the recall to include most of the important information, be it important story elements (narrative text) or main idea information (expository text). We ordinarily expect the recall to roughly mirror the order the information was presented in the text. Any significant divergence from either inclusion of important information or text order is a cause for concern. Some children recall information haphazardly, as if they were picking out random facts, suggesting poor recall and the need for work in this area.

A word of caution is in order. Some children, because of a shy nature or a lack of understanding of the task, simply do not recall text well. In other words, their response may lead a teacher to underestimate how well they have comprehended. Interpretation of poor recall should involve considering whether a limited response may have been the result of reticence or failure to grasp the task.

STRATEGIC KNOWLEDGE

Consider how you, as a proficient reader, are probably reading this text. Chances are, you are in a comfortable, but not too comfortable, place, one you typically reserve for studying. The lighting is good. As to the actual process of studying, there is considerable variation. Some people study with music; others need quiet. Some people use highlighters; others write in the margins, use note cards, or nothing at all. Some people gain an overview by skimming the whole text; others read it carefully, from start to finish. Whatever approach you are taking, chances are that it is the same approach you have taken to reading textbooks in the past. You have found a set of strategies that work for you while studying.

Contrast this set of strategies with those used for reading a recreational novel. You probably read the novel in a different place, possibly in bed or in a noisier environment. The contrast between the two activities shows how you, as a proficient reader, have different strategies for reading different types of texts for different purposes. Prior to reading, you decided what your purpose was and chose a set of strategies to help you achieve your purpose. The strategies are both related to environment and learning set (i.e., place to work, quiet or noise) and cognitive strategies for remembering (i.e., highlighter, note cards, reading end of chapter summaries first).

We find that children with reading problems often have difficulties assimilating different strategies and knowing which should be used for a given purpose. For example, Cameron is a sixth grader with severe reading difficulties. His primary problems involve his slow reading rate and his ponderous process of word recognition. When given the textbook interview (in Chapter 8) and asked how he would study a chapter for a test, he replied that he would read it straight through. Because of his slow reading rate, we doubted he would be able to finish it in a week, or that he would remember much of what he had read because of his labored focus on the individual words. When we asked him, he confirmed that he rarely finished half of his weekly reading assignment. When asked what kind of grades he got, he replied, "D's and F's." Cameron was not successful at studying and did not know how to modify his behaviors so that he could be successful. There are techniques that can be used to help children who have reading problems study more effectively, even material they might have difficulty reading straight through (see Schumaker, Deshler, Alley, Warner, & Denton, 1982), and we did teach him to use these techniques, which improved his grades somewhat.

The first question we ask is:

♦ What concepts of print does the child have?

We want to know about the child's knowledge of basic print concepts, including the purposes and functions of written language.

♦ Does the child have a set of strategies that he or she can apply to achieve different purposes in reading?

This question is largely answered by interviews and self-assessments. We have provided a textbook interview, but, with older children, we often spend a great deal of time talking about how the child deals with content area texts. Older children often have a great deal of insight into their difficulties and we try to take advantage of that insight.

Not only do children with reading problems often not know specific strategies, but they often do not understand general purposes for reading. In one study, proficient readers were asked, "If I gave you something to read, how would you know you were reading it well?" They responded that they would know they were reading it well if they understood what they read, if they "got the big ideas," etc. Struggling readers, on the other hand, often responded that they were reading well when "they said the words correctly" or when they were not corrected by the teacher. Worse yet, many struggling readers were unable to identify how they knew they were not reading a passage successfully. If readers do not know that the general purpose for reading is to get meaning from print, but instead view reading as a decoding act, they will experience difficulties.

To ascertain the child's understanding of the general purposes of reading, we need to ask a question such as:

♦ What does the child view as the goal of reading, in general?

Even before they understand the general purposes for reading, children develop basic print concepts. Some of these concepts concern the function of print: that we read for pleasure or information. Some of these concepts concern the form of print, such as the fact that English writing goes from left to right, and top to bottom, that sentences begin with a capital letter and end with a period, and so on. Extremely important is the concept of a printed word: that a word is a collections of letters separated by spaces. For example, Andrew, a second grader who had repeated first grade, was still puzzled by the difference between a word and a letter, despite his experience of 2½ years in primary school. When asked to slide two cards together to show a word, he slid them together to reveal one letter. When asked to show two words, he showed two letters. When asked to show one *letter*, he was puzzled, thinking that he had already done that. This child would have been extremely confused during lessons that talk about the "first letter in the word _____." If his teachers had spotted his confusion and dealt with it early, it is likely that many of Andrew's current problems would not have developed. We have provided several measures that evaluate children's concept of what a word is in this book.

PUTTING IT ALL TOGETHER

Listing all the questions that we ask, we arrive at the following:

♦ Is the child able to read texts at his or her grade placement level with automatic word recognition and adequate expression?
  ♦ Does the child make use of context to monitor his or her reading?
  ♦ Is the child fluent?

- ◆ Does the child have adequate sight-word knowledge?
- ◆ Does the child have adequate knowledge of decoding strategies?
- ◆ Does the child have adequate phonological awareness?
- ◆ Is the child able to comprehend the language of the text?
  - ◆ Does the child have an adequate vocabulary for his or her age and grade?
  - ◆ Does the child have the background knowledge necessary to understand the particular passage that he or she is reading?
  - ◆ Is the child able to use common text structures to aid in comprehension?
- ◆ Does the child have adequate knowledge of the purposes for reading and possess strategies available to achieve those purposes?
  - ◆ What concepts of print does the child have?
  - ◆ Does the child have a set of strategies that can be used to achieve different purposes in reading?
  - ◆ What does the child view as the goal of reading in general?

These questions can be used to guide us through the assessment process. By the time we finish a complete assessment of a child, we should have answered each of these questions.

Form 1.1 (p. 22) is a modified version of Figure 1.2, with larger boxes for note taking. Many teachers have found it useful to make notes about a child in each of the boxes. Having to fill out the chart forces one to examine all aspects of the child's reading.

Now let's return to our three cases. For Josh, we are concerned about his decoding ability. The first questions we would ask concern his ability to decode and his phonological awareness, because we suspect that difficulties in this area underlie difficulties in automatic word recognition and reading connected text. We also would want to know about his ability to use context, his comprehension ability, and his listening comprehension. As for Latrelle, we suspect that her decoding skills are adequate, though we would want to assess them nevertheless. We are more concerned about her automaticity and her ability to use context. We also want to know about her comprehension, and since she is required increasingly to read different kinds of text in fourth grade, we would want to know about her knowledge of strategies. For Sean, we are not as concerned with his word recognition as we are with his comprehension and strategic knowledge.

Chapter 2 focuses on general issues in assessment. Chapter 3 introduces the informal reading inventory, the keystone of classroom reading assessment, since it is so important in answering many of the questions we have raised here. The remainder of the book deals with more fine-grained assessment in the particular areas we have discussed.

FORM 1.1. Modified cognitive model.

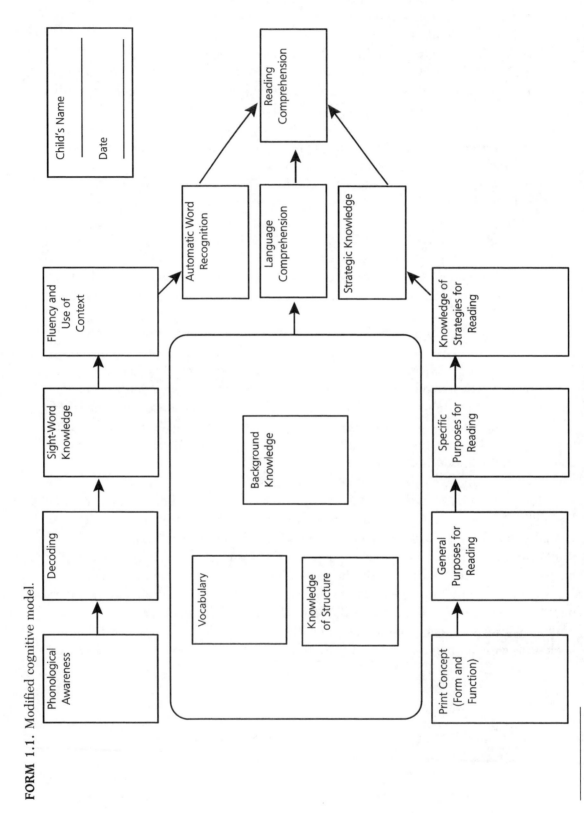

2

General Concepts of Assessment

There are many means of acquiring the information necessary to make appropriate instructional decisions with respect to your students. Some of these methods involve conventional tests, whereas others involve less structured methods of gathering information. We'll look at tests first, then consider the alternatives.

TYPES OF TESTS

It is useful to categorize tests along four dimensions. Most of the commercial and teacher-constructed tests currently available can be readily categorized according to these four dimensions:

- ◆ Group versus individual tests
- ◆ Formal versus informal tests
- ◆ Norm-referenced versus criterion-referenced tests
- ◆ Survey, screening, and diagnostic test

Group versus Individual Tests

Some tests are designed to be administered to a group of students simultaneously whereas others must be administered individually. The primary reason for individual administration is that oral responses are required of the child. Needless to say, individually administered tests tend to provide more dependable results than group assessments because the teacher can command the mental engagement of the student, to some extent, during the testing process. On the other hand, of course, group tests are far more efficient, even if their results are less dependable.

Formal versus Informal Tests

Tests differ with respect to how rigidly they are administered and interpreted. A formal test is one in which the directions for administration are clear-cut and allow little, if any, discretion on the part of the teacher. Moreover, formal tests are scored in a carefully prescribed manner. A group standardized achievement test, such as those often mandated by state or local education agencies, is a good example of a formal test. An informal test, on the other hand, is one in which teacher discretion plays a major part. The teacher, for example, may decide to modify how the test is given, based on early responses given by the student. Moreover, the teacher may exercise wide latitude in determining how to interpret the results. An essay test is one example of an informal test, and so is an informal reading inventory, which we discuss in Chapter 3.

Norm-Referenced versus Criterion-Referenced Tests

There are two major ways of bringing meaning to test scores. One way is to compare one child's result with the results of other children. In other words, we can compare one child's performance with what might be normally expected of other children. Hence, the word *norm*. Norms such as percentile ranks, grade equivalents, stanines, normal curve equivalents, scale scores, and many others are commonplace in educational parlance. (We discuss norms in greater detail later in this chapter.)

A second way to interpret a child's performance is to compare his or her test score against a preestablished criterion or benchmark. A good example is the written portion of the state driver's examination. An examinee is permitted to miss a predetermined number of questions and still pass the exam. This criterion has nothing to do with how others performed on the same test. The comparison is between the individual driver and the criterion established by the Department of Motor Vehicles.

As a general rule, norm-referenced tests are useful in determining the overall developmental level of a child with respect to others. Criterion-referenced tests are useful for mastery-level learning or competency-based assessment. A curriculum that consists of many specific skills to be learned is probably well served by a series of criterion-referenced tests (one per skill).

Survey, Screening, and Diagnostic Tests

Another useful way to categorize tests is by the use that is made of them. Three types are particularly important; survey, screening, and diagnostic tests. Survey tests attempt to provide a broadly defined estimate of a student's overall achievement level in a given area. The Stanford Achievement Test, the Iowa Tests of Basic Skills, and the Comprehensive Tests of Basic Skills are good examples of survey tests. They provide broadly based results that are not very useful in planning instruction but that might provide clues about program effectiveness on a large scale.

Screening tests are generally administered individually and are used to identify areas where more fine-grained assessments should be administered. These tests are brief and fairly general. Above all, the results indicate the next step to be taken in reading assessment: the administration of diagnostic instruments.

Diagnostic tests provide detailed information useful in planning instruction. These tests may involve multiple dimensions, possibly represented by subtests or by a variety of tasks a student is asked to perform. By the same token, a test designed to tell whether a student has mastered a particular objective is also an example of a diagnostic test. This is because the result documents progress in terms specific enough to help in planning instruction.

INTERPRETING NORM-REFERENCED READING TESTS

Perhaps the most important part of giving a test is making sense of the scores. In the case of a norm-referenced testing, interpretation is guided by comparing a student's raw score (the number of items correct) with the scores of other students. In other words, we are interested in what a "normal" score might be and to what extent the score for a particular student differs from it. To make such a comparison, the student's raw score is converted into another score, called a norm. Many types of norms are in common use today; some of the most frequently encountered are presented in Table 2.1.

Figure 2.1 illustrates how some of these norms are related to one another in terms of the normal (what else?) curve. Notice, for example, that the fifth stanine always contains 20% of the group used to norm the test and extends from the 40th through the 59th percentile ranks. Also note that the nine stanines are perfectly symmetrical, so that the

TABLE 2.1. Common Norms and What They Mean

Norm	Definition
Percentile rank	Percentage of children the same age whose scores a given child's equals or exceeds. (This is an approximate definition, not the one used in computation.) Percentile ranks cannot be averaged.
Stanine	One of nine statistically comparable divisions of the population tested, with the fifth positioned in the middle of the normal curve and accounting for 20% of those tested. (Short for "standard nine.")
Grade-equivalent score	An estimate of the grade level corresponding to a given student's raw score—a highly dubious norm whose and its use is officially discouraged by the International Reading Association.
Normal curve equivalent	The score resulting from partitioning the normal distribution into 99 statistically equivalent sections. NCEs can be averaged, unlike percentile ranks.
Scale score	A statistically converted score, usually computed to combine the results of different tests or to weight items differentially.
Quartile	One quarter of the norming group, permitting a given child's score to be grossly categorized as falling in one of four sections.

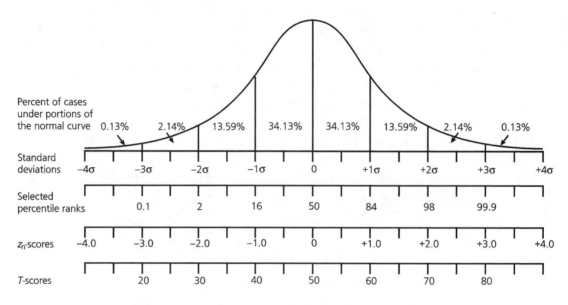

FIGURE 2.1. Common norms in relation to the normal distribution.

first and ninth stanine always contain 4% of the population, the second and eighth always contain 7%, and so on.

The lower graph in Figure 2.1 illustrates how a population of students varies from its own mean (average) score. The Greek letter *sigma* (σ) is used to represent the standard deviation of the group (that is, the extent to which the scores made by group members tend to vary). You will observe that over 68% of the population (about two-thirds) has scores that fall within one standard deviation of the group mean. The farther we get from this mean, the fewer individuals we find. For example, only 13.59% of those tested typically score more than one standard deviation above the mean and far less than 1% score more than three standard deviations above it.

Not all tests produce these symmetrical, bell-shaped curves. Imagine a weekly spelling test of 20 words, on which all of the students in a gifted class score either 19 or

20. Results of such a test would be skewed to the right, which should be of no concern to the teacher. The results of classroom tests of this nature are usually interpreted not by comparing students with one another but against a criterion for mastery or a simple grading scale. Publishers of commercial norm-referenced tests, however, often go to great lengths to ensure that scores do tend to produce a normal distribution, such as those depicted in the diagrams. This goal is accomplished by field testing potential test items and ultimately selecting only those that contribute to a normal distribution of scores.

Most teachers associate norm-referenced tests with the group achievement measures they may be required to administer and for which they are often held accountable. However, many norm-referenced tests are individually administered, such as those used by special educators to classify students. Another minor misconception about norm-referenced tests concerns the word *standardized*. This term is frequently used as a synonym for *norm-referenced*. In fact, however, a standardized test is any test for which the procedures for administration and scoring are rigorously prescribed. Even a criterion-referenced test (e.g., the written portion of the state driver's examination) could be thought of as standardized in this sense.

Standard Error of Measurement

How much confidence can we have that a student's score accurately reflects what the student knows or can do? In the best of worlds, test scores would provide perfect indicators of student learning. But in the real world, both predictable and unpredictable factors influence scores in unpredictable ways. A typical class about to take a norm-referenced achievement test in reading may well contain individuals who skipped breakfast, argued that morning with their parents, are unmotivated to perform well, or who failed to get a good night's sleep. It also may contain students who have been offered inducements by their parents to do well, or who enjoy the self-competition made possible by the norms. Such factors contribute to what is called measurement error, which reduces the reliance teachers can justifiably impute to the test scores. All tests, even those constructed by teachers, suffer from measurement error. In the case of norm-referenced tests, however, it is possible to estimate just how large this error may be.

A simple equation may help us conceptualize the error factor. This equation depicts the relationship between a student's "true score" (that is, the score the student should have received based on the area being assessed) and the student's "actual score" (the score the student actually makes on the test).

Actual score = True score ± Error

The true score can never be directly measured, only estimated. Hopefully, the actual score is reasonably close to the true score, but we can never be certain that this is the case. The standard error of measurement provides a way of estimating how far "off" the actual score may be. This we can accomplish by creating a zone, or interval, around the actual score. First we add the standard error of measurement to the actual score to form the high point of the interval. Then we subtract the standard error from the actual score to find the low point. Because of the statistical properties of a test that has a normal distribution, we can conclude that there is roughly a 67% chance that the individual's true score falls somewhere within this interval. We call this region a "confidence interval," because it permits us to make a statement, with reasonable confidence, about the true score. To say that there are roughly two chances in three that an individual's true score lies within one standard error of the actual score sounds appealing, but it also means that there is one chance in three that the true score is either above the interval or below it—with no way to tell which!

If you desire to have more confidence in your conclusion, you simply construct a larger confidence interval by adding and subtracting twice the standard error from the actual score. The result is a 95% interval. In other words, we can be 95% certain that an individual's true score lies within two standard errors of the actual score. This seems very useful, indeed—except that the 95% interval can be so large that the statement is virtually meaningless.

As an example, consider the diagram in Figure 2.2. In this case, a student has earned a raw score of 20 on a test that has a standard error of measurement of 2 raw score points. The 67% confidence interval is constructed by adding and subtracting 2 points from the raw score of 20, so that the interval extends from 18 to 22. The 95% interval is constructed by doubling the standard error before adding and subtracting, so that this interval extends from 16 to 24. When the end points of the interval (that is, 16 and 24) are translated into norms such as percentile ranks, the range is disappointingly large.

One may well wonder, given the difficulties involved in attempting to estimate the true score, just why group achievement tests are given. Surely there is so much error involved that the results cannot be meaningfully interpreted. The response to this objection is that group achievement tests are not designed to assess individual students with a high level of accuracy. Rather, they are designed to assess groups and to answer educational questions concerning the achievement of groups. When large numbers of scores are averaged, the measurement error is diminished. A question such as "How well is the

FIGURE 2.1. Examples of confidence intervals (standard error of measurement = 2).

fifth grade doing in our school district?" is far better suited to group achievement testing than a question such as "How well is Johnny doing in reading?" Such tests provide us with only the most tentative measures of an individual student's learning.

Which Norms Are Best?

For the purpose of interpreting the results of group achievement testing, percentile ranks and stanines are perhaps the most useful norms for teachers. Percentile ranks give an indication of where an individual student's performance falls relative to other students the same age. Stanines do this as well, but since there are only nine possible stanine scores, they are not as precise as percentile ranks. Why, then, report stanines at all? The reason is that stanines are statistically equivalent, allowing certain conclusions to be reached. It takes as much effort to move from the first to the second stanine as it does from the sixth to the seventh, for example. This is not true of percentile ranks, however, rendering stanines preferable for making pretest–posttest comparisons or for comparing the results of two subtests.

The Two-Stanine Rule

If the difference between the scores made by a student on two different subtests (or on the pre- and postadministrations of the same test) is two stanines or greater, the difference is probably real. A difference of two stanines is typically sufficient to overcome measurement error. For example, if a child scores at the fourth stanine on a subtest of Reading Comprehension, and at the sixth stanine on a subtest of Vocabulary, it is reasonable to conclude that achievement in the area of reading comprehension is lower than achievement in vocabulary, compared with the norming group. On the other hand, if the stanine for one of these two areas is three and, for the other area, fourth we are statistically prevented from concluding that there is any real difference whatsoever.

A Limitation of Percentile Ranks

Some educators make the mistake of computing class or school averages using percentile ranks. Doing so is not statistically appropriate because percentile ranks are not on an equal-interval scale. That is to say, the "distance" between the second and third percentile ranks is not the same as the "distance" between the 32nd and 33rd percentile ranks. The closer a score is to the 50th percentile rank, the more volatile it becomes and the easier it is for the score to change from one administration to the next.

Because of this difficulty, statisticians rely on normal curve equivalents and scale scores (see Figure 2.1) in order to compute averages and other statistics. In fact, this is virtually the only use that norms of this kind serve. They are hard to interpret in themselves. It is best to rely on percentile ranks and stanines to bring meaning to achievement test scores. The percentile rank of a class or some larger group can be ascertained, if desired, by first computing the average scale score or NCE and *then* locating the percentile rank that corresponds to this average.

Which Norms Are Worst?

Without question, the worst norm typically reported on group achievement tests is the grade-equivalent score. This norm purports to indicate the grade level at which the student has performed on a particular subtest. A common way of interpreting a grade-equivalent score is by relating it to that of "average children" at a particular level. For example, if a seventh grader produces a grade equivalent score of 2.6 on a subtest of Reading Comprehension, it is common for teachers to conclude that this student comprehends as well as the average second grader who is in the sixth month of school. This conclusion is very difficult to defend, however. For one thing, a test that is appropriate for middle schoolers is unlikely to have been given to second graders simply in order to establish norms. Indeed, many grade-equivalent scores are merely statistical projections that permit a student to be compared with students of other ages.

Another difficulty of grade-equivalent scores is that for most tests they have "floors" and "ceilings." A floor is simply the lowest grade-equivalent score it is possible to make, because grade equivalents have not been projected below a certain level. For example, if the floor for a Reading Comprehension subtest is 2.0, then even a student who is a nonreader may be judged to be reading as well as the average beginning second grader (Silvaroli, 1977). Problems with floors are not as troublesome as they once were, but the potential for difficulties still exists.

A ceiling, on the other hand, is the highest grade-equivalent score a student can earn. It is rare for an achievement test to have a ceiling higher than 12th grade. Although ceilings could lead us to underestimate the achievement of advanced students, this possibility is not as troublesome as that of overestimating the achievement of struggling readers due to the effects of floors.

The International Reading Association, in a 1980 Board of Directors position statement that is still in effect, officially condemned the use of grade-equivalent scores for all of these reasons. You may well ask, if such scores are so bad, why are they computed by test publishers in the first place? The answer publishers often give is that educators demand grade-equivalent scores. The publishers are well aware of their limitations, of course, but contend that eliminating them would put them at a competitive disadvantage. Perhaps the solution to this dilemma lies in fostering better awareness in educators, policy makers, and other stakeholders who make use of test results. Until awareness is heightened, however, the best advice that can be offered to practitioners in the position of interpreting test results is simply to ignore grade-equivalent scores.

Suggestions for "Reading" a Student Profile

The array of data contained in the score report for an individual student can be perplexing. The following suggestions are offered as a means of navigating through this maze of data.

1. Ignore grade-equivalent scores. For all of the reasons we have discussed, such scores offer no usable information to teachers.
2. Consider the Reading Comprehension score as the best indicator of overall reading achievement.

3. In the case of low scores, note whether the number of items attempted is the same as the number possible, especially for subtests that are out of line with the general profile.
4. Be skeptical of specific skill results based on very few items. It is common for skill breakdowns to include results based on only a handful of items corresponding to a particular skill. The reliability of these embedded subtests is extremely low, and daily classwork constitutes a far better indicator of skill deficits. (See the sample contained in Figure 2.3.)
5. Use the national stanine to interpret achievement for each subtest. The percentile rank is more precise in some ways, but stanines can be more easily interpreted, as follows:

> Stanines 7–9 = Above average
> Stanine 6 = Borderline
> Stanine 5 = Average
> Stanine 4 = Borderline
> Stanine 1–3 = Below average

6. Use the two-stanine rule to compare subtest scores. Remember that if the difference is at least two stanines, there is a statistically good chance that a real difference exists. You cannot know precisely how large the difference is, however.
7. Use group achievement scores for broad-based screening purposes only. Be prepared to reinterpret results based on other evidence that may be more de-

Student: Joe Kelly

School: Kashinkerry Elementary

Grade: 03

Test Date: March

	Reading Subtests		
	Total Reading	Reading Vocabulary	Reading Comprehension
Number Possible	84	30	54
Raw Score	45	17	28
Scaled Score	590	582	595
National Percentile Rank	23–4	23–4	26–4
National Stanine	4	4	4
National NCE	34.4	34.4	34.4
Grade Equivalent	2.7	2.7	2.7

FIGURE 2.3. Sample reading profile from a fictitious nationally norm-referenced group achievement test.

pendable. Such evidence might include classroom performance, results of individual assessments, and teacher observations.

8. Be on the lookout for students who do not take the testing seriously. It is unfortunately commonplace for some students to expend only minimal effort in taking achievement tests. The scores they produce are virtually worthless, and it is important to know who these students are. Otherwise, mistakes can be made when evaluating the extent (or lack) of their achievement. Make a point of giving their names to next year's teachers if the results of the testing arrive too late in the year for you to make any use of them yourself.

The National Assessment of Educational Progress

The National Assessment of Educational Progress (NAEP) in reading is "our nation's report card," an assessment periodically given to students across the country to assess growth in reading achievement over time. It has been administered since 1969, allowing policy makers to examine trends in achievement. The scores on the NAEP are reported on a scale from 0 to 500. These scores are developed separately for each subject area.

The NAEP does not report individual student scores, and it does not report schoolwide scores for participating schools. Since 1990, scores have been reported for individual states, so that states who participate (and not all states do) can compare their achievement to that of other states and to the national averages.

If the test cannot be used for individual assessment, since the results are never reported that way, why discuss it here? We do so for two reasons. First, these results are widely reported in newspapers and other media, and it is important to understand what they are, and are not, so that teachers can respond intelligently. Second, the NAEP provides some benchmarks for judging children's performance, rather than only discussing how children scored in relation to a norming sample.

The NAEP reports scores in two ways. The first is the average scale score for the nation and for the states. A state's average can be compared with the nation's or with that of other states. For example, Table 2.2 indicates that Georgia's statewide average for grade 4 was below the national average in 1992, 1994, and 1998, whereas Connecticut was above average all 3 years. Connecticut also made significant gains between 1994 and 1998.

The second way results are reported are by benchmarks. The NAEP governing board has divided performance into three levels—basic, proficient, and advanced—as defined in Table 2.3. These performance levels are translated into specific benchmarks for each grade.

Although these are listed as "benchmarks," they were designed as high standards for children to reach. The point of setting standards so high was that teachers would push their students toward these standards, rather than a more modest level of attainment. But children can fail to reach the "basic" level for fourth grade, for example, and still demonstrate a literal understanding of what they read, understand a main idea from expository text, or follow a simple plot (Donahue, Voelkl, Campbell, & Mazzeo, 1999). These are all listed as "below basic" skills at the fourth-grade level. At the eighth- and twelfth-grade levels, "below basic" implies an even higher level of skill. We need high

TABLE 2.2. Average 1998 NAEP Grade 4 Scale Scores for the States (Public Schools Only)

	Average scale score		
	1992	1994	1998
Nation	215	212	215
Alabama	207	208	211
Arizona	209	206	207
Arkansas	211	209	209
California	202	197	202
Colorado	217	213	222
Connecticut	222	222	232
Delaware	213	206	212
Florida	208	205	207
Georgia	212	207	210
Hawaii	203	201	200
Iowa	225	223	223
Kansas	—	—	222
Kentucky	213	212	218
Louisiana	204	197	204
Maine	227	228	225
Maryland	211	210	215
Massachusetts	226	223	225
Michigan	216	—	217
Minnesota	221	218	222
Mississippi	199	202	204
Missouri	220	217	216
Montana	—	222	226
Nevada	—	—	208
New Hampshire	228	223	226
New Mexico	211	205	206
New York	215	212	216
North Carolina	212	214	217
Oklahoma	220	—	220
Oregon	—	—	214
Rhode Island	217	220	218
South Carolina	210	203	210
Tennessee	212	213	212
Texas	213	212	217
Utah	220	217	215
Virginia	221	213	218
Washington	—	213	217
West Virginia	216	213	216
Wisconsin	224	224	224
Wyoming	223	221	219
District of Columbia	188	179	182

TABLE 2.3. NAEP Performance Level Definitions and Descriptions

Achievement-level policy definitions

Basic   Partial mastery of prerequisite knowledge and skills that are fundamental for proficient work at each grade.

Proficient   Solid academic performance for each grade assessed. Students reaching this level have demonstrated competency over challenging subject matter, including subject-matter knowledge, application of such knowledge to real-world situations, and analytical skills appropriate to the subject matter.

Advanced   Superior performance.

Fourth grade

Basic   Fourth-grade students performing at the Basic level should demonstrate an understanding of the overall meaning of what they read. When reading text appropriate for fourth-graders, they should be able to make relatively obvious connections between the text and their own experiences and extend the ideas in the text by making simple inferences.

Proficient   Fourth-grade students performing at the Proficient level should be able to demonstrate an overall understanding of the text, providing inferential as well as literal information. When reading text appropriate to fourth grade, they should be able to extend the ideas in the text by making inferences, drawing conclusions, and making connections to their own experiences. The connection between the text and what the student infers should be clear.

Advanced   Fourth-grade students performing at the Advanced level should be able to generalize about topics in the reading selection and demonstrate an awareness of how authors compose and use literary devices. When reading text appropriate to fourth grade, they should be able to judge text critically and, in general, to give thorough answers that indicate careful thought.

Eighth grade

Basic   Eighth-grade students performing at the Basic level should demonstrate a literal understanding of what they read and be able to make some interpretations. When reading text appropriate to eighth grade, they should be able to identify specific aspects of the text that reflect overall meaning, extend the ideas in the text by making simple inferences, recognize and relate interpretations and connections among ideas in the text to personal experience, and draw conclusions based on the text.

Proficient   Eighth-grade students performing at the Proficient level should be able to show an overall understanding of the text, including inferential as well as literal information. When reading text appropriate to eighth grade, they should be able to extend the ideas in the text by making clear inferences from it, by drawing conclusions, and by making connections to their own experiences—including other reading experiences. Proficient eighth-graders should be able to identify some of the devices authors use in composing text.

Advanced   Eighth-grade students performing at the Advanced level should be able to describe the more abstract themes and ideas of the overall text. When reading text appropriate to eighth grade, they should be able to analyze both meaning and form and support their analyses explicitly with examples from the text; they should be able to extend text information by relating it to their experiences and to world events. At this level, student responses should be thorough, thoughtful, and extensive.

12th grade

Basic   Twelfth-grade students performing at the Basic level should be able to demonstrate an overall understanding and make some interpretations of the text. When reading text appropriate to twelfth grade, they should be able to identify and relate aspects of the text to its overall meaning, extend the ideas in the text by making simple inferences, recognize interpretations, make connections among and relate ideas in the text to their personal experiences, and draw conclusions. They should be able to identify elements of an author's style.

Proficient   Twelfth-grade students performing at the Proficient level should be able to show an overall understanding of the text which includes inferential as well as literal information. When reading text appropriate to twelfth grade, they should be able to extend the ideas of the text by making inferences, drawing conclusions, and making connections to their own personal experiences and other readings. Connections between inferences and the text should be clear, even when implicit. These students should be able to analyze the author's use of literary devices.

Advanced   Twelfth-grade students performing at the Advanced level should be able to describe more abstract themes and ideas in the overall text. When reading text appropriate to twelfth grade, they should be able to analyze both the meaning and the form of the text and explicitly support their analyses with specific examples from the text. They should be able to extend the information from the text by relating it to their experiences and to the world. Their responses should be thorough, thoughtful, and extensive.

standards to propel our students (and us) to higher achievement, but we are concerned that statements such as "40 percent of our fourth graders are reading below the basic level" can be misinterpreted.

Finally, the NAEP is a measure that is both standardized and formal, with aspects of a criterion-referenced measure. Item difficulties are calculated by comparing the numbers of children who got each item correct, creating a scale score. The test is formally administered, by a set of administration rules, but there also are criteria that were used to develop the test (the achievement level definitions). Many state tests have been based on this model, being both formal and criterion-referenced.

RELIABILITY AND VALIDITY

Perhaps the most important statistical evaluators associated with tests are reliability and validity. These two related criteria are frequently confused. *Reliability* refers to the consistency of results—the general dependability of a test: A test that produces similar results under similar conditions is said to be reliable. *Validity* refers to the degree to which a test measures what it purports to measure and what examiner wishes to measure. Reliability is a prerequisite of validity, but validity is not needed for reliability. To put it another way, a valid test is always reliable, but a reliable test is not necessarily valid.

Consider an everyday analogy: McDonald's hamburgers. McDonald's hamburgers, we suggest, are reliable but not valid. If you walk into a McDonald's anywhere in the world, from Savannah to Hong Kong, you receive precisely the same product. Now, that's reliability! But are these sandwiches what you really want when you think of a good hamburger? In our view, they are not. In other words, they are not valid examples of "true" hamburgers. To put it in testing terms, there is high reliability and low validity. The same can be true of a test. To use an extreme example, a math test may be highly reliable, but if used to assess reading ability, it would produce results that are clearly invalid.

Reliability is computed in various ways and is usually expressed as a decimal. The closer the reliability coefficient is to 1.0, the more reliable the test. Reliability coefficients of .90 or higher are considered extremely high and are hallmarks of reliable testing. Reliability is influenced by such factors as (1) the length of the test (the longer the test, the more reliable it is), (2) the clarity of directions, and (3) the objectivity of scoring.

Validity is a murkier concept and has no numerical translation. Rather, the producers of a commercial test simply make a case for its validity by presenting the evidence they have accumulated. It is up to consumers (i.e., teachers and administrators) to decide whether the test is truly valid for their purposes. Several types of validity are important; a quick overview may help clarify the general concept of validity.

Content Validity

A test that reflects the curriculum that is taught is said to possess *content validity*. The process of curriculum alignment, advocated by Fenwick English and others (English & Frase, 1999), is designed to ensure a good match between what is taught and what is tested, and is a popular means of improving content validity. Imagine a teacher who invests many hours trying to foster critical reading comprehension ability merely to find that students will be given only low-level questions on an achievement test. Such a test would have limited content validity for that teacher.

Construct Validity

When a test produces results that conform well to real-world applications, it is said to possess *construct validity*. For example, assume that the results of a reading achievement test show that students who did well had already been placed in advanced reading groups by their teachers, that students who performed poorly had been placed in below-average groups, and so forth. This would be evidence of construct validity.

Predictive Validity

Some tests are expressly designed to predict future performance or success. Results of the SAT and ACT, for instance, correlate well with the later college GPAs of the students who take them. College admissions officers use the results in the confidence that they do a good job of predicting success. That is to say, the tests possess good predictive validity.

Concurrent Validity

If a new measure and an established measure are administered at about the same time to the same students, and if the two scores turn out to be highly correlated, this result could be regarded as evidence of validity for the new test. Since the two measures are administered at almost the same time, we call a strong relationship evidence of *concurrent validity*. When, for example, a convenient, easy-to-give measure, such as the San Diego Quick Assessment, is shown to provide reading-level estimates that are the same or similar to those provided by more complex tests, evidence of concurrent validity is established.

WHEN IS A TEST NOT A TEST?

Information useful in planning reading instruction does not always come in the form of test results. In fact, many teachers would argue that the most important information about students does not come from tests at all, but from other sources. These sources include written work, classroom observations, parent input, and portfolios.

Written Work

The products of written class assignments can provide important clues to a student's literacy development. Such products include compositions, journal entries, worksheets, emails, class notes, and many others. For younger children, written work samples may include scribbling and early writing, potentially rich in data about spelling development and phonological awareness.

Classroom Observations

As students engage in reading and writing activities during the school day, observant teachers often discern patterns useful in monitoring growth and identifying needs. Yetta Goodman has called this process *kidwatching* (e.g., Owocki & Goodman, 2002). In some cases, structured observations can be helpful, such as checklists of key behaviors. Unstructured observations are useful as well, especially for experienced teachers who know what they are looking for in terms of behavioral cues. In this case, the teacher notices a revealing pattern and either makes a mental note of it or (better yet) makes a brief anecdotal record for later reference.

Parent Input

Calls to parents and remarks they make during face-to-face conferences can provide insights into a child's behaviors. Documenting such input by making quick, dated notes for later use can be useful. Occasionally, parent input also comes in written form, as notes or letters sent to the teacher or other educators.

Portfolios

A literacy portfolio is a collection of evidence that enables a teacher to document progress over time. The evidence might include:

- ♦ Samples of daily work
- ♦ Coded passages read orally by the student
- ♦ A chart of reading rate over time
- ♦ A record of reading interests and books read
- ♦ Journal entries by the teacher (or anecdotal notes)
- ♦ Journal entries by the student
- ♦ Test results

This list is far from exhaustive. Creative teachers can make portfolios a telling glimpse into the literacy growth and development of individual students. Following are guidelines and suggestions for getting starting with portfolio projects.

1. All of the evidence should be dated so that progress over time can be interpreted. Leafing through a portfolio from start to finish can provide an occasional long-term perspective that would otherwise be hard to gain.

2. Unless a teacher is fairly selective about what is included in the portfolio, it can rapidly become cumbersome, difficult to store, and hard to use.

3. Roger Farr (1992) recommends keeping two portfolios for each student. One he terms the *working* portfolio, as described above. This is the portfolio used to monitor progress and guide instructional decision making. The other is the *show* portfolio, a dated collection of the student's best work. It is far smaller than the working portfolio and is used to signal progress during student conferences and to discuss a student's strengths and needs during parent conferences. If you think keeping two portfolios would be unmanageable, a compromise might consist of keeping only the working type and using stickies to identify specific entries prior to a conference so that they can be quickly located.

4. Consider passing portfolios along to next year's teachers. Logistics can be troublesome, but putting a well-maintained portfolio into the right hands can provide a wealth of information at the start of a new school year. Think how you might feel if you were on the receiving end of such a policy!

5. Use portfolios during postobservation conferences with an administrator. Their contents can enrich the discussion considerably and also document why you might have used certain instructional techniques with particular students. The observing administrator will not fail to be impressed, for portfolios are clearly one mark of a reflective teacher intent on using evidence of student performance to guide instructional planning.

SUMMARY

There is a wide variety of options available for assessment and a wide variety of users of educational assessment. From the highest levels, policy makers in the state and federal government might use information from the NAEP to judge the effectiveness of reading instruction in an entire state or the nation. These results can provide a rough estimate of whether policies are improving achievement. Standardized norm- or criterion-referenced tests can provide a school superintendent the same type of data on a smaller scale. These tests can tell the superintendent or the school board about the overall effectiveness of curriculum in a district, or how well individual schools are performing. Used correctly, standardized tests can provide important information about reading programs used in a district.

For an individual teacher, however, such measures usually do not provide much information above and beyond that available through informal measures and observations. Because of the standard error of measurement, scores on norm-referenced tests are rarely sufficiently accurate, by themselves, for individual diagnosis. At best, they may be used to screen children. If a child does particularly poorly or particularly well, the teacher might want to retest, using an informal reading (IRI) to confirm the score of the norm-referenced test. If the IRI produces divergent results, the teacher should at least question the results of the norm-referenced test. IRIs, running records, and other measures are closer to the child's curriculum and may be more relevant for individual diagnosis.

3

Informal Reading Inventories and Other Measures of Oral Reading

In reading assessment, we are always asking questions and using the results of our assessments to answer these questions. At the end of Chapter 1, we asked a series of questions about children's reading skills. From our model, we are concerned globally about the child's abilities in the areas of automatic word recognition, language comprehension, and strategic knowledge. An expanded list of questions follows.

WHAT DO WE WANT TO LEARN FROM A READING ASSESSMENT?

Questions	Sources of information
Automatic word recognition	
Does the child read fluently and naturally?	Oral reading sample, observations
What level material should the child use for instruction?	Oral reading sample, level
Does the child use context to decode unknown words?	Miscue analysis of oral reading
Does the child self-correct?	Oral reading sample, observations
What words can the child read accurately?	Word lists

Does the child read words better in context or in isolation?	Word lists, oral reading sample
With which spelling patterns is the child familiar?	Criterion-referenced decoding test, invented spellings
Can the child decode words in isolation that he or she cannot decode in context? Or vice versa?	Comparison of decoding test with oral reading sample
Does the child have an adequate level of phonemic awareness?	See Chapter 4

Language comprehension

What level material can the child comprehend when reading silently?	Silent reading sample, informal reading inventory (IRI)
What level material can the child comprehend when reading orally?	Oral reading sample, IRI
Does the child comprehend better when reading orally than silently?	Comparison of oral and silent reading
Does the child comprehend what he or she can read accurately?	Oral reading sample, IRI
What types of questions give the child trouble?	Examination of literal, inferential, etc., questions on IRI
Does the child understand material at his grade level when presented orally?	Listening comprehension passage
Does the child have an adequate vocabulary for understanding?	See Chapter 3; informal observations during reading
Does the child use story structure to aid in comprehension?	Retellings
Does the child have adequate background knowledge?	Background knowledge measures (varies with each story read)
What does the child do when he or she lacks background knowledge?	Analysis of IRI

Strategic control

Does the child use varied strategies flexibly during reading?	See Chapter 10
Does the child understand the purposes of reading?	See Chapters 9, 10
What is the child's attitude toward reading?	See Chapter 9
What is the child's knowledge of basic print concepts?	See Chapter 4

A quick review of this table suggests that a great many of the questions we raise about children's reading can be answered through the sensitive use of on oral reading sample. Such a sample can come from an informal reading inventory or running records. Many of the other questions can be answered through the use of other parts of the informal reading inventory—the silent reading and listening comprehension sections and the word list. For that reason, we consider the IRI to be the cornerstone of the reading assessment process. Many of the other assessments in this book are used to confirm or explicate the results garnered from observation of an IRI. Relatively easy to administer (once you have learned some simple notations) an IRI in the hands of a well-trained practitioner provides a great deal of information about a child's reading strengths and weaknesses. In addition, the same processes involved in interpreting an IRI can be used by teachers in their everyday observations of children's reading.

What Is an Informal Reading Inventory?

An IRI mainly consists of a sequence of graded passages, typically beginning at the preprimer level. Each passage is followed by comprehension questions and occasionally, a retelling scoring guide. Most IRI also are equipped with graded word lists for estimating where to begin in the passages.

For each passage the child reads, the teacher makes a judgment as to whether the passage is on the child's independent, instructional, or frustration level. (We will define these levels more precisely in a moment.) This judgment is based on both accuracy of word recognition and success in answering the comprehension questions posed orally by the teacher. The teacher shows the child a copy of the passage and makes notations on a separate copy that includes the questions and scoring guides. Once the child completes a passage, the teacher must decide which, if any, of the remaining passages in a sequence should be given next. Following the IRI administration, the teacher must consider the child's performance on all of the passages read and then make an overall judgment as to the child's instructional reading level.

Form 3.1 (p. 68) presents the teacher's version of a sixth-grade passage that we have developed as an illustration. The student version of this passage (Form 3.2, p. 69), of course, contains no questions and is printed in larger type. The summary form (Form 3.3, p. 70) is a generic table used to record some of the most important data produced by an IRI administration in an organized manner.

Reading Levels

Traditionally, children were assigned a reading level by means of an informal reading inventory. These levels were based on those determined by Emmett Betts in the 1930s (Betts, 1946). A passage of a particular readability level was judged to represent a child's independent, instructional or frustration level, as defined below:

- *Independent level* is the highest level at which a child can read the material without assistance.
- *Instructional level* is the highest level at which a child could benefit from instructional support.
- *Frustration level* is the lowest level at which a child is likely to be frustrated, even with instructional support.

How are these levels estimated using an IRI? When the results of an IRI are quantified into percentages of questions answered correctly and percentages of words read accurately aloud, these percentages can be used to estimate a child's reading levels. Conventionally, the independent level has been defined as the highest level at which a child can read with 99% accuracy and with at least 90% comprehension. The instructional level has been defined as the highest passage a child can read with 95–98% oral accuracy and with at least 75% comprehension. The frustration level has been defined as the lowest level at which the child can read with 90% or lower oral accuracy and with 50% comprehension or below. These criteria are presented in Table 3.1.

This classification has been used to the present day. Nearly all commercial informal reading inventories and textbooks use these levels. There are problems with the leveling, however. First, comprehension is dependent on the questions used. Some questions are more difficult; some are easier. A child's performance depends on the difficulty of the questions.

Others have questioned the accuracy levels. Clay (1993a) uses a 90% accuracy level for the early reading books in Reading Recovery. This level makes sense for the predictable picture books used in early first grade. It also makes sense, given the level of support in Reading Recovery.

It is also not clear whether the 95% for instructional level should include self-corrections or how semantically acceptable miscues should be handled. Some informal reading inventories regard semantically acceptable miscues as acceptable; others count all miscues. Some commercial IRIs, such as the Qualitative Reading Inventory (Leslie & Caldwell, 2001), provide two ways of determining the instructional level: (1) counting all miscues, and (2) counting only those that significantly change the meaning of the text.

Hoffman (personal communication, December 1994) suggested that instructional level depends on the level of the instruction given. Betts based his notion of instructional levels on the instruction typical of the time. During that era, the directed reading activity (also developed by Betts) was the most commonly used instructional model. In this model, prior to reading, the teacher provides background information, preteaches vocabulary, and provides a purpose, or focus, for reading. Children read segments of the text silently, stopping to discuss teacher-posed questions. Children reread the text that addresses the answer of the question orally. Following the reading of the whole selection, children answer a series of postreading questions. The directed reading activity provides relatively minimal instruction compared to more recent models. In fluency-oriented reading instruction (Stahl, Heubach, & Cramond, 1994), first the entire text is

TABLE 3.1. The Betts Criteria for Interpreting the Level of an IRI Passage

Level	Word recognition		Comprehension
Independent	99–100%	*and*	90–100%
Instructional	95–98%	*and*	75–89%
Frustration	90% or lower	*or*	50% or lower

read and discussed, followed by a number of repeated readings of the text. In this approach, children receive considerably more support in reading the text and thus should be able to benefit from reading more difficult text. Stahl and his colleagues found that children could benefit from reading text with 85% accuracy—texts that would conventionally be considered at the frustration level—at the beginning of instruction.

This finding does not imply that all children can read all texts. Consider Vygotsky's (1978) notion of the zone of proximal development. Vygotsky suggests that children can do work in a zone. The bottom end of the zone (the easiest material) is the level at which children can work independently. The top end of the zone (the most difficult material) is the most difficult level at which children can work with teacher support. Above that level, a child cannot work with material under any circumstance. Our experience is that children can be supported in working with material that is relatively difficult, if the teacher plans to provide extra support. Sometimes this support is provided through repeated readings or assisted reading of various kinds; at other times it can be provided through direct comprehension support, such as through reciprocal teaching.

We do not have precise guidelines for determining a zone of proximal development for each child. Our rough and ready guess is that, if you are using intensive teaching techniques, such as those described above, you might try starting 1 year above the child's instructional level, as measured by a conventional informal reading inventory. This is a guess, but it has worked well in our clinic. If you are using classroom techniques, such as directed reading activities, which do not provide as much support, then you might stay at the instructional level. Either way, you need to monitor what the child is doing and make sure that the child is successful, but somewhat challenged, by the level of material you are using.

GUIDELINES FOR ADMINISTERING AN IRI

There is no *single best way* to give an IRI. Much depends on what you want to know. The IRI is like a toolkit that can be used for a variety of purposes—not all of it may be appropriate on a given occasion, and the way you use it will vary.

This does not mean that there is no consensus about useful approaches to giving IRIs, however. If your goal is to estimate a child's instructional reading level and, in the process, gather data about how the child decodes words, then the following general steps may be helpful. But, remember, as a teacher you are empowered to "veto" any of these steps if the specific circumstances appear to warrant it.

Overall Strategy for Giving the IRI

1. *Estimate the child's independent reading level.* One way of doing this is by examining any available evidence you may have, such as classroom performance, results of a previous IRI, etc. Another way is to give the graded word lists of the IRI and to consider the highest word list on which no words are missed to be a tentative estimate of the independent reading level.

2. *Administer the passage corresponding to your estimate of the independent level.* Have the child read this passage orally while you code miscues. Then ask the comprehension questions. At this point you must judge whether the passage is at the independent reading level by considering both the word-recognition accuracy (number of oral reading errors) and the child's comprehension performance (number of questions missed).

3. *Decide which passage to administer next.* If the initial passage is above the independent reading level, you must proceed to simpler passages until the independent level is reached. If the initial passage is judged to be at the independent reading level, you should proceed to more difficult passages until frustration is reached or appears to be imminent. In any case, each time you complete a passage, you must decide which passage to give next or whether to discontinue the IRI.

Strategy for Giving Each Passage

1. Briefly prepare the student by asking the question about prior knowledge or identifying the topic.
2. Ask the student to read the passage aloud.
3. If you are interested in reading rate, note the exact beginning time.
4. Code oral miscues as the child reads.
5. If the child hesitates too long, supply the word.
6. Discontinue the passage and do not ask the questions if
   a. the passage is so difficult that you are reasonably sure it would be judged at the frustration level, or
   b. you have had to supply, in your judgment, too many words.
7. If you are interested in reading rate, note the exact ending time.
8. Ask the comprehension questions, giving partial credit where you feel it is warranted and rewording questions if you think it will help communicate what a given question asks.
9. Use the scoring guidelines to determine the level of the passage in terms of (a) oral accuracy and (b) comprehension.
10. Come to an overall judgment as to whether the passage is at the child's independent, instructional, or frustration level. Sometimes this judgment may not be clear-cut.

Coding Oral Reading

As the child reads a passage, the teacher marks departures from the printed text. The goal is to create a record that can be "played back" later. These departures are often called *miscues* rather than errors because the reader may be using certain "cues" about a word (such as phonics, structure, and context) and ignoring or underutilizing others. Major types of miscues include the following:

1. *Omission.* A word is skipped during oral reading.
2. *Insertion.* A word or phrase not in the text is spoken by the reader.
3. *Substitution.* The printed word is replaced with another.
4. *Reversal.* The order of the printed words is changed by the reader. (Changing the order of letters within a single word, such as saying *was* for *saw*, is a type of substitution.)
5. *Teacher-supplied word.* The reader hesitates long enough that the teacher steps in and pronounces the word in order to keep the process moving.
6. *Repetition.* A word or phrase is repeated, sometimes for better enunciation, sometimes to monitor comprehension.
7. *Ignoring punctuation.* The reader ignores commas, periods, question marks, and so forth, so that the oral reading is not meaningful and fluent, even though word accuracy may be quite high.
8. *Hesitation.* The reader hesitates but not long enough that the teacher pronounces the word.
9. *Self-correction.* The child rereads one or more words in order to correct an error.

Not everyone agrees on how these miscues should be coded by the teacher. The following examples represent conventional practice. In the end, it matters very little as long as (1) the teacher is consistent, and (2) teachers with whom coded passages may be shared are familiar with the system being used.

1. Text: Jim called me yesterday.
   Child: Jim called me.
   Coding: Jim called me (yesterday.)

2. Text: Jim called me yesterday.
   Child: Jim called me up yesterday.

   Coding: Jim called me ⌃ yesterday.
            (up inserted above ⌃ between "me" and "yesterday")

3. Text: Jim called me yesterday.
   Child: Jim called me today.

   Coding: Jim called me yesterday.
            (today written above "yesterday")

4. Text: Jim called me yesterday.
   Child: Jim called me me yesterday.
   Coding: Jim called <u>me</u> yesterday.

5. Text: Jim called me yesterday.
   Child: Jim called me *(brief pause)* yesterday.
   Coding: Jim called me | yesterday.

6. Text: Jim called me yesterday.
   Child: Jim called me *(pause, word pronounced by teacher)* yesterday.

                                            P
   Coding: Jim called me yesterday.

7. Text: Jim called me yesterday.
   Child: Yesterday Jim called me.
   Coding: Jim called me yesterday.

8. Text: Jim called me yesterday.
   Child: Jime called me yesterday.

                       —   *Jime*
   Coding: Jim called me yesterday.   OR   Jim called me yesterday.

9. Text: Jim called me yesterday.
   Child: John phoned me sometime yesterday.
             John phoned sometime
   Coding: Jim called me yesterday.
                        ^

10. Text: Jim called me yesterday.
    Child: John Jim called me yesterday.
             John √
    Coding: Jim called me yesterday.

11. Text: Jim called me yesterday. We talked for an hour.
    Child: Jim called me yesterday we talked for an hour.
    Coding: Jim called me yesterday. We talked for an hour.

Counting Miscues

Which miscues are tallied after the child finishes? The answer to this question may alter the results and lead to different conclusions about whether the passage is on the child's independent, instructional, or frustration level. The question is really twofold. First, can certain types of miscues be disregarded in counting the total? Conventional wisdom suggests that hesitations and ignoring punctuation should not be counted. This policy leaves the following:

1. Omissions
2. Insertions
3. Substitutions
4. Reversals
5. Teacher-supplied words
6. Repetitions

Authorities (including the authors of commercial IRIs) agree on the first five but remain split on the issue of repetitions. Some studies indicate that counting them lends validity to the scoring criteria developed by Emmett Betts, who created the first IRIs (McKenna, 1983). Others argue that repetitions are healthy signs of comprehension monitoring and, in any case, involve no departure from the printed text. Perhaps the best advice is to adopt the policy recommended by the instrument a teacher is actually using, since it has probably been field tested using that guideline.

The second question is whether to consider the semantic acceptability of a miscue in deciding whether to count it. When a child says *crimson* for *scarlet*, for example, it seems unjust to count it as an error. Unless the passage is from *Gone with the Wind*, the original meaning seems to have been preserved. Some authorities therefore recommend that the acceptability of any departure from the printed text be considered in arriving at an error tally. Our view is that the nature of miscues should be considered subjectively, as a source of potentially useful qualitative evidence, but that semantic acceptability should not be considered in arriving at an error count. There are several reasons for this policy. First, considering semantic acceptability is subjective; different examiners are likely to arrive at different tallies. Second, such a policy is time consuming; IRIs require a fair amount of time to administer and interpret, as it is, without compounding matters unnecessarily. Third, counting semantically acceptable miscues correct would invalidate the Betts scoring criteria, and although alternate criteria are offered by IRI authors, these certainly do not enjoy the research validation of those recommended by Betts.

Applying Scoring Criteria

At the end of the examiner's copy of each passage are criteria for judging the child's performance. Separate criteria pertain to comprehension and oral accuracy. Simple charts make it possible to arrive at rapid judgments, so that a teacher can decide which passage to administer next. These charts represent the error tallies and are tied to percentage criteria. Although authors differ about which criteria lead to the best estimates of reading levels, the most enduring are those suggested by Emmett Betts (see Table 3.1).

The Betts criteria are somewhat strict. Keep in mind that if more lenient criteria were used, the resulting estimate of a child's instructional level might be higher. Note also that the conjunction (*and* versus *or*) is critically important in Table 3.1. For example, for a passage to be judged on a child's independent reading level, the criteria for both comprehension *and* word recognition would need to be met. On the other hand, if either criterion for the frustration level is met, the passage is assumed to be at the frustration level. Later in this chapter we reexamine how these criteria are applied.

GUIDELINES FOR INTERPRETING THE RESULTS OF AN IRI

The following guidelines may be useful for estimating a child's independent, instructional, and frustration level after the IRI has been given.

1. Classify the student's performance on each passage given as independent, instructional, or frustration level. You might find it convenient to use the abbreviations *IND*, *INST*, and *FRUS* for this purpose. Use the lower level of word-recognition accuracy and comprehension, unless you are convinced to the contrary, for reasons that are apparent during the testing. Borderline results may cloud the picture, but that is a natural consequence of IRI assessment.

Examples:

Word recognition	Comprehension	Overall
IND	IND	IND
INST	INST	INST
FRUS	FRUS	FRUS
IND	INST	INST
INST	IND	INST
FRUS	IND	FRUS
INST	FRUS	FRUS

2. Estimate the independent level to be the highest level at which the overall judgment is IND.

3. Estimate the instructional level to be the highest level at which the overall judgment is INST.

4. Estimate the frustration level to be the lowest level at which the overall judgment is FRUS.

Example 1

Passage	Word recognition	Comprehension	Overall
PP	IND	IND	IND
P	INST	INST	INST
1	FRUS	FRUS	FRUS

Independent level: PP
Instructional level: P
Frustration level: 1

Example 2

Passage	Word recognition	Comprehension	Overall
PP	IND	IND	IND
P	IND	INST	INST
1	INST	INST	INST
2	INST	FRUS	FRUS

Independent level: PP
Instructional level: 1
Frustration level: 2

Example 3

Passage	Word recognition	Comprehension	Overall
2	IND	INST	INST
3	IND	IND	IND
4	IND	INST	INST
5	INST	FRUS	FRUS

Independent level: 3
Instructional level: 4
Frustration level: 5

Example 4

Passage	Word recognition	Comprehension	Overall
PP	INST	IND	INST
P	INST	INST	INST
1	FRUS	FRUS	FRUS

Independent level: Not Determined
Instructional level: P
Frustration level: 1

MISCUE ANALYSIS

Considering the nature of miscues can sometimes lead to (1) insights about how reading is developing, and (2) indications of the kind of instruction a child needs. Looking for trends within and across passages is a subjective process, one that is informed by experience. Research can help too, and becoming knowledgeable about some of the major findings from studies of miscue analysis is useful. Here are just a few:

1. About half of first graders' miscues are omissions.
2. As children mature, substitutions become more common.
3. Initially, substitutions may amount to mere guesses, often with a word beginning with the same letter.
4. Substitutions gradually become more sophisticated, bearing greater phonic resemblance to the actual word.
5. Substitutions begin as real words (for beginning readers) but often become nonwords (i.e., phonic approximations).
6. Insertions are always rare (10% or less of all miscues).
7. Letter reversals (such as *was* for *saw*) are common in first grade but typically disappear during second grade.
8. Reliance on context is heaviest for beginning readers and older poor readers.
9. Repetitions can be a mark of comprehension monitoring—that is, of a reader's attempt to make print make sense.

10. Word-perfect reading does not always mean good comprehension.
11. Miscues made on passages at the frustration level can give a misleading view of a child's ability to use context.

Form 3.4 (p. 71) is a worksheet that can be used to examine children's miscues. Basically, we take each substitution and ask ourselves questions about it. First, we ask whether the miscue was graphically similar to the text word at the beginning (B), middle (M), or end (E) of the word. Next we ask whether the word is syntactically similar to the text word, or whether it was the same part of speech as the text word. Then we ask whether the word has a similar meaning to the text word. For this, we use a fairly liberal criterion: whether the substitution would force the child to go back and correct the meaning. Thus a word can make sense, even if it is not a synonym for the text word. Finally, we ask whether the word was self-corrected. We expect children to monitor their reading, and if a miscue does not make sense, we expect a child to notice and at least attempt to correct it. If a miscue does not make sense and the child does not attempt to correct it, it is likely that the child is not monitoring the reading for sense.

In the example given in Figure 3.1, taken from a first grader reading a preprimer passage at his frustration level, six of the seven miscues were graphically similar in the first position, two were syntactically similar, and one was semantically similar to the text word. This pattern suggests (1) that the child is relying on the first letter to identify words (because of the predominance of correct first letters), and (2) that the child is not using context to support or monitor word identification (since few of the words are syntactically or semantically acceptable). This pattern is especially troublesome, since the passage had a clear predictable pattern.

Text says	Child says	Graphically similar?			Syntactically similar?	Semantically similar?	Self-corrected?
		B	M	E			
lost	like	√			√		
inside	in	√			√	√	
looked	lood	√		√			
was	w–	√					
he	him	√			√	√	
under	your			√			
same	school	√					
pony	horse				√	√	

FIGURE 3.1. Sample miscue analysis.

RUNNING RECORDS*

Running records are coded notations of text reading, used as a vehicle for error analysis. After coding the student's reading, the errors are evaluated to determine the type of error or the reason for the error. Although used widely in classrooms today, running records were originally used as a daily assessment procedure in Reading Recovery lessons (Clay, 1993b). Running records share several similarities with informal reading inventories and the Reading Miscue Inventory (Goodman, Watson, & Burke, 1987). However, running records can be generated from any text, not only prepared text.

Functions of Running Records

Teachers and researchers can use all three assessments as authentic process measures of children's reading. In this case, *authentic* means that the measure duplicates reading that the child is likely to be doing in a classroom or independently. The one-on-one setting required for these measures may contribute to increased focus by some readers or performance anxiety for others. The student is asked to read aloud, and the examiner records the examinee's reading of the text using a coding system. This procedure enables the researcher or teacher to get a "snapshot" of the reader engaged in the reading process, rather than the product evaluation obtained with commercially produced theme tests or standardized reading tests.

Errors are analyzed in relation to the reader's use of the semantic, syntactic, and graphic cues, called "meaning, syntactic, and visual (graphophonic) cueing systems" by Clay (1993a). Although the examiner may ask a few comprehension questions after the reading, the error analysis constitutes the primary evaluation of meaningful reading. This information may be used to make immediate teaching decisions or at a later time to develop a plan of instruction.

Teachers who use leveled texts in reading instruction can use running records to track progress over time. By *leveled* texts we mean any texts that increase in difficulty along a gradient that is sensitive to characteristics that reflect reading challenges. Teachers can use running records over time to demonstrate children's increasing competencies with increasingly difficult texts. Running records provide evidence of children's developing knowledge of the reading process (see examples in Figures 3.2, 3.3, and 3.4).

Taking a Running Record

Texts

Two advantages of running records are the ease and flexibility of administration. The coding format of running records enables teachers to use them without a typescript.

*This section was written by Katherine A. Dougherty Stahl.

FIGURE 3.2. Running record taken at the beginning of the year.

FIGURE 3.3. Running record taken near midyear.

FIGURE 3.4. Running record at the end of the year.

However, because a typescript is not used, the coding of a running record is slightly more complex than the coding system employed for informal reading inventories.

Text length is not dictated, but generally a sample should have between 100 and 200 words. This length enables teachers to conduct running records with a wide variety of texts. Running records can be taken more frequently than a miscue analysis or an informal reading inventory because of the ease and adaptability of the measure to an authentic setting in which a variety of materials are in use. Clay (1993a, 1993b) recommends that running records be administered using any texts that children can read with 90–95% accuracy. Typically, authentic texts are used. "Little books" that contain complete, cohesive stories or informational text that has been leveled using qualitative criteria (Peterson, 1991; Rhodes, 1981) are often selected as benchmark texts for systematic assessment.

Recording the Reading

Competence in recording running records requires time and practice. Clay (2000) advises beginners to practice tracking running records with average readers first. The fluency of good readers and the complex error patterns of struggling readers may be difficult for a novice to record. It is a good idea for teachers to practice making running records with texts that are overly familiar to them. Although the examiner sits next to the child and looks at the text with him or her, it is less of a juggling act if the examiner has prior experience with the text and its challenges. Clay (2000, p. 6) advises teachers to practice making running records until the teacher feels comfortable and can get a "true account" of student reading with "any text, any time."

A teacher sets the stage for making a running record by asking a child to read to him or her and informing the child that he or she will be writing down some notes. For assessment purposes, the text should be completely unfamiliar to the child; the examiner gives a brief introduction to the story and then asks the child to read. In an instructional setting, the selected book would more likely be a book previously introduced by the teacher and perhaps read once or twice the preceding day. For instructional decision making, children should be able to read a text at between 90 and 95% accuracy. This level enables the child to maintain fluent reading, but also enables the teacher to see what material challenges the child and how the child solves any difficulties with text.

Coding the Reading

Coding becomes easier with time and practice. The ability to code becomes refined with each running record made on a child. It is okay to ask a child to hesitate before starting a new page if the examiner needs to catch up. While learning how to make running records, focus on recording the child's reading; you can go back later and record the text that was omitted or substituted. Among the variety of codes used to record errors, we use Clay's (1993a, 2000). Standard coding procedures are important so that teachers can share information about a child. Coding can be done on a blank piece of paper, index card, or running record sheet. The book *Rosie's Walk*, by Pat Hutchins (1968), is used to demonstrate the coding system.

1. Mark every word read correctly with a check. Make lines of checks correpond to lines of text. Clay uses a solid line to indicate page breaks.

Rosie the hen went for a walk	√√√√√√
Across the yard	√√√
Around the pond	√√√
Over the haystack	√√√

2. Record an incorrect response with the text under it. Each substitution is scored as an error.

Rosie the hen went for a walk	√√ chicken √√√√ hen
Across the yard	Around√√ Across
Around the pond	√√√
Over the haystack	√√ hay haystack

3. Record an omission with a dash over the omitted word. Each omission is scored as an error.

Rosie the hen went for a walk	√ — — √√√√ the hen
Across the yard	√√√
Around the pond	√√√
Over the haystack	√√√

4. Record insertions by writing the word on top and putting a dash beneath. Each insertion is scored as an error.

Rosie the hen went for a walk	√√√√√√long √ —
Across the yard	√√√
Around the pond	√√fish √ —
Over the haystack	√√√

5. A self-correction occurs when a child has made an error and then corrects it. This self-correction is usually evidence that a child is cross-checking one set of cues against another (Johnston, 2000). A self-correction is recorded by using the letters *SC* and is *not* considered an error.

Rosie the hen went for a walk	√√ <u>chicken/SC</u> √√√√ hen
Across the yard	<u>Around/SC</u> √√√ Across
Around the pond	√√√
Over the haystack	√√√

6. A repetition is recorded with a line above the repeated segment of text but is *not* scored as an error. Repetitions may be demonstrations that a child is sorting out a point of some confusion, either because something did not make sense or was a difficult word or to gain fluency and meaning (Clay, 2000; Johnston, 2000). A numerical superscript may be used to show multiple repetitions.

Rosie the hen went for a walk	$\overline{√√}$√√√√
Across the yard	$\overline{√R^2}$ √√
Around the pond	$\overline{Across/SC √√R}$
Over the haystack	√√√

7. If a child hesitates for longer than 5 seconds because he or she has made an error and does not know how to correct it, or if the child stops and makes no attempts, he or she is told the word. This pause is coded with a *T* (for *told*) on the bottom and scored as an error.

Rosie the hen went for a walk	√√√√√√
Across the yard	<u>In</u>　√√ Across/T
Around the pond	—　√√ Around/T
Over the haystack	√√√

8. If a child asks (A) for help, the teacher responds, "Try something" and waits 3–5 seconds for an attempt before telling the child the correct word. This strategy enables the teacher to observe what problem-solving strategies the child is likely to use when facing challenges in text.

Rosie the hen went for a walk	√√√√√√
Across the yard	— /A/ — √√ Across/ /T
Around the pond	— /A/Across √√ Around/ /T
Over the haystack	√√√

9. Sometimes a child loses his or her place or goes off on a tangent that is far re-moved from the text. In such a case, the teacher should say "Try that again" (TTA), and indicate the line, paragraph, or page where the child should restart. Record by putting brackets around the faulty section of reading and code *TTA*. The entire section is only coded as one error.

Rosie the hen went for a walk	[√√√wanted to get away] went for a walk TTA √√√√√
Across the yard	√√√
Around the pond	√√√
Over the haystack	√√√

10. Other behaviors may be noted but not scored. Pausing, sounding out parts of the word, finger pointing, unusually fast or slow reading rates, and word-by-word reading should be noted on the running record and considered in the analysis but not included in quantitative scoring. If there are alternative ways of scoring responses, one would usually choose the method that gives the few-est possible errors. According to Clay's (1993a) system, with the exception of proper names, repeated errors are scored as errors each time. For example, if a child substitutes *will* for *would* multiple times, each counts as a separate error. However, it only counts once if a child substitutes *Joey* for *Jerry* throughout a story.

Table 3.2 provides a review of the scoring of errors in a running record.

TABLE 3.2. Scoring of Errors in a Running Record

Scored errors	Non-error behaviors
Substitutions	Self-corrections
Omissions	Repetitions
Insertions	Hesitations
Told the word or told to "try that again"	Ignored punctuation
Repeated errors	

Analysis and Interpretation of the Running Record

Quantifying the Running Record

The accuracy rate, error rate, and self-correction rate are calculated. First, the number of running words (RW) in the text (excluding the title), the number of errors (E), and the number of self-corrections (SC) are counted. The accuracy rate is the percentage of words read correctly, or $100 - (E/RW \times 100)$. We prefer the use of an accuracy rate rather than an error rate. An accuracy rate allows one to see the positive skills that readers have instead of focusing on the errors they make. This rate relates to the independent, instructional, and frustration levels described earlier. The error ratio is the ratio of errors to running words (E/RW). According to Clay (2000), error rates lower than 1:10 provide the best opportunities for observing children interacting with text. Students who have error rates higher than 1:9 with the text selection may be too frustrated to demonstrate their typical reading processes.

The self-correction ratio is the ratio of self-corrections to the total of errors and self-corrections (SC/E + SC). Self-corrections may indicate the degree to which a reader is monitoring his or her reading or using multiple cueing systems to process text. Self-corrections can provide an important window into the reader's thinking. Which errors does the reader think need fixing? Some readers fix errors that interrupt meaningful reading. Other readers are more in tune to the visual system and only correct errors that don't look right. Typically, if readers have a low error ratio, they are able to use multiple sources of information to self-monitor. However, as error rates become higher, they may neglect information that they would normally be able to use to monitor and adjust their reading.

Miscue Analysis

Typically the miscue analysis of an IRI or the Reading Miscue Inventory (Goodman, Watson, & Burke 1987) are done on a separate worksheet. However, a running record worksheet usually includes columns for the miscue analysis. When an error is made, write the letters *MSV* (i.e., meaning, structure, visual) in the error column and circle the letters that indicate the source of information most likely used by the child up to the point of error. Miscues are analyzed by asking a series of questions about the miscues and any self-corrections. The questions may be asked about acceptability at the passage level, sentence level, partial sentence level, and the word level. The question areas include:

- *Meaning (M)*. Did the reader choose a substitution or phrasing that makes sense in the passage or sentence or part of the sentence?
- *Structure cues (S)*. Did the reading sound like language that follows a grammatical form? (The grammatical form may be a dialect form used by the reader.) Did the reader follow the structure of the text? (Sometimes the reader continues with the earlier pattern in a predictable text, even when the structure of the text has changed.)

◆ *Visual.* Did the child read a word that has graphic similarity or sound similarity to the word in the text? Was the graphophonic system being used?

◆ *Self-correction column (write the letters* MSV). What cueing systems did the reader use to fix the error?

Interpretation of Errors and Self-Corrections

The pattern of errors and self-corrections provides important insights into a child's developing awareness of the reading process. Do the child's errors reflect that he or she is reading for meaning or simply sounding out the words? Does the child's awareness of the graphophonic system extend to scanning the entire word and chunking, or is he or she limited to saying the first sound and making a wild guess? A brief summary of observations and interpretations can be included on the running record sheet. The teacher who can observe these patterns in a written format possesses a powerful guide to instruction. Lesson plans for a child or small group of children should be based on behaviors represented in the running records.

Memories of even the most experienced, capable reading teachers are not always accurate. Observing by listening without recording may make it difficult to detect patterns of errors. Furthermore, undocumented observations cannot be shared or used to trace changes over time. In a period of time when teacher accountability is becoming increasingly important in the lowest grade levels, running records can be an effective tool for documenting student progress.

One measure that has adapted the procedures for making running records but given them the structure of an informal reading inventory is the Developmental Reading Assessment (DRA; Beaver, 2001; for a similar test, see Rigby, 2001). This measure uses a set of leveled texts, similar to those used in running records, but provides a single text for each level. It also provides a printed version of the text, similar to an IRI, so that a teacher not trained in giving running records can administer the test. It does contain guidelines and a rubric for judging recall. Comprehension questions are used only to prompt recall, not as the primary means of judging comprehension. Functionally, the DRA works like an informal reading inventory but uses leveled texts. The leveled texts may resemble more closely the little books that children use in their classrooms.

ESTIMATING A CHILD'S LISTENING LEVEL

The listening level is conventionally defined as the highest passage at which comprehension of the passage read aloud to the child is at least 75%. Generally, the teacher first estimates the frustration level from the passages administered and then selects the next-higher passage to administer on a listening basis. Both the passage and the questions are read aloud to the child. As with the reading passages, the teacher may need to administer more than one listening passage, either above or below the starting point, in order to determine the listening level.

Knowing a child's listening level can be useful in discerning whether comprehension difficulties are the result of decoding problems. In the following example, the listening level of this fourth grader is fourth grade, whereas the instructional level is only second grade. The teacher might justifiably conclude that this child's low reading level is primarily the result of inadequate word-recognition skills.

Example 1

Passage	Word recognition	Comprehension	Overall	Listening
1	IND	IND	IND	
2	INST	IND	INST	
3	FRUS	INST	FRUS	
4				80%

Independent level: 1
Instructional level: 2
Frustration level: 3
Listening level: 4

On the other hand, consider a hypothetical second grader whose listening level is no higher than the instructional level. In this case, the teacher has first administered the second-grade passage on a listening basis. This task was clearly too difficult, however, so the teacher readministered the first-grade passage and then the primer passage, this time reading them to the child. (An alternate form at these levels might have been used.)

Example 2

Passage	Word recognition	Comprehension	Overall	Listening
PP	IND	IND	IND	
P	INST	INST	INST	80%
1	FRUS	INST	FRUS	60%
2				50%

Independent level: PP
Instructional level: P
Frustration level: 1
Listening level: P

For this student, it would be incorrect to conclude that merely improving decoding ability would lead to a substantial gain in reading level. More must be done. This student will require work in comprehension strategies and perhaps oral language development in order to make good progress.

ISSUES CONCERNING IRIs

IRIs are one of the best tools available for estimating reading levels. However, a number of issues surround their structure and use. The questions that follow continue to provoke debate, and authorities undoubtedly will continue to differ.

1. *Which question types should be included?* Studies have shown that different question sets covering the same passage can lead to very different interpretations of a child's comprehension. Field testing of the questions that are actually chosen for use can help, but there are no commonly accepted guidelines for question selection.

2. *How high should the word lists extend?* As a general rule, the higher the grade level, the less sure we can be that the words on a particular list are representative of that grade level. This uncertainty arises from the fact that the number of words in use by older children multiplies dramatically and is difficult to sample. Word lists past the primary grades become increasingly suspect.

3. *Are the questions dependent on having read the passage?* Sometimes children can answer questions on the basis of prior knowledge rather than having understood the content of a passage. Ideally, each question should only be answerable after having read the passage, but it is difficult for test developers to predict what a child might or might not know. We explore this issue further in Chapter 7.

4. *Which scoring criteria should be used?* Through the years, debate has centered on the best criteria for use in interpreting IRI results. Johns (2001) argues that alternatives to the Betts criteria have proved unsatisfactory, and indeed they have. As long as we view the criteria as guidelines that can be overruled by teacher judgment, this issue will remain in perspective.

5. *Which readability levels should be represented?* As with word lists, the higher the passage, the more difficult it is to assert that a given passage represents a particular grade level. The difference, for example, between a sixth- and a seventh-grade passage is less than the difference between a second- and a third-grade passage. Again, we rely on field testing to assure an ordered sequence of passage difficulty, but the higher the passage, the greater the likelihood that anomalous results might occur. For example, if a child has more prior knowledge of the topic discussed in the sixth-grade passage than the topic in the fifth-grade passage, it might appear from the IRI that the child comprehends better at the sixth-grade level than at the fifth-grade level. Teachers must not be discouraged by anomalies of this kind, but they do need to interpret such results subjectively. Of course, anomalies are less likely to occur in the lower grades, where differences in difficulty level are clearer.

6. *How long should the passages be?* The passages on some IRIs gradually increase in length as grade level increases, on the rationale that fluency and attention span enable the student to handle longer samples of text. Authors of other instruments have elected to maintain the same length, except perhaps for the simplest passage, so that it is easier to apply scoring criteria and to compare a child's performance across passages of different difficulty levels.

7. *Are IRIs sufficiently situated?* Because the experience of an IRI is so different from classroom activities, some have argued that IRI results may not be very predictive of what a child is likely to do in the classroom. According to this argument, it would be preferable to observe and interpret reading performance during day-to-day classroom activities. We contend, however, that the IRI reveals the child's proficiency under more favorable circumstances (one-on-one engagement with the teacher, few distractions) and is therefore more likely to display what the child is truly capable of than classroom activities.

8. *Should IRIs include pictures?* Including pictures might provide the child with clues that lessen the need to read carefully and comprehend. That is, pictures may threaten to inflate scores and lead us to overestimate a child's reading levels. On the other hand, pictures are very much a part of the reading children do, especially younger children. Is it reasonable to ask them to read passages without illustrations? Is a pictureless environment likely to be too unnatural? Authors of commercial IRIs have come down on either side of this issue.

9. *Should a number of teacher prompts lead to discontinuing a passage?* When a child pauses at a difficult word, the teacher steps in to keep the process moving. The more times a teacher supplies unfamiliar words, however, the less representative the results will be of the child's ability. In extreme cases, the passage is more akin to a listening than a reading experience. The teacher must judge when this line is crossed and either halt the administration or discount the results afterward.

10. *Should semantically acceptable miscues not be counted in word-recognition accuracy?* Many commercial IRIs provide dual systems of scoring, affording a choice to the teacher about whether to count all miscues or only those that depart from meaning. As we noted earlier in this chapter, considering the semantic acceptability of miscues has a number of drawbacks: (a) increased administration time, (b) unreliable scoring criteria, and (c) overly subjective standards for judging. Looking to semantic acceptability also hearkens back to a model of reading that has been repudiated by research. For all of these reasons, we discourage it.

11. *Should IRI passages be narrative or expository?* Research tells us that, other factors being equal, expository prose is more difficult to process and comprehend than narrative prose. Some IRI developers approach this problem by intermingling narrative and expository passages, so that both types are represented in the inventory. (As we noted in Chapter 2, this approach is also the one taken by developers of group achievement tests.) IRI authors who intersperse the two types rely on field testing to ensure a clear sequence of passage difficulty. An alternative approach is to separate expository and narrative passages into distinct strands. In the Qualitative Reading Inventory 3 (Leslie & Caldwell, 2001), for example, the teacher can choose, in advance, which passage type to present.

12. *Are questions of reliability and validity adequately addressed by IRI developers?* It is a concern that IRIs do not generally report reliability and validity evidence. Often their reliability is contingent on trust in the author rather than standardization. One study (Paris et al., in press) found different forms of one popular IRI to be so different that the authors needed to create their own scaling of the results. Teacher consumers of IRIs should examine, in advance, the evidence the authors provide of the psychometric properties of their instruments.

STEPS TO A SHORTENED IRI

An IRI can be given on an abbreviated basis by limiting the assessment to a single passage. For example, a second-grade teacher might wish to know which students are reading at or near grade level by the end of the year. By administering only the second-grade passage to each child, the teacher can tell whether it falls at a given child's instructional or independent level. Administering an IRI on this basis, of course, will not lead to estimates of the independent, instructional, and frustration levels. More than a single passage would be needed for that purpose.

In order to quickly categorize your students by administering on IRI on a shortened basis, we recommend the following steps:

1. Select the passage corresponding to your grade level. If you teach first grade and will be testing during the spring, use the grade-1 or First Reader passage.
2. Duplicate one copy of the examinee's version per child. (You'll need these for marking the coding and notes.)
3. Assess each child individually.
4. Begin by reading the "prior knowledge" questions, if any. Make a judgment call as to whether limited knowledge of the passage topic may prevent adequate comprehension. Usually, the topics are relatively commonplace, and background knowledge is not an issue. If prior knowledge is too limited, in your judgment, make a note of this absence.
5. Explain that you want the child to read a story aloud and give him or her the examinee's copy (the one containing only the passage and not the questions).
6. Code the miscues the child makes on the examiner's copy.
7. Use the scoring guide at the bottom of the examiner's copy to determine whether oral reading accuracy is at the independent, instructional, or frustration level.
8. If oral reading accuracy is at the frustration level, stop. Do not ask the questions; the passage is assumed to be at the frustration level.
9. If oral reading accuracy is above the frustration level, ask the comprehension questions.
10. Give full credit, partial credit, or no credit, at your discretion. Reword questions to make them clearer, if you wish, but stop short of prompting.
11. Use the scoring guide at the bottom of the examiner's copy to determine whether comprehension is at the independent, instructional, or frustration level.
12. Compare the results of oral accuracy and comprehension. The passage is judged to be at the lower of these two results. For example, if oral accuracy is independent and comprehension is instructional, the entire passage is judged to be instructional.
13. On your class roster, note each child's performance level on the passage. That is, was it at the child's independent, instructional, or frustration level?

USING IRIs IN PROJECT AND SCHOOL EVALUATION

IRIs tend to provide more reliable information about reading growth than group standardized measures. The fact that they are individually administered, and in a manner that is responsive to student performance, tends to produce valid results. Moreover, they can be administered much more flexibly than achievement tests, so that pre–post comparisons can be made with reasonable confidence.

Several options are available for project evaluation, depending on the questions project personnel are interested in answering. The two options presented here offer a wide variety of evaluation opportunities.

Option 1: Full Pre–Post Administration

In this option, IRI testing is done at the beginning and end of the project implementation. Our example is from Kashinkerry Elementary, a pre-K–5 school. We will assume that grades 1–5 have been involved in reading-related activities throughout the year. For grades 2–5, this reading activity includes one assessment in early fall and another in late spring. For first graders, however, the preassessment should be delayed until midyear so that more children will be capable of reading at least a preprimer passage.

Two methods can be used to interpret the data. The first approach is to convert IRI instructional reading levels into continuous grade-level terms by using the following standard equivalencies, used in studies conducted at the National Reading Research Center:

Below preprimer	=	1.0
Preprimer	=	1.3
Primer	=	1.6
1st reader	=	1.8
2nd grade	=	2.5
3rd grade	=	3.5
4th grade	=	4.5
5th grade	=	5.5
6th grade	=	6.5
7th grade	=	7.5
8th grade	=	8.5

The advantage of this method is that parametric statistics, both descriptive and inferential, can be computed. Hence growth can be plainly charted in terms of years gained. This indicator is far superior to the grade-equivalent scores produced through standardized achievement testing, because of the individual administration of the IRI and the fact that the data for children of differing chronological ages are not pooled, as they are in achievement testing.

The results for Kashinkerry are summarized in Table 3.3. (These results are for a real school, located in an inner-city area and serving predominantly high-risk children.) In grades 2–5, the average gain is in the vicinity of 1 year. Growth at grade 1 reflects only the half year since the January pretesting. Inferential statistics can be computed, if desired. In the case of Kashinkerry, growth at each grade was statistically significant ($p < .001$), and effect sizes (delta) ranged from .43 to .72. Such effects are considered moderately large and attest to the educational significance of reading growth at

TABLE 3.3. IRI Instructional Level Results for Kashinkerry Elementary

Grade	N	Instructional reading level					
		Fall		Spring		Mean gain in years
		M	SD	M	SD	
1	123	1.4	0.7	1.9	0.9	0.5
2	106	2.0	1.1	3.3	1.8	1.3
3	79	2.9	1.8	4.3	2.2	1.4
4	97	4.7	1.9	5.7	2.3	1.0
5	92	5.0	1.9	6.1	2.0	1.1

Kashinkerry. (Similar statistics might have been used to compare Kashinkerry with a contrast school in which project activities did not occur.)

A second method of data analysis is to represent the distribution of instructional reading levels at each grade and then, from these distributions, compute the proportion of children at each grade level who finished the school year reading at or above grade level. These results for Kashinkerry are presented in Table 3.4.

Option 2: Single-Passage Administration

In this approach, each child is given only one passage, the one at grade level. Only about 5 minutes per child are needed, compared with up to 20 minutes for a full IRI. (See the previous section for suggestions about how to administer an IRI in this way.) Although this approach does not reveal each child's instructional reading level, it can still be used to estimate the percentage of children who are reading at or above grade level versus the percentage who are reading below grade level.

Let's assume that Ms. Johnson, a third-grade teacher, administers the third-grade passage of an IRI to each child in the spring of the year. A child whose performance is judged to be instructional or independent on that passage is counted among those read-

TABLE 3.4. End-of-Year IRI Instructional Levels for Kashinkerry

Grade	None[a]	Preprimer	Primer	1st reader	2	3	4	5+
	Percentage of children at each level							
1	16	15	18	20	19	8	2	1
2	2	7	10	11	23	21	7	18
3	0	5	6	4	19	19	11	35
4	1	0	3	4	8	11	9	63
5	0	1	1	1	8	8	9	73

[a]No level could be determined.

**TABLE 3.5. IRI Results for Project
and Nonproject Students**

	Percentage of students reading below grade level	
Class	Fall	Spring
Project	72.3	30.3
Control	75.6	52.1

ing at or above grade level. A child whose performance falls below the criteria for the instructional level is counted among those children reading below grade level.

Let's further assume that Ms. Johnson's students have been involved in a reading-related project, whereas Mr. Williams's students, who are demographically similar, have not participated. Mr. Williams' class can be used as a control group by means of the IRI assessment. Table 3.5 presents a hypothetical comparison.

These results favor the class that took part in project activities, since fewer students were reading below grade level at year's end. These proportions can be compared statistically, if desired.

It should be noted that the teacher factor in this design has not been controlled. There is a possibility that Ms. Johnson's students might have produced similar results without benefit of the project. This possibility might have been countered by including more than one teacher in each group or by comparing two of Ms. Johnson's classes in successive years (such as the year before the project with the implementation year).

LIST OF COMMON INFORMAL READING INVENTORIES

Bader, L. A. (1997). *Bader reading and language inventory* (3rd ed.). Englewood Cliffs, NJ: Prentice Hall.

Burns, P. C. (1998). *Informal reading inventory: Preprimer to twelfth grade* (5th ed.). Boston: Houghton Mifflin.

Colvin, R. J., & Root, J. H. (1999). *Read: Reading evaluation-adult diagnosis: An informal inventory for assessing adult student reading needs and progress* (5th ed.). Syracuse, NY: Literacy Volunteers of America.

Flynt, E. S., & Cooter, R. B. (1999). *English–Español reading inventory for the classroom*. Englewood Cliffs, NJ: Prentice Hall.

Johns, J. (2001). *Basic reading inventory* (8th ed.). Dubuque, IA: Kendall-Hunt.

Leslie, L., & Caldwell, J. (2001). *Qualitative reading inventory 3*. Boston: Allyn & Bacon.

Shanker, J. L., & Ekwall, E. E. (1999). *Ekwall/Shanker reading inventory* (4th ed.). Boston: Allyn & Bacon.

Silvaroli, N. J., & Wheelock, W. (2000). *Classroom reading inventory* (9th ed.). New York: McGraw-Hill.

Stieglitz, E. L. (1997). *Stieglitz informal reading inventory* (2nd ed.). Boston: Allyn & Bacon.

Woods, M. L., & Moe, A. J. (1998). *Analytical reading inventory* (6th ed.). Englewood Cliffs, NJ: Prentice Hall.

FORM 3.1. Sample IRI passage, teacher version.

Togo

Togo is a small country in Africa, just north of the Equator. In area, it is about the same size as West Virginia. The people who live there produce coffee, cocoa, cotton, and other crops. The capital of Togo is called Lomé a city of about a half million.

Togo has three neighbors. To the east is the country of Benin, to the west is Ghana, and to the north is Burkina Faso. Togo's fourth border is the Atlantic Ocean.

The main language of Togo is French, but four African languages are also spoken. Most of the people in Togo belong to one of 37 tribes. Togo is an interesting place, filled with variety and life.

Comprehension Check

____ 1. Where is Togo? (Africa)

____ 2. Name a crop grown in Togo. (Accept coffee, cocoa, or cotton)

____ 3. What country is west of Togo? (Ghana)

____ 4. How many tribes live in Togo? (37)

____ 5. What is the main language of Togo? (French)

____ 6. If you were in Togo, you'd have to travel in what direction to reach the Atlantic Ocean? (south)

____ 7. Is Togo as big as the United States? Why? (No. Togo is only as big as one of the states in the United States)

____ 8. Do more people live in Togo or Lomé? Why? (Togo, since Lomé is entirely within Togo.)

____ 9. Do more people live in Togo or West Virginia? (Impossible to say. If the student ventures a guess, ask why. Give credit only for a logical idea.)

____ 10. Name a crop you think might be grown in Ghana or Benin.

(Accept coffee, cocoa, or cotton, since these two countries are probably similar to Togo. If the student suggests another crop, ask why. Give credit for a reasonable response, such as equatorial crops.)

Scoring Guide

INDEPENDENT LEVEL	**0–2**	Comprehension Errors	AND	**0–2**	Oral Errors
INSTRUCTIONAL LEVEL	**2.5–3**	Comprehension Errors	AND	**3–7**	Oral Errors
FRUSTRATION LEVEL	**5+**	Comprehension Errors	OR	**12+**	Oral Errors

Togo

Togo is a small country in Africa, just north of the Equator. In area, it is about the same size as West Virginia. The people who live there produce coffee, cocoa, cotton, and other crops. The capital of Togo is called Lomé, a city of about a half million.

Togo has three neighbors. To the east is the country of Benin, to the west is Ghana, and to the north is Burkina Faso. Togo's fourth border is the Atlantic Ocean.

The main language of Togo is French, but four African languages are also spoken. Most of the people in Togo belong to one of 37 tribes. Togo is an interesting place, filled with variety and life.

FORM 3.3. IRI summary form.

Student _____   Date _____

Examiner _____   Grade _____

Level	Word Lists	Word Recognition	Comprehension	Overall Judgment	Listening
PP					
P					
1					
2					
3					
4					
5					

Estimated Levels

Independent Level	
Instructional Level	
Frustration Level	
Listening Level	

FORM 3.4. Miscue analysis chart.

Text says	Child says	Graphically similar?			Syntactically similar?	Semantically similar?	Self-corrected?
		B	M	E			

4

Fluency

If fluency were once the "neglected reading skill" (Allington, 1983), it is no longer. There has been an increased interest in developing fluency, as indicated by the findings of the National Reading Panel on the effectiveness of guided oral reading approaches to developing comprehension (National Reading Panel, 2000) and by research (e.g., Kuhn & Stahl, 2003).

There are three components to fluency: Fluent reading should involve *accurate* and *automatic* word recognition, with appropriate *prosody* or inflection. Each component affects comprehension in its own way.

Obviously, if children cannot read the text relatively accurately, their comprehension will suffer. As noted in Chapter 3, the reading does not have to be word-perfect. A child can misread five words out of 100 (or 95% accuracy) and still be within the instructional range. With more instructional support, such as that found in some of the fluency-oriented approaches discussed at the end of this chapter, the child can read initially with less accuracy. However, word-recognition accuracy will continue to affect comprehension.

Automaticity is also important for comprehension. By *automaticity* we mean the ability to read words without conscious effort, as you are doing now. Unless we throw in a word in a crazy font, like `ketchup`, your reading proceeds without your having to think about the words; instead you continue to focus on comprehension. If a child reads accurately but has to sound out or stumble over every word, his or her comprehension also will suffer. People have just so much mental energy to devote to a cognitive task such as comprehension. If they have to put extra mental energy into decoding the words, that energy or focus will not be available for comprehension. We find that many struggling readers who have experienced successful remediation of their word-recognition skills often have difficulty with automaticity.

Prosody is the ability to read with some sort of inflection. When we read aloud, our voice goes up and down, depending on the part of the sentence we are reading. We tend to drop our voice (slightly, but perceptively) at the ends of sentences and raise our inflection at the end of questions. We see prosody as an indicator that children are understanding the parts of speech in a sentence—in essence, a low-level type of comprehension.

JUDGING ORAL FLUENCY

When we consider fluency, we are interested in all three components: accuracy, automaticity, and prosody. We can judge accuracy by applying the procedures of informal reading inventories, as discussed in Chapter 3. Automaticity is usually assessed using rate of reading. We provide guides for reading rates later in this chapter. Prosody is the most difficult of these components to assess. For example, in IRIs we have found that it is difficult to get agreement on whether readers left out periods or ran sentences together when reading. Judging whether a child uses inflection well can be even more difficult. A few years ago, a colleague of mine and I (Stahl) tried to use a number of scales to assess fluency, in general, and prosody, specifically. We could not achieve sufficient agreement on nearly all the scales we tried. The only scale that we could agree on sufficiently was the one developed for the National Assessment of Educational Progress (NAEP), below. This is a simple 4-point scale that can only give the broadest indication of a child's fluency, but it can be used easily. This scale can be used on any oral reading sample, either from an IRI or classroom reading. You can tape-record individual students to observe growth over time, or your whole class. Taped reading samples can be used for parent–teacher conferences and can be a powerful demonstration of a child's progress over time.

NAEP Rubrics

Table 4.1 shows the fluency scale used in the National Assessment of Educational Progress oral reading study, given as part of the 1992 NAEP (Pinnell, 1995). This study of children's ability to read aloud is scheduled to be redone based on data gathered in 2002. The scale also may be redone for this study.

  We have found this scale to be fairly easy to apply to a child's oral reading sample. To do so, tape a sample of the child's oral reading. Listen to the entire selection and give an overall rating, using the four levels described in Table 4.1. We strongly recommend that you meet with another person who is doing the same thing and that you try to establish interrater agreement before doing this on your own. Our experience is that interrater reliability is easy to establish on this scale, since it is straightforward—and it is an important part of the process.

  Table 4.2 shows the average numbers of words per minute and accuracy levels for fourth graders involved in the NAEP oral reading study. They should be used as guidelines of what to expect of children. Younger children might be expected to read somewhat more slowly, but the rates for children reading at Levels 3 and 4 seem appropriate for older children as well.

TABLE 4.1. The NAEP Oral Reading Fluency Scale

Level 4	Reads primarily in larger, meaningful phrase groups. Although some regressions, repetitions, and deviations from text may be present, these do not appear to detract from the overall structure of the story. Preservation of the author's syntax is consistent. Some or most of the story is read with expressive interpretation.
Level 3	Reads primarily in three- or four-word phrase groups. Some smaller groupings may be present. However, the majority of phrasing seems appropriate and preserves the syntax of the author. Little or no expressive interpretation is present.
Level 2	Reads primarily in two-word phrases with some three- or four-word groupings. Some word-by-word reading may be present. Word groupings may seem awkward and unrelated to larger context of sentence or passage.
Level 1	Reads primarily word-by-word. Occasional two-word or three-word phrases may occur, but these are infrequent and/or they do not preserve meaningful syntax.

Note. U.S. Department of Education, National Center for Education Statistics (1995, p. 15).

CURRICULUM BASED ASSESSMENTS

Another way of using oral reading to determine a child's achievement is through curriculum-based measurements (CBMs). This approach uses short passages, usually 100 words, taken from texts that are used in the child's class. The child is asked to read the passage and is judged on the basis of rate and accuracy. The procedures for developing and administering CBMs are presented in Table 4.3.

Hasbrouck and Tindal (1992) developed norms for CBMs that can be used for judging fluent oral reading using other materials. To use these norms, calculate the number of words correctly read per minute: (% accuracy × number of words × 60)/reading time in seconds. Hasbrouck and Tindal give the median score at the 25th percentile, the 50th percentile, and the 75th percentile (see Table 4.4). Compare the score you obtained to the scores on the table. Scores between the 25th and 75th percentiles would be considered roughly average; scores above or below would be considered as above or below av-

TABLE 4.2. Percent Accuracy and Words per Minute, by Fourth Graders' Oral

	Reading fluency			
	Nonfluent		Fluent	
	Fluency Level 1	Fluency Level 2	Fluency Level 3	Fluency Level 4
Percent accuracy	94	94	96	97
Words per minute	65	89	126	162

From U.S. Department of Education, National Center for Education Statistics (1995, p. 44).

TABLE 4.3. Curriculum-Based Measurement Procedures for Assessing and Scoring Oral Reading Fluency

Say to the student: *"When I say 'start,' begin reading aloud at the top of this page. Read across the page* [demonstrate by pointing]. *Try to read each word. If you come to a word you don't know, I'll tell it to you. Be sure to do your best reading. Are there any questions?"*

Say, *"Start."*

Follow along on your copy of the story, marking the words that are read incorrectly. If a student stops or struggles with a word for 3 seconds, tell the student the word and mark it as incorrect.

Place a vertical line after the last word read and thank the student.

The following guidelines determine which words are counted as correct:

1. *Words read correctly.* Words read correctly are those words that are pronounced correctly, given the reading context.
    a. The word *read* must be pronounced *reed*, not as *red*, when presented in the context of "He will read the book."
    b. Repetitions are not counted as incorrect.
    c. Self-corrections within 3 seconds are counted as correctly read words.
2. *Words read incorrectly.* The following types of errors are counted: (a) mispronunciations, (b) substitutions, and (c) omissions. Further, words not read within 3 seconds are counted as errors.
    a. *Mispronunciations* are words that are misread: *dog* for *dig.*
    b. *Substitutions* are words that are substituted for the stimulus word; this is often inferred by a one-to-one correspondence between word orders: *dog* for *cat.*
    c. *Omissions* are words skipped or not read; if a student skips an entire line, each word is counted as an error.
3. *Three-second rule.* If a student is struggling to pronounce a word or hesitates for 3 seconds, the student is told the word, and it is counted as an error.

Note. Adapted from Shinn (1989, pp. 239–240).). Copyright 1989 by The Guilford Press. Adapted by permission.

TABLE 4.4. Curriculum-Based Norms in Oral Reading Fluency for Grades 2–5 (Medians)

| | | WCPM | | | |
Grade	Percentile	Fall	Winter	Spring	SD of raw scores
2	75	82	106	124	39
	50	53	78	94	
	25	23	46	65	
3	75	107	123	142	39
	50	79	93	114	
	25	65	70	87	
4	75	125	133	143	37
	50	99	112	118	
	25	72	89	92	
5	75	126	143	151	35
	50	105	118	128	
	25	77	93	100	

Note. From Hasbrouck and Tindal (1992, p. 4). Copyright 1992 by the Council for Exceptional Children. Reprinted by permission.

erage. These are somewhat lower than the NAEP norms, listed in Table 4.4. The scores shown here reflect words correct per minute; the NAEP scores are based on rate alone, with accuracy accounted for separately. The NAEP norms, though a little higher than the Hasbrouck and Tindal norms, are roughly in the same ballpark. Use of either one is fine.

DYNAMIC INDICATORS
OF BASIC EARLY LITERACY SKILLS

Another approach to fluency assessment is the Dynamic Indicators of Basic Early Literacy Skills (DIBELS), developed at the University of Oregon. These assessments can be used to assess progress over time, since they can be given at different points in the school year.

The DIBELS assessments begin in kindergarten and progress to third grade. Unfortunately, DIBELS uses the term *fluency* to mean *proficiency*. Thus they speak of "fluency of letter recognition," and so forth. Our concern in this chapter is with oral reading fluency, so we focus on the DIBELS approach to its assessment at grade 2.

For each passage, the child is asked to read the passage aloud and is stopped after a minute. There are norms available from their website (*http://dibels.uoregon.edu/ index.php*). Since DIBELS were developed by a federal grant, the use of these materials and the website is free. Administration is easy and time-efficient. Again, they can be used individually to track a student's progress over time, or applied to an entire class. Sample materials are in Form 4.1 (pp. 82–84).

FLUENCY-ORIENTED APPROACHES

A rule in our clinical work is that children need to spend the majority of the time during tutoring reading connected text aloud; if beneficial, the tutor can read one page and the student, the next page, in alternating fashion. Repeated readings or any variation of fluency-oriented instruction can be employed. We find that repeated or assisted reading gives children the support they need to read increasingly difficult texts. Our research (Kuhn & Stahl, 2003) suggests that assigning children a passage to read repeatedly is not as effective as assisted reading, in which an adult actively models reading. In a clinic, repeated reading can be monitored closely. In the classroom, we prefer a more assisted reading model.

Several approaches to fluency development are described below. These approaches are most useful for children who already have good oral language comprehension but either poor or slow word-recognition abilities.

We suggest that you choose material that is relatively difficult for the child, though not beyond his or her level of comprehension—perhaps one level above his or her instructional level, but not so far above it that the child cannot cope. We have found that children can benefit from reading material with as low as 85% accuracy, if they are given adequate support.

A desired criterion for fluency is (1) reading a passage at 100 words per minute, with (2) zero or one insignificant errors and (3) adequate inflection.

Some suggested activities follow:

Echo Reading

In echo reading, the teacher reads a section of the text aloud. This section could be a sentence, a paragraph, or a longer passage. Students "echo" the section back, pointing to each word as they say it. This is a useful introduction to a difficult text.

Repeated Readings

Students read the same text repeatedly, until a desired level of fluency is attained. We use a specific procedure in the reading clinic, as follows:

1. Choose a passage to read that is slightly above the child's instructional level, but one that the child might be interested in reading. (This method may be used, with grade-level materials, for a child who is reading significantly below grade level.)

2. Take a 100-word excerpt from this passage. (You may use different lengths, but the math is more difficult!)

3. Have the child read the passage aloud, marking all his or her miscues. Tape-record and time the reading (using a stopwatch or watch with a sweep second hand). Mark the child's speed and error rate on a chart.

4. Review the child's miscues with him or her, using the tape or through discussion.

5. Have the child reread the passage, and mark his or her errors and time on the chart.

6. Have the child continue until a speed of 100 words per minute, with zero or one miscue, is achieved. If achieving this goal takes more than seven tries, you might want to try an easier passage. This process usually takes more than one session; chart each attempt.

7. Proceed to another section at the same level. When the child can read relatively fluently for the first time, select a more difficult passage.

An Alternate Approach

This instructional method can be used with small groups or an entire class as well as with an individual child. Take a book or passage and have child(ren) read orally for 3 minutes. At the end of 3 minutes, have the child(ren) mark the last word he or she read with a pencil. You might discuss words with which the child had problems. Then have the child(ren) reread the passage, again for 3 minutes. Have the child(ren) mark the last word read. He or she should have been able to read more in the second attempt. This procedure can be repeated a third time.

Tape Reading

The teacher records a longer passage or uses a commercially available tape. The student reads along with the tape until he or she can read the story comfortably and fluently. Then the student reads to the teacher, who judges whether or not the reading is adequate. Make sure that students are responsible for reading the text themselves. Too often these "read-along" opportunities turn into listening opportunities. Children who need fluency practice generally have good language abilities and do not benefit as much from listening as they do from reading practice. We cannot stress too strongly that *unless students are responsible for reading what they have practiced to an adult, taped reading is a waste of time.*

Partner Reading

Students choose partners and read an entire story, taking turns. Usually turn taking proceeds page by page, but partners can negotiate differently. During reading, one partner reads while the other monitors the reading and helps, if needed.

A related alternative to partner reading is paired repeated readings. Students divide themselves into pairs. The teacher selects short, interesting passages at the students' instructional or independent (98%+ accuracy) level. Each student reads his or her passage three times. The other student in the pair comments on how well it was read.

Still another alternative is a team effort in which partners or a group work together as problem solvers. The children work on a difficult text, sentence by sentence, striving together to understand the meaning of the text. In such a group, you might have three older children with reading problems working with a text that might be far too difficult for any one of them working alone. One child would read a sentence of the text, and the group would discuss any difficulties they might have with that sentence, such as difficulties with words, with the meaning, or with specific vocabulary. After the sentence is discussed, the student who read it now paraphrases the sentence. The next student reads the next sentence, and so it goes.

Choral Reading

Choral reading, which involves the simultaneous reading of a passage, can be done individually or in groups. . In classes, it is often fun to use the choral-reading format with poems. Anthologies of poems by authors such as Shel Silverstein and Jack Prelutsky are popular choices. In a choral-reading session it is important to monitor children's reading to ensure that *all* children are participating.

For individual work, choral reading can be applied to any passage, and can be done repeatedly. In repeated choral reading, the tutor might lower his or her voice with each repeated reading, thus phasing him- or herself out. (This approach used to be called the "neurological impress method" for reasons best forgotten.)

Plays and Reader's Theater

Plays are another approach to engaging children in reading practice. Having children practice parts is an excellent way of getting them to read text repeatedly, until they reach a desired level of fluency. One guideline: It may be the weakest readers who would benefit from this activity the most. Give them substantial parts, and then make sure they have adequate practice prior to performance.

Oral Recitation

The oral recitation lesson (Hoffman, 1987) format is an approach that combines a number of these procedures into a single lesson plan. An oral recitation lesson has two parts: A direct teaching phase and a mastery phase.

Direct Teaching

1. For a regular length story, the teacher begins by reading the entire story to the group. Then the teacher discusses the story as a whole, either using questions or developing a group story map.

2. Then the teacher rereads the story, either sentence by sentence or paragraph by paragraph (use your judgment), as students follow along in their books, after which students echo back the portion read. Teacher and students proceed through the story in this way.

3. The teacher divides the story into parts and assigns a section to each student. Students practice their assigned section and perform it for the group. As an alternative, students can choose their parts, based on interest.

4. Teacher and students proceed to the next story. You may assign worksheets, work on skills, and so on here.

Mastery Phase

Students practice stories covered in the direct teaching phase until they are able to read them with 99%+ accuracy and at a rate of at least 85 words per minute (or another acceptable level of fluency). This practice is done on their own. The teacher works with them when they feel they are ready.

Students progress more quickly through the direct teaching phase than the mastery phase, so that a child may be on a fifth story in the direct teaching phase but only have mastered the first three stories. Students engage in mastery work during independent work time, in place of some seat work.

Paired Reading

Paired reading, a program developed by Keith Topping (1987) in Scotland, is widely used in the United Kingdom and Canada. In paired reading, a more capable reader, usually an adult, works one-on-one with a struggling reader. A paired reading session begins with the tutor and child choosing a book together. The only selection requirement is that the book be of interest to the child. There should be no readability limits (although our experience is that children rarely choose material that is far too difficult). They begin by reading in unison, until the child signals the tutor, by touching the tutor or raising a hand or some other prearranged signal, when he or she wants to read solo. The solo reading continues until the child makes an error. The tutor provides the word, they repeat the sentence in unison, and the procedure begins again. (See Topping, 1987, for more details. A video is available from Filmwest Associates, 702-883-8090.)

Buddy Reading

Children with reading problems benefit from working with younger children as readers or tutors. Reading to younger students is a good way for children to practice their reading in a natural setting. Pick a book that might be interesting to younger children. It should be short, colorful, with few sentences on a page. The student practices the book until he or she feels comfortable. Then he or she reads the book to a younger child or to the class, to the benefit of both. In the case of older children who read at a very low level (e.g., a sixth grader reading at a first-grade level), allowing them to select books to read to kindergartners, say, is a practical way of allowing them to practice appropriate material while maintaining their self-esteem.

Tutoring a younger child is potentially a richer experience. As opposed to merely reading to a child, tutoring involves instructional interactions that can lead the tutor to greater awareness of the processes involved in learning to read. In a tutoring situation, we recommend the following steps:

1. *Choose a book at an appropriate level.* Prior to the tutoring session, the tutor (the older child with reading problems) chooses a book at an appropriate level for the tutee to read. Initially, this selection might be made with the help of the younger child's teacher. The tutor should read and practice the book to be used prior to the tutoring session.
2. *Make lesson plans and review them with the teacher.* The tutor should make lesson plans, including words that he or she needs to preteach. The teacher can review a rationale for teaching words. The lesson plans also might include a comprehension activity, writing activity, etc.
3. *Tutor the child.*
4. *Keep a journal about the tutoring experience.* A reflective journal can be used to discuss with the teacher how the session went, what worked, what did not work, etc.

In preparation for tutoring, students should be taught procedures for responding to oral reading errors, such as: If the tutee misreads a sentence, ask "Does that make sense?" If the child says no, then ask him or her to make a correction so that it does make sense. Every so often, also ask if the sentence makes sense when, in fact, it does. Otherwise, your question becomes a statement. If the child is unable to correct him- or herself or hesitates at a word (for over 5 seconds), just give the word to the child, then have him or her reread the entire sentence. Note the word that was missed and, *after the reading lesson is over*, provide extra help with that word. For example, the word can be added to a set of word cards and used in a paired drill.

Tutoring and reading to children can be done with middle school and high school children as well, provided transportation can be arranged. We suggest contacting an elementary school with an after-school program and working 1 or 2 days a week.

Closed-Captioned Television

According to research, children's word identification improves from watching closed-captioned television (Koskinen, Wilson, & Jensema, 1985). We are not sure how effective this "method" is, but it is relatively easy to suggest that children with reading problems watch TV with the captions on at home. It does not hurt and might help.

FORM 4.1. Sample materials from DIBELS.

Dynamic Indicators of Basic Early Literacy Skills™ 6th Ed.
University of Oregon
Second Grade – DIBELS Oral Reading Fluency

Name:_____   Teacher:_____

(continued)

DIBELS measures are free to download and use. See the website *http://dibels.uoregon.edu*. Reprinted by permission of Dr. Roland Good. The Summary of Decision Rules technical report is available at *http://dibels.uoregon.edu/techreports/ decision_rule_summary.pdf*. The description of readability analysis and standards is available at *http://dibels.uoregon.edu/ techreports/DORF_Readability.pdf*. Systemwide percentile ranks for DORF scores are available at *http://dibels.uoregon.edu/ techreports/DIBELS_Percentiles.pdf*. Relations to statewide reading assessment performance for Colorado are avaialble at *http:// dibels.uoregon.edu/techreports/shaw_csap_technical_report.pdf*. Relations to statewide reading assessment performance for Florida are available at *http://dibels.uoregon.edu/techreports/fcrr_fcat_report.pdf*.

<u>DIBELS Oral Reading Fluency</u>
Short Form Directions

Make sure you have reviewed the long form of the directions and have them available. Say these specific directions to the student:

Please read this (point) *out loud. If you get stuck, I will tell you the word so you can keep reading. When I say, "stop" I may ask you to tell me about what you read, so do your best reading. Start here* (point to the first word of the passage)*. Begin.*

Start your stopwatch when the student says the first word of the passage.

At the end of **1 minute**, place a bracket ( ]) after the last word provided by the student, stop and reset the stopwatch, and say,

Stop. (remove the passage)

If the student reads more than 10 words correct, proceed with the retell part. Say,

Please tell me all about what you just read. Try to tell me everything you can. Begin. Start your stopwatch after you say "begin".

The first time the student does not say anything for 3 seconds, say *"Try to tell me everything you can."* This prompt can be used only once.

If the student does not say anything or gets off track for 5 seconds, circle the total number of words in the student's retell and say, *"Stop."*

At the end of **1 minute**, circle the total number of words in the student's retell and say, *"Stop."*

(continued)

DORF Progress Monitoring 1

Riding the Bus to School

I ride a big yellow bus to school. I stand on the corner of our	15
street with my friends and we wait for the bus. My friend's	27
grandma waits with us. When it's raining, she holds an umbrella	38
to keep us dry. Sometimes when it's cold she brings us hot	50
chocolate.	51
I leave my house to walk to the bus stop after my parents go	65
to work. I watch the clock so I know when to leave. Sometimes	78
mom phones me from her office to remind me. Sometimes she	89
can't call, so I have to be sure to watch the time.	101
Our bus driver puts his flashing yellow lights on and then	112
stops right next to us. When he has stopped he turns the red	125
lights on so all the cars will stop. He makes sure we are all	139
sitting down before he starts to go. He watches out for us very	152
carefully.	153
My friends and I are the first ones to be picked up by the bus.	168
We like to sit right behind the bus driver and watch while he	181
picks up all the other kids. We know where everyone lives. By	193
the time we get to our school, the bus is almost full. Sometimes	206
the kids get noisy and the driver has to remind us to keep it	220
down. He says their noise makes it hard for him to concentrate	232
and drive safely. I am glad that our bus driver is so careful.	245

Retell: _____ Total: _____

```
0  1  2  3  4  5  6  7  8  9  10 11 12 13 14 15 16 17 18 19 20 21 22 23 24 25
26 27 28 29 30 31 32 33 34 35 36 37 38 39 40 41 42 43 44 45 46 47 48
49 50 51 52 53 54 55 56 57 58 59 60 61 62 63 64 65 66 67 68 69 70 71
72 73 74 75 76 77 78 79 80 81 82 83 84 85 86 87 88 89 90 91 92 93 94
```

5

Emergent Literacy

During the years prior to school, and into the primary grades as well, we expect to see the development of behaviors in young children that signal an adequate foundation for formal reading instruction. In order to monitor the development of these emerging literate behaviors, teachers can apply simple, informal assessment techniques.

What do we expect children to be able to master prior to formal reading instruction? At one time, children were expected to have mastered certain prerequisite perceptual skills before they began a formal reading program. These discretely conceptualized skills—such as auditory discrimination, visual discrimination, visual figure–ground— are now seen as relics of the past. Instead, we view the child as learning continuously about reading from the first exposure to print as an infant. This increasing knowledge of both print and oral language provides the foundation upon which success in reading is built.

Specifically, we examine some ways of assessing three of the major components of emergent literacy: concepts of print, alphabet recognition, and phonological awareness.

CONCEPT OF PRINT

It is easy to take for granted some of the conventions that surround how books are printed and how we read them. These conventions, or common understandings, have little or nothing to do with the processes of word recognition and comprehension. Instead, they are more basic than that, and we hope to see them developed long before formal reading instruction begins. Without them, children will be at a serious disadvantage and are sure to suffer frustration and confusion.

What are these concepts about print? As fluent readers, it has become second nature to us that when we hold a book the spine is on our left. But this is not an inevitable, "natural" state of affairs. For example, books in Arabic or Hebrew are read with the spine to the right. Moreover, when we read a line of print, we start from the left and progress toward the right. Again, however, this is an arbitrary convention, and readers of Arabic and Hebrew, among other languages, begin at the right of each line. Furthermore, when we encounter a page of print, we know from long experience that we must begin reading the uppermost line and proceed downward. Also we must understand that it is the letters and words that convey the message and not the illustrations. A young child's first inclination is to focus on the pictures, which are the only components of a page that seem to have any meaning. Finally, in order to read a line of print, we must know that the white spaces between letter clusters mark the boundaries between *words*. This particular convention is extremely useful in the process of word recognition: Imagine how much more laborious reading would be if words were printed without spaces between them.

None of these understandings comes automatically. Children must learn them either through direct instruction or extensive teacher modeling. It is important to assess children's knowledge of these concepts. The following procedure quickly provides a great deal of information through a single, nonthreatening, informal encounter.

As the child is seated at a table, place a picture book in front of him or her. Make sure that the book is not positioned in the traditional way. That is, don't place the book with the spine at the left and the front of the book uppermost. Ask the child to show you the front of the book. Then open the book to any page having both a picture and at least two lines of print. Ask the child where you would begin reading. Hopefully, the child will point to the left-most word of the top line. (Do not be surprised, however, if the child points to the illustration or to some vague area within the text.)

Next open the book to any page containing only a single line of print and place two blank index cards at either end of the line. Using both hands, slide the cards toward each other and say to the child, "I want you to push these cards together until only one word shows. Show me one word." Repeat the process, asking the child to show you one letter.

This entire procedure might last only a minute but can give you a great deal of useful data. Simply record the child's responses in a convenient checklist form, making sure to date your entries. Such a checklist might look like the one on Form 5.1 (p. 100). Rather than using a single checkmark, however, it is a good idea to write the date that a child has successfully demonstrated knowledge of a given concept and to write nothing if the child fails to demonstrate it.

A more comprehensive approach involves the book-handling guidlines presented in Form 5.2 (pp. 101–103).

Another approach to examining children's concept of print is through the use of a wordless picture book, which enables the teacher to examine the child's knowledge of how books work. Paris and Paris (2001) constructed a narrative comprehension assessment out of wordless picture books that consists of three parts: a "picture walk," story retelling, and prompted comprehension. To do this assessment, first choose a book that has a clear narrative that can be followed just by looking through the pictures. Paris and

Paris used *Robot-bot-bot* by Fernando Krahn, but there are any number of similar books that could be used. The picture walk evaluates how the child approaches the text and handles the book, the language he or she uses, and his or her general familiarity with literate and "book-like" language and conventions. A convenient form for evaluating the picture walk appears in Form 5.3 (p. 104).

The picture walk is an effective, informal way of observing the child's familiarity with books and literate language. Paris and Paris (2001) use the picture walk to evaluate five behaviors:

◆ *Book-handling skills*—or whether the child has a sense of the appropriate speed and order of reading, and whether pages are skipped or skimmed.

◆ *Engagement*—whether the child appeared engaged in the story, as indicated by appropriate affect, attention, interest, and effort.

◆ *Picture comments*—whether the child makes comments about the pictures, including descriptions of objects, characters, emotions, actions, and so on (refers to looking at pictures individually).

◆ *Storytelling comments*—whether the child makes comments that integrate information across pictures, indicating that he or she is using the pictures to create a coherent story. Comments might include narration, dialogue, or the use of storytelling language.

◆ *Comprehension strategies*—whether the child uses strategies that indicate monitoring of comprehension. These strategies can include looking back or looking ahead in order to make sense of something, self-correction of story elements or narrative, asking questions for understanding, or making predictions about the story.

Although there are scores given for each skill, this procedure is better used as an informal means of assessing children's familiarity with books. Used with an individual child, it can give insights into the child's knowledge of the function of books, his or her experience being read to, and his or her knowledge of book conventions. These are the five categories provided by Paris and Paris; however, we suggest that one also look at the use of literary language. For example, does the child begin with "Once upon a time . . . " and conclude with "The End"? Does the child use language that sounds like story language, or does the child tell the story in vernacular terms? These observations also can be useful.

The retelling is given immediately after the picture walk. It is a free retelling, in which the child is asked to retell as much of the story as possible. When the child has finished, the teacher can give a neutral prompt, asking the child if he or she remembers anything else about the story. The teacher should not point to specific pictures or ask specific questions about the story. During the retelling, the teacher should note what is said, possibly tape recording it later for transcription. The retelling is evaluated by the number of story grammar elements included; settings, characters, goal/initiating events, problem/episodes, solution, and resolution/ending. We have provided an evaluation chart in Form 5.4 (p. 105).

Again, this retelling can provide some information about the child's experience with narratives. Children who have a strong story sense, as evidenced by their use of story grammar elements in their retelling, are likely to do better in reading stories than children who lack such a sense. Further, the retelling should be evaluated for overall coherence. Is the child clearly telling a story, or is the child merely recalling bits and pieces of unrelated information? Children without a clear story sense will need additional practice in listening and responding to stories.

Paris and Paris (2001) provide a set of comprehension prompts. Although these prompts are specific to the story that Paris and Paris used, they might be useful in guiding recall for most stories. They are listed below, with directions.

Explicit questions

1. [Book closed, characters] Who are the characters in this story? (replacement words: *people*, *animals*)
2. [Book closed, setting] Where does this story happen? (replacement words: *setting*, *take place*)
3. [Open book to initiating event, usually the first page] What happens at this point in the story? Why is this an important part of the story?
4. [Open to problem] If you were telling someone this story, what would you say is going on now? Why did this happen?
5. [Go to ending] What happened here? Why does this happen?

Implicit questions

1. [Feelings] Tell me what the people are feeling in this picture. Why do you think so?
2. [Causal inference] Why do you think this happened?
3. [Go to page with people speaking] What do you think the people would be saying here? Why would they be saying that?
4. [Go to last page of the book] This is the last picture in the story. What do you think happens next? Why do you think so?
5. [Close the book, theme] In thinking about everything you learned after reading this book, what have you learned from this story?

Overall, this evaluation will give you a sense of the skills that precede being able to read with comprehension. The information from this set of assessments complements the word-level and print-concept measures discussed elsewhere in the chapter. Paris and Paris found that children's scores on the various measures improved through the grades. On the picture walk, the average kindergartner scored a little less than 7, the average first grader about 7, and the average second grader about 8. In the retelling, average scores improved from about 2 in kindergarten, to about 3 in first grade, to about 4–4.5 in second grade. These are guidelines, not absolute norms, since they were based on a small sample.

Although Paris and Paris (2001) conducted this assessment using wordless picture books (and we recommend that it be used that way), it can be adapted for use with storybooks that have a similar narrative line. The picture walk would be conducted in the same way as with a wordless picture book. After the picture walk, the teacher could read the book to the child, and the retelling would be based on that reading. This sequence would yield a measure of language comprehension.

Emergent Storybook Reading

Another approach to evaluating children's knowledge of storybooks is Sulzby's (1985) Emergent Storybook Reading scale. By observing emergent readers, she noted clear developmental trends in how children approach storybooks, moving from picture-governed attempts at reading to print-governed attempts, with the child finally moving toward near-accurate rendering of the text. Observing a child attempt to read a storybook can provide valuable insights into the child's knowledge about how books work and can provide direction when considering how to help the child develop the knowledge needed to handle print.

The Emergent Storybook Reading scale can be used in a formal or informal setting. In a formal setting, the teacher might take the child to the side, tell the child to pick a favorite book, and then ask the child to "read" the book. It is important that the child be familiar with the book, so that more mature behaviors can be seen. If the child protests that he or she cannot read, then tell him or her to "read as best you can" or "to pretend to read the book." You can encourage the child by making neutral comments, such as "What can I do to help? What do you want me to do? How will that help?" The scale also can be used informally while the teacher observes a child pretend-read in a natural setting. Either way, understanding the stages that children go through as they learn to handle books will inform the teacher's instruction, by indicating the "next step" in the emergent reading process.

Sulzby (1985) found that children appear to go through nine stages in their approach to storybook reading, as they move from emergent to formal reading levels. This nine-stage scale has been validated repeatedly in her work. For ease of administration, we have compressed the scale to the format shown in Form 5.5 (p. 106).

Picture-Governed Attempts

1. *Labeling and commenting.* In this stage, the child looks at each picture and provides a name or descriptor, such as "doggie," "horse," or "bed," or makes a comment, such as "Go to bed," "That's ugly," or "He's a monster." Sometimes these comments are accompanied by a gesture or by slapping the page. Typically, the speech is less mature than the speech used in other contexts and may represent a storybook reading routine used by parents. In this stage (and the following stage), each page is treated individually, and there are no attempts to link pictures to make a story.

2. *Following the action.* In this stage, children remark upon the action in each picture as if it were occurring in the present moment. Comments might be similar to "There he goes. He's gonna get that monkey." The verbs used are typically present tense, present-progressive tense, or "gonna." Again, there is no attempt to link pictures to make a story.

3. *Dialogue storytelling*. This stage is a transition between the "labeling and commenting" and "following the action" stages and the more mature storytelling seen later. It may contain elements of the earlier stages but also includes an attempt to bridge the pages, using dialogue between the adult and child. The "story" may seem disjointed, but a listener can perceive that the child is trying to make a story. Here is an actual example:

CHILD: The children are looking for—for the other children (*turns page*) for one more children. And (*pause*) they looked all over the place (*pause*) for that little children (*turns page*). He went off to the _____. (*Turns page.*) He writed a note to—to the king—and they, uh (*pause*).

ADULT: They wrote a note to the king and then—

CHILD: Then they would. Then the boy bring the note to the king, and then he said to bring it back to here. (*Turns page.*) And then the little girl got peanuts and threw them at everybody.

ADULT: —Oh —

CHILD: And they're making stuff. And that, and that.

ADULT: —Oh—

CHILD: Pushed her into the peanuts.

4. Monologue storytelling. At this point, the child is clearly telling a story and uses a storytelling intonation that takes the form of an extended monologue stretching across the pages. The child makes reference to the picture content, but the major emphasis is on a continuous story. Sulzby (1985, p. 468) provides an example of this type of storybook reading:

> "This is his house and he is going to sleep. He was reading a book and then after he was reading the book he saw pictures of the mountains up here. Here (*pause*) there's some pictures, here, and then he thought he was going exploring the mountains, he's going to, yeah, about the mountains and he thought I'm going to explore the mountains tomorrow. And then he asked his daddy . . . then he got out of the gate and he saw the mailman coming on the street. And then he went (*pause*) and then he went (*pause*) and then he said to him (*pointing to dog in picture*), Angus. Angus, 'cause that's his name, I know. After this we're gonna come to the mountains (*pause*) and then he got one of his, and then he stuck one flag in there and then this is gonna be his tree."

The story here is primitive, but there is a clear attempt to connect an ongoing plot across the different pages.

Print-Governed Attempts

5. *Print awareness*. This stage is a transition between the purely oral story, governed by picture interpretation, and reading. In this type of reenactment, the child inserts parts that sound like written language, either in intonation or in wording or in

both, into parts that sound like oral language. The story may depart from the actual story, but the pretend reading shows a clear sense of audience and a concern with coherence that is missing in the above excerpt. This type of reading also contains parts that are decontextualized or are specified well enough that they could be understood without the pictures. At his stage, the child may refuse to read a section because he or she does not know the words. This stage is similar to Biemiller's (1970) conceptualization of the refusal stage, in which the child knows that print carries the information in the text and knows that she or he cannot read the print. In earlier stages, children may refuse to read, but in this stage the refusal is based clearly on the belief that they need to know more about the print in order to read.

6. *Aspectual reading.* In this stage, the child often uses the patterns of the original story or those in similar books. The child may focus on particular words that he or she knows or may overrely on a particular pattern. One child in Sulzby's study went through the book and read, pointing, "a" "the" "Grandpa" "and," page after page. Other children focus their attention on sounding out individual words. Compared to the earlier stages, this may seem like a regression, but it is an important one. In this stage, the child is trying out new repertoires that will be integrated later on with story knowledge.

7. *Text-governed reading.* In this reading, the child is clearly trying to create a verbatim rendering of the text. Sulzby divides this stage into two parts—reading with strategies unbalanced and reading independently—but we have merged these because both informal reading inventories and running records made of children reading text are better approaches to assess children's use of strategies during text-governed reading. What is significant here is that the child is clearly reading the text, not the pictures, often using finger pointing. The child may skip unfamiliar words or insert nonsense words, but most of the words are text words, and the child is using a reading intonation.

This emergent reading scale can provide a great deal of information about a child's knowledge of how books work. If the child's "reading" does not fit clearly into one category or another, assume that the reading is in the lower of the two categories and instruct the child in the next-higher category. Thus, if the child's reading is between dialogue and monologue forms of storytelling, assume that the child is in the dialogue stage and prompt him or her to tell extended stories by asking for elaborations and clear the transitions between pages.

Concept of "Word"

An aspect of print concepts is the child's concept that a word is represented by the marks between the spaces. This is a crucial concept, since it enables children to learn about letters and words through exposure to print. Several studies have found that acquiring the word concept, as measured by accurate finger pointing, is an important marker on the child's road to reading proficiency. Ehri and Sweet (1991), Morris (1993), and Uhry (1999) suggest that children need to have some word knowledge and/or some phonological awareness before they are able to accurately finger point. Other studies have found that finger pointing seems to be a prerequisite for learning about words from text (Clay, 1993b).

The acquisition of the word concept in text, as indicated by finger pointing, is generally measured by having a child memorize a simple rhyme, such as nursery rhyme (e.g., *Bah, Bah, Black Sheep*) or a simple song (e.g., *I'm a Little Teapot*). After the rhyme is memorized, the child is asked to read it in a book, pointing to each word as it is spoken.

ALPHABETIC RECOGNITION

It is vital for young children to learn letter names if they are to become proficient readers. Why is this true? It is certainly possible to learn to recognize words by memorizing them as whole units. For example, children with no alphabet knowledge at all could learn to say *cat* whenever they encountered the word in print. But learning words in this way would exert crippling demands on memory, and it would ignore the alphabetic nature of our language. Specifically, there are two important reasons for teaching children letter names at an early age. First, fluent readers do not recognize words as whole units. Rather, they do so by identifying the component letters. This process occurs at an unconscious level, but research leaves no room for doubt. The second reason is that teachers must have some means of referring to the letters during instruction. Although it may be theoretically possible to learn the letters and not their names, this approach would hardly be practical.

Assessing alphabetic knowledge is best accomplished by presenting a child with letters, one at a time, and asking the child to say the name of each. Several questions arise about how best to implement this procedure.

1. *In what order should the letters be presented?* The best way to answer this question may be in the negative. That is, it is important only to avoid presenting the letters in alphabetical order. Doing so would provide the child with a built-in prompt that could lead to inaccurate results. Randomly ordering the letters is preferable.

2. *How should the letters be presented to the child?* Flashcards could be used, but remember that a teacher must have one hand free in order to record results. Another way is to present all of the letters on a single sheet of paper in a grid format. The teacher can then simply point to each letter with one hand and record the child's response on a separate copy of the grid, using the other hand. In this way, the entire assessment requires only one sheet of paper rather than a flashcard deck.

3. *Should capital letters or lower-case letters be assessed?* Because both forms of letters will be encountered continually in printed materials, both forms must be assessed. The random arrangement of letters on the grid should also randomize the appearance of each form. In other words, it would be a poor idea to put the capital and lower-case form of the same letter next to each other. Keep in mind that, for many letters, the upper- and lower-case forms are identical (or very nearly so). These letters include *c, k, o, p, s, u, v, w, x,* and *z.* It would be a waste of time to present children with both cases of these letters.

4. *What font should be used?* There is probably no answer to this question on which everyone would agree. However, common sense suggests that a font that is plain and free of seraphs (those extra, decorative marks, such as the short horizontal lines at the top and bottom of a capital *I*) would be less likely to mislead the child. A related issue concerns the letters *a* and *g*. The lower-case forms of these letters often occur in two very different formats, so that children need to be assessed on their knowledge of both. They may encounter a or *a*, g or *g*.

Addressing all of the issues that we have just discussed results in a one-page grid displaying all of the letters, most of them in both their upper- and lower-case forms, plus an extra lower-case form for the letters *a* and *g*. This means that alphabet assessment should tap children's knowledge of 44 symbols. Using such a grid as a method of recording a child's responses is a convenient means of record keeping. By using different markings for repeated assessments, a teacher can document growth in alphabetic recognition on a single sheet of paper over the course of many months. Form 5.6 (p. 107) presents such a grid.

PHONEMIC AWARENESS

It is vital that prereaders become aware of the sounds that comprise spoken words. *Phonemes*, the smallest sounds we hear in words, are the building blocks of our spoken language, and becoming aware of their presence is vital to later successful phonics instruction. It is important to understand, however, that phonemic awareness is not directly linked to phonics. In fact, it is not connected with written language in any direct way. A child may be phonemically aware and yet have no knowledge of the alphabet. Phonemic awareness is entirely an auditory matter.

The word *cat* contains three phonemes, each represented by a letter. Learning about how these letters represent phonemes is a matter of phonics. Becoming sensitive to their presence in spoken words is something far more basic. Phonemic awareness should develop prior to school entry or in kindergarten.

How can we tell if a child is aware of the component sounds of spoken words? How can we assess a child's phonemic awareness? Here are a few assessment formats that are regularly used to do so:

1. See if the child can identify words that rhyme.
2. Say three words to the child, two of which have a common phoneme, such as an initial sound (e.g., *dog, horse, duck*). Ask the child tell which of the three words does not belong with the other two.
3. Tell the child that you are going to say a word in your own "secret code." Then pronounce the word by saying each phoneme in succession. For example, say *cuh—ah—tuh*. The child must blend these sounds to form the word *cat*.
4. Provide the child with a common rime, such as *ake*. Ask the child to make a word by adding a sound to the beginning of *ake*. Provide an example or two first to make the task clear.

5. Say a common one-syllable word, such as *cake*. Ask the child to remove the beginning sound, so that the child says *ake*.

Notice that none of these formats involves the use of printed words or letters. Each one is entirely an oral activity, which is why such assessments can be done so readily with 4- and 5-year-olds. Phonemic awareness activities often have game-like formats, and a child's responses can provide a teacher with useful information about the extent of that child's phonemic awareness, even though the child is scarcely aware of being assessed.

Note that in the Stahl–Murray Test of Phonemic Awareness (reproduced later in this chapter in Form 5.7, pp. 108–109), several of these testing formats are incorporated in the same informal instrument. You may copy and use this assessment with your own students, if you like.

The research into phonemic awareness instruction is compelling. Findings clearly show that (1) children can be taught to become phonemically aware, and (2) there is a strong causal link between phonemic awareness and later phonics learning. This second finding makes perfect sense. After all, it is difficult to learn letter–sound correspondences if you are unable to hear the component sounds of a spoken word. A certain level of phonemic awareness is a prerequisite to successful phonics instruction.

The increased emphasis on phonemic awareness has led to the development of commercial assessment instruments. The Test of Phonemic Awareness (TOPA; Torgesen & Bryant, 1994) is one such instrument. It is individually administered and can take more than half an hour to give, however, so that its cost-effectiveness is an issue.

Finally, let's examine a minor issue of terminology. Some experts prefer the term *phonological* awareness to *phonemic* awareness. The former term is broader and includes not just speech phonemes but larger units of sound, such as rimes. For example, a teacher might ask a child to blend the following two sounds: *cuh* and *at*. The child would then say the word *cat*. Technically, such an assessment activity is not purely a matter of phonemic awareness. This is because the rime, *at*, is larger than a single phoneme. It is a chunk of sound comprising two phonemes. Working with rimes and other chunks of sound that are larger than a single phoneme has led some to use the broader phrase, *phonological awareness*. You are likely to encounter either phrase in the literature. It is a small but interesting distinction.

We have included two measures of phonological awareness. The first (Form 5.7, pp. 108–109) is a measure taken from Stahl and Murray (1994). This is a purely oral measure, validated by research. We did not include the full segmentation and deletion measures taken from the same study, however. Subsequent research has indicated that segmentation and deletion tasks *reflect* rather than *predict* a child's spelling knowledge. A mental experiment might illustrate this point. Try the following deletion task, taken from Rosner (1975). "Say *stale*" (do not look at the print). "Now say it again, but don't say /t/" (again, do not look at the print). Everyone with whom we've tried this experiment first makes a mental spelling and then manipulates the letters in order to delete the sound. It is possible to do this task purely auditorily, but our experience and research strongly suggest that children need to be spellers in order to delete phonemes. The same is true for total segmentation. If you need spelling knowledge to complete a task, then, not surprising, the task is highly correlated with other measures of word recognition. But it is not a useful task for diagnosing reading problems. Nevertheless, this task is included in many measures of phonological awareness, such as the C-TOPP (Comprehensive Test of Phonological Processing; Torgesen & Wagner, 1999). We feel that such measures should be interpreted carefully.

The second measure called Dictation for Phonological Awareness (Form 5.8, p. 110) is an adaptation of Hearing Sounds in Words, from the Observation Survey (Clay, 1993a). We include this instrument because invented spelling can be a useful way of evaluating phonological awareness. Although this dictation task includes both phonological awareness and alphabetic knowledge, it can be a useful supplement to a "pure" test of phonological awareness. Further, it can be given to small groups, as well as individually, thus making it an efficient screening tool.

In planning instruction, it is useful to assess different aspects of a child's phonemic awareness. For example, can the child blend individual phonemes into a word or separate the initial phoneme from a complete spoken word? The Test of Phonemic Awareness (Form 5.7, pp. 108–109) is a useful tool for providing information about progress in these components. It takes only about 2 minutes to administer.

WHAT TO DO WITH ASSESSMENT RESULTS?

Now that you have the results, what are you going to do with them? General guidelines for teaching children in the emergent literacy stage involves providing experience with books and book handling as well as direct instruction in the skills needed for the next stage. It is important that children develop a foundation in print concept and book handling, since that foundation is the basis for learning how to read connected text. Although we believe very strongly in decoding instruction, placing too much emphasis on decoding early on will lead to confusion later. Instead, we believe that a program for the early reader should involve a balance between word work and text experience. A typical program for children reading at the emergent level would involve experience with predictable books, general book handling, phonological awareness instruction, and word-recognition work. We offer suggestions in the following material.

Predictable Books

Predictable books are books that have a repetitive pattern. This pattern serves to support the child in learning print conventions (concept of word in text, finger pointing, left-to-right progression, and so on) and to provide what we call "booksuccess." Experiencing booksuccess is essential for children who have initially failed to learn to read, because it convinces them that they *can* learn to read.

Consider a book like *Brown Bear, Brown Bear, What Do You See?* (Martin, 1983). It is a simple pattern, with the pictures supporting the text. On one page is the pattern "[color animal], [color animal], what do you see?" (the animals include a brown bear, a goldfish, a red bird, etc.). These animals are pictured. On the following page is "I see a [color animal] looking at me." Thus, reading is propelled by the pattern, which provides an excellent opportunity to teach both directionality and finger pointing during the joint reading. It is easy to memorize the book, so that children can bring it home and demonstrate their "reading" skills to their parents.

Following the reading of a predictable book, the teacher can put some of the words on word cards and use these as the basis of word reading or word sorting lessons (see Chapter 6). Over the course of the child's program, the teacher works with progressively less predictable books. One metric for predictability is the Reading Recovery levels, now widely used to gauge book levels.

In addition to predictable books, we recommend that each session include some exposure to a nonpredictable storybook, used for comprehension. It is important for children with reading problems to develop the vocabulary and comprehension skills needed for success in the later grades, once word recognition is mastered. Facilitating the acquisition of these skills might involve an interactive reading session, wherein the teacher reads the book and asks questions or elicits a discussion about the story. Here one should be aware of the child's emergent reading level, as measured by the Sulzby scale. The teacher should try to nudge the child along the scale, so that the child is encouraged to work at the next-higher level, if possible.

Developing Phonological Awareness

Phonological awareness stems from the insight that words can be thought of as an ordered set of sounds. In normal development, this is learned through play or experimentation. For the child with reading problems, however, this experimentation needs to be directed through activities that encourage the child to think actively about sounds in words. Some of these activities are described in the following material.

Nursery Rhymes

Teaching common nursery rhymes should be part of every kindergarten class. We recommend that nursery rhymes be presented on charts, so that the child can learn basic print concepts as well as the rhyme. Rhymes can be chanted chorally by groups or memorized individually. Children should be encouraged to predict rhymes, write (or orally compose) another line in the rhyme, and so on.

Picture Sorting

Sorting pictures is an effective phonological awareness task. Teachers can gather pictures of objects that begin with the same sound, or, after children are proficient in beginning sounds, end with the same sound. For example, children can sort pictures that begin with the same beginning as *bear* or *mom*. Begin with sorting two sounds, then move to three sounds. This exercise can be integrated with letter work, so that after a letter has been taught, the child can sort pictures that begin with the new sound from pictures that begin with previously taught sounds.

Oddity Tasks

Tasks that require students to identify the "odd man out" from a set of words can also improve phonemic awareness. One might begin with rhyming words but progress to words that differ in beginning consonants, then final consonants. Words that differ in medial consonants can be used but may be too difficult at this level.

Stretch Sounding

Teach children to stretch a word out so that phoneme changes can clearly be heard. For example, *dog* might be stretched to *d-d-d-o-g-g-g-g*. This can be done by first modeling it, then having the students repeat what you have vocalized. Once students are proficient at stretching out words, try having them clap as they hear new sounds or place a token in a box. For example, if the word is *sad*, you would draw a row of three boxes. Students put a token into a box (moving from left to right, of course!) when they hear the phonemes change. This effective technique was introduced by the Russian psychologist Elkonin (1973).

Caution: We are using the term *phoneme* for clarity. Please do not teach it, or any other technical term, to students. Use *sound* instead, but be clear in your own mind what you mean.

Invented Spelling

Stretch sounding should serve as a natural bridge to invented spelling, since one must stretch a word out in order to spell it. Invented spelling appears to improve phonemic awareness, among other skills. This point is discussed more thoroughly in Chapter 6.

Tongue Twisters

Have students repeat a tongue twister (from Wallach & Wallach, 1979), first in a regular fashion, then separating onset and rime. For example, for the *h* sound, the tongue twister *Harry had a horrible headache and hated to hear Henry howl* might be separated out as *H-arry h-ad a h-orrible h-eadache and h-ated to h-ear H-arry h-owl.*

Adding Sounds

Take a common rime (-ear, -ake, -all, etc.) and have students add and subtract sounds. For example, one might start by saying, "If I have *ear* and I add /h/, what do I have now? Then, if I take away the /h/ and add /w/, what do I have?" And so forth. This can be done later, using words on the blackboard.

Deletion Tasks

Similar to those described in class, you might have students say *burn* without the *b*, *pink* without the *p*, and so forth. Rosner (1975), who invented this task, chooses words so that the result is a real word, but we do not employ this limitation—especially after the children get the hang of it.

The Troll

One might use a troll puppet (or any other type of puppet) and say that "the troll will only allow people whose name begins with [ends with, or has in it] the sound of ____ to cross the bridge." Then give names (from the class or outside) and have students determine whether the troll will let this person cross the bridge. If this task proves too difficult, begin with syllables, using the same type of activities. Begin with continuant consonants (*m, s, n, f, z, v*) and vowels, because these can be sounded by themselves. Save stop consonants (such as, *t, d, b, c*) until later.

Alphabetic Work

Although research is not clear as to whether a child needs to know the alphabet prior to learning to read, we recommend that children learn the names and sounds of letters. There is a clear progression in how children normally acquire alphabetic knowledge, at least in the United States. First, they learn the alphabet song. Then they learn to pick out letters from an array of letters in order. Then they learn individual letters. This process can be translated into an instructional sequence.

1. If a child does not know the alphabet song, teach it.
2. If a child knows the alphabet song, ask the child to pick out letters from a letter strip, using the song as a guide.
3. Teach the letters individually.

There are literally hundreds of approaches to teaching letters individually. We do not know how to distinguish among them. Many teachers use a "letter of the week" approach. Teaching one letter a week seems fine, although we would start with common consonants rather than *a*. We would also continually review all the letters taught, rather than allocating them to the backburner, in essence, at the end of each week. While teaching the letter of the week, we would emphasize the sound of the letter as well as the name. We would have the child cut out pictures of items that contain the letter from old magazines, do picture sorts (see above), do the troll activity using letters rather than sounds, and so on. We also would integrate writing into these lessons, since learning to write the letters provides writing practice as well as important reinforcement for the letter name.

Word Work

Finally, at this emergent stage, we feel that some word learning is useful. This activity might involve asking the children to pick out words that they want to learn or words from their storybooks, either predictable or not. These words can be printed on index cards to be practiced at home and in school. For older children, we have found that the "Three Strikes and You're Out" procedure, described in Chapter 4, works well. Recall that in this procedure the child reads the word cards. If a word is read correctly in three separate sessions, the word is "retired" or put into a "learned" pile. Word cards also can be used for word sorting (see Chapter 6). In using these sorts, we want the child to notice the features of words, not necessarily be able to spell those words.

We also want children to write using invented spelling. This "writing" might be a sentence or a story. In the typical classroom setting, the teacher might encourage the children to attempt to write daily about a topic of their choice. When time permits, a more structured approach might be used. In Reading Recovery (Clay, 1993a), for example, the teacher and student agree on a sentence and they work on writing the sentence together. On a practice page, the child writes what she or he can. If the child cannot write a word, the teacher may ask the child to write what is known on the practice page, with the teacher filling in what the child does not know, or use Elkonin boxes (see above) to break the word into sounds and add letters for the sounds that fit in the boxes. Again, the child can be encouraged to do this by him- or herself or with teacher assistance.

It is important to remember that we want to provide a foundation for the child so that later reading will be successful, while, at the same time, prepare the child quickly for formal reading instruction. For children at the emergent stage in first grade and beyond, we want to be time-efficient, so that we can get the children at this stage ready to work with their peers; often the children need to make more than a year's progress in a year's time. Indeed, they need to make "accelerated progress," in Clay's (1993a) words, learning more material than they ordinarily might in the same amount of time. Programs such as Reading Recovery are designed to help children make such progress and should be considered as potential learning resources for the child with reading problems at this level.

FORM 5.1. Checklist for concepts of print.

Concept	Date / /	Date / /	Date / /	Date / /	Date / /
Book orientation					
Left-right directionality					
Top-to-bottom progression					
Word boundaries					
Concept of letter					

FORM 5.2. Book-handling knowledge guidelines.

NAME: AGE: GRADE: DATE:

Before you begin, make sure that you are familiar with the test and the book you will be using. Make sure you select a book that has both pictures and a written story that includes the required punctuation marks. When you begin, be sure to make the child feel comfortable. If you quickly establish rapport, the results will be more valid. If a child shows mastery of a concept, check the provided space. If a child does not show mastery of a concept, leave the space blank or write what the child did.

Say: **I'm going to read you this story, but I want you to help me.**

1.   Test: For orientation of book.
     Pass the book to the child. Hold the book vertically by its outside edge,
     spine toward the child. Say:
     Show me the front of the book   Orientation of book

     Concept _____

2.   Test: For the concept that print, not pictures, carries the message.
     Turn to the first page of the story. Say:
     I'll read this story. You help me. Show me where to start reading.
     Where do I begin?   Print carries message

     Concept _____

     Read the page. Turn to the next page.

3.   Test: For directional understanding (left to right, return sweep). Say:
     Show me where to start.
     (If child goes back to the beginning of the book, turn back to the page under
     discussion and provide the next prompt.)
     Show me where to start on this page.
     Which way do I go? (Child should indicate left-to-right motion.)
     Where do I go after that? (Child should go to beginning of next line.)
                                          Directional understanding

     Concept _____

     Read the page.

(continued)

4. Test: For speech-to-print match/word-by-word pointing. Say:
   Point to it while I read it.

   Read the page slowly but fluently.   Speech-to-print match

   Concept _____

5. Test: For concept of first and last.

   Read the page. Say:
   Show me the first part of the story.
   Show me the last part of the story.   First and last (must have both)

   Concept _____

6. Test: A left page is read before a right page.
   Read text until you come to a page that has print on both left and right sides
   of the page. Then ask:
   Where do I start reading? Left page read before right

   Concept _____

7. Test: Punctuation.
   Read text, then point to period and ask:
   What is this for?   .   **Period recognition**

   Concept _____

   Point to comma and ask:
   What is this for?   ,   Comma recognition

   Concept _____

   Point to quotation marks and ask:
   What is this for?   " "   Quotation mark recognition

   Concept _____

8. Test: For speech-to-print match/word-by-word pointing. Say:
   Point to it while I read it.

   Read the page slowly but fluently.   Speech-to-print match

   Concept _____

(continued)

9. Test: Lower-case letters.
    Point to a capital letter. Say:
    Find a little letter, or a lower-case letter, like this.
    Demonstrate correct match if child does not succeed.
    Point to a different capital letter. Say:
    Find a little letter, or a lower-case letter, like this.   Lower-case letter

    Concept _____

10. Concept of letter, word, first and last letter, capital letter.
    Use two index cards or small pieces of paper that a child can slide easily.
    To start, lay the cards on the page, but leave all the print exposed. Open the
    cards between questions.

    Read the last page of the book, then say:

    I want you to push the cards across the story like this. Demonstrate how
    you can move the cards across the page, coming from opposite directions.
    **Now I want you to push the cards across the page so all you can see is
    just one letter.**

    Now show me two letters.

    Letter concept _____

    Now show me just one word.
    Now show me two words.

    Word Concept _____

    Take the cards again and show me the first letter of a word.

    Now show me the last letter of a word.   First and last _____

    Show me a capital or upper-case letter.   Capital letter _____

FORM 5.3. Picture walk scoring guidelines.

Picture walk element	Score description	Score
1. Book-handling skills: Orients book correctly, has sense of appropriate viewing speed and order; viewing errors include skipping pages, speeding through pages, etc.	Incorrectly handles book and makes more than two viewing errors.	0
	Makes one to two viewing errors.	1
	Handles book appropriately, making no viewing errors.	2
2. Engagement: Displays behavioral and emotional involvement during the picture walk, as indicated by attention, interest in book, affect, and effort.	Displays off-task behavior or negative comments.	0
	Displays quiet, sustained behavior.	1
	Shows several examples of attention, affect, interest, or effort (i.e., spontaneous comments).	2
3. Picture comments: Makes discrete comments about a picture, including descriptions of objects, characters, emotions, actions, and options, as well as character vocalizations.	Makes no picture comments.	0
	Makes one picture comment or verbalization.	1
	Makes two or more comments or verbalizations about specific pictures.	2
4. Storytelling comments: Makes comments that encompass several pictures, demonstrating an understanding that the pictures tell a coherent story—can include narration, dialogue, using book language, and storytelling voice	Makes no storytelling comments.	0
	Provides storytelling elements, but not consistently.	1
	Through narration or dialogue, connects story events and presents a coherent story line.	2
5. Comprehension strategies: Displays vocalizations or behaviors that show attempts at comprehension, such as self-correcting, looking back/ahead in book, asking questions for understanding, making predictions about story.	Demonstrates no comprehension strategies.	0
	Exhibits one instance of comprehension strategies.	1
	Demonstrates comprehension strategies at least two or more times.	2

FORM 5.4. Retelling evaluation guidelines.

Did the child include . . .	Yes/No
Setting	
Characters	
A goal or initiating event	
A problem faced by a character, or episodes involving that character	
A solution to the problem	
A clear ending	

FORM 5.5. Emergent Storybook Reading Scale (after Sulzby, 1985).

	Stage	Characteristics?	Notes
Picture governed	Labeling and commenting	1. Each page is treated as a separate unit. 2. Child either names or describes person/animal on each page or comments on it.	
	Following the action	1. Each page is treated as a separate unit. 2. Child describes the action on each page.	
	Storytelling in dialogue format	1. Child begins to make links between pages. 2. Overall, the listener can perceive a story, although it is disjointed. 3. Storytelling is in dialogue form, propelled by prompts from adult.	
	Storytelling in monologue format	1. Child bridges plot between pages. 2. Tends to take the form of a monologue.	
Print governed	Print awareness	1. Child may refuse to read based on lack of print knowledge. 2. Child points with finger.	
	Aspect-governed reading	1. Child inserts parts that sound like written language. 2. Child may overrely on sounding words out or only read words that are known.	
	Text-governed reading	1. Child attempts to render a verbatim reading of the print.	

FORM 5.6. Alphabet recognition chart.

B d x m v c

r s l f J z

G q e M R h

i L b A F g

H n j p T y

a g Q u N w

E k t o a I

D Y

FORM 5.7. Test of Phonemic Awareness.

Administration

For each subtest, give feedback only for practice words. Use additional examples if necessary. When the idea is clear, discontinue feedback and continue with test items.

I. Blending

Explain to the child: "I'm going to say some words in a secret code, spreading out the sounds until they come out one at a time. Guess what word I'm saying. For example, if I say h-a-m, you say *ham*." (For each item, pronounce the segments with as little additional vowel as possible.) If the child gives the correct answer, place a checkmark on the line. Leave incorrect answers blank.

Practice words: f-un; k-ing; s-o-me; p-u-t; s-e-n-d

1. Simple rime:

    m-a-p   _____

    t-e-n   _____

    s-e-t   _____

    d-i-d   _____

    sh-ee-p   _____

2. Cluster onset:

    f-l-a-t   _____

    c-r-a-ck   _____

    s-p-a-ce   _____

    p-l-ai-n   _____

    s-t-e-p   _____

3. Cluster rime:

    f-i-n-d   _____

    p-i-n-k   _____

    c-a-m-p   _____

    w-i-l-d   _____

    l-a-s-t   _____

    Blending _____ /15

    Mastery = 12/15

II. Isolation

Explain to the child: "This time I want you to listen for just one sound in a word. Tell me the sound you hear at the beginning of each word I say. For example, if I say *fix*, you say /f/."

Practice words: no (n); ship (sh); time (t); hot (h); jump (j)

1. Onset rime:

    food (f) _____

    came (k) _____

    side (s) _____

    pad (p) _____

    seal (s) _____

2. Cluster onset:

    flood (f) _____

    cross (k) _____

    speak (s) _____

    please (p) _____

    state (s) _____

(continued)

Adapted from Stahl and Murray (1994). Copyright 1994 by the American Psychological Association. Adapted by permission. From *Assessment for Reading Instruction* by Michael C. McKenna and Steven A. Stahl. Permission to photocopy this form is granted to purchasers of this book for personal use only (see copyright page for details).

Explain to the child: "Now I want you to listen and tell me the sound at the very end of each word I say. For example, if I say *watch*, you say /ch/."

Practice words: off (f); fish (sh); egg (g)

3. Simple rime

    room (m) _____

    not (t) _____

    gas (s) _____

    sled (d) _____

    cross (s) _____

    Isolation ____ / 20   Mastery 16/20

4. Cluster rime

    sand (d) _____

    junk (k) _____

    limp (p) _____

    build (d) _____

    best (t) _____

FORM 5.8. An adaptation of Hearing Sounds in Words (after Clay, 1993a).

Dictation for Phonological Awareness

After children are ready with their pencils and paper, say, "I'm going to read this story to you, and you are going to try to write it as best as you can." First read the story in a normal intonation, then read it word by word, so that the children are able to attempt to record each word.

1. The dog saw Sam. He crossed the road and ran into his arms. (39 phonemes)
2. I ate a big slice of cake with some ice cream at the party. (37 phonemes)
3. Dad went to his job at the mill. He is working late today. (39 phonemes)

1. Th e d o g s aw S a m. H e c r o ss ed th e r o a d a n d r a n
   1 2 3 4 5 6 7 8 9 10 11 12 13 14 15 16 17 18 19 20 21 22 23 24 25 26 27 28

   i n t o h i s a r m s
   29 30 31 32 33 34 35 36 37 38 39

Mastery = 31

2. I a te a b i g s l i ce o f c a ke w i th s o m e i ce c r ea m a t
   1 2 3 4 5 6 7 8 9 10 11 12 13 14 15 16 17 18 19 20 21 22 23 24 25 26 27 28 29 30

   th e p a r t y. (37)
   31 32 33 34 35 36 37

Mastery = 30

3. D a d w e n t t o h i s j o b a t th e m i ll. H e i s w o r k i ng
   1 2 3 4 5 6 7 8 9 10 11 12 13 14 15 16 17 18 19 20 21 22 23 24 25 26 27 28 29 39 31 32

   l a te t o d ay. (39)
   33 34 35 36 37 38 39

Mastery = 31

To score the dictation test, count as correct each phoneme (/th/, /s/ /aw/) appropriately represented. It is not necessary that the phoneme be spelled correctly, only that it is represented. Remember that our goal for this measure is phonological awareness. The scoring should be based on an 80% mastery criterion, so for sentence 1, 31 of the 39 phonemes should be correctly represented, even if they are misspelled.

6

Word Recognition and Spelling

Monitoring the development of word-recognition ability is one of the most important tasks of teachers in the primary grades and teachers of struggling readers in the upper grades. The broad area of word recognition is complex, however. There are many contributing skills to track, so it is important that teachers have a solid understanding of the skill areas underlying a student's ability to recognize words.

A useful way of organizing both assessment and instruction in this complex area is to divide it into four components: sight words, context usage, structural analysis, and phonics. Let's look at each one of these areas in turn.

SIGHT-WORD KNOWLEDGE

A sight word is any word that can be pronounced automatically, without conscious analysis. There is a tendency to confuse the notion of sight words with that of high-frequency words (such as *of*, *but*, *can*, etc.). It is true that all high-frequency words must eventually become sight words if a reader is to be fluent. However, a reader's sight vocabulary may well include many words that are of low frequency, such as his or her last name. Sight vocabularies therefore differ considerably from one student to the next, although every teacher hopes that they have many words in common.

In order to assess sight words, the teacher must begin with a target list. Primary teachers typically use the Dolch (1936) or Fry (1980) lists or some other compilation of high-frequency words. Next, the teacher must decide on an assessment format in order to gain knowledge about how many of these words each child can pronounce at sight.

One way—a very efficient one—is to assess children as a group. The format presented below is designed for such a group assessment. The children are presented with row after row of words, each row containing four words. In the first example, the teacher leads the children from one row to the next, instructing them to circle one of the words.

Example 1
Teacher says, "Circle *book*." Child sees row of four words.

pear   book   bolt   napkin

The time saved through group assessment is considerable, of course. However, the accuracy of the results maybe compromised, as it often is in group assessments. For example, a child who is familiar with the sound made by the letter *b* will be able to eliminate the first and fourth words of the sample item, even though the word *book* may not yet be a sight word for that child.

In contrast, consider the format presented in Example 2, designed for individual administration. In this case, the teacher shows the child a word and asks for a pronunciation. The words may be presented on flashcards, in list form, or even by means of computer.

Example 2
Teacher says, "Say this word." Child sees flashcard.

book

It is important that the teacher remember that the sight word is one that can be pronounced immediately, without analysis. If a student takes more than a second to produce the pronunciation or perceptibly "sounds it out," then that word cannot reasonably be judged a sight word.

It is easy to construct a sight-word inventory once you have decided on which target words to include. Many lists are available. Some include shorter, high-frequency word lists (e.g., the Dolch 220 or Fry lists of 300 and 600 "instant" words). Some are longer lists that include words of lower frequency. Form 6.1 (p. 130–136) presents Fry's list of 300 instant words in the form of a sight-word inventory. Form 6.2 (p. 137) displays Dolch's list of 220 words categorized by approximate level. You may prefer to construct a simple sight-word inventory on the basis of Dolch's words.

Regardless of the list you use, it is important to keep in mind that sight-word knowledge consists of individual words. That is to say, each word is a separate skill! Were you to administer a sight-word inventory, it would therefore make little sense to tally the number of words a child can pronounce at sight. Rather, each of the words represents a distinct skill, a word worth knowing in its own right.

CONTEXT USAGE

Children should be able to use context for two principal reasons. First, it may help them determine the identity of a word that is in their listening vocabulary but not yet in their sight vocabulary. Second, context may help them decide among multiple meanings of a particular word. If we read, for example, that "the clock had a broken minute hand," we would use context to determine that the word *hand* does not refer to the appendage at the end of one's arm.

Cloze Formats

There are many ways to assess context use, and there is little agreement on which is best. Here we give a brief overview of five formats based on the cloze procedure (a method of deleting information from prose and replacing it with blanks).

She bought a _____ dress.
She bought a b____ dress.
She bought a _ _ _ _ dress.
She bought a b _ _ _ dress.
She bought a b _ _ e dress.

These five formats are all based on the same sentence. They are arranged in order of difficulty (with the hardest format at the top), according to research. It is more difficult to supply a word when all of it is missing, as in the first sentence. A far easier format, by contrast, is represented by the last sentence, in which the first and last letters of the word have been provided. Cloze formats vary considerably, as can be seen by these examples, and represent a flexible means of ascertaining whether or not a student can use context in the course of reading.

Maze Formats

The maze procedure is a cousin to cloze assessment and provides children with multiple choices within sentence contexts. A maze exercise is similar to a true maze, in which only one route leads to success. Maze assessments are somewhat difficult to process by word, but they are easier to complete than cloze passages for primary-age children, because demands on spelling and fine motor development are less. Here's an example:

in.
He climbed a paper.
tree.

Pseudowords in Context

An interesting alternative is the use of pseudowords, as illustrated in the following sentence:

For a snack I peeled a zum.

Using a pseudoword in a sentence context that is carefully crafted to provide a strong hint is perhaps a more natural alternative to cloze and maze formats. After all, when we use context in real reading situations, we are targeting actual words, not blanks or three-word "pile-ups." If a child is presented with a sentence such as the one above, the teacher might ask what the child thinks a *zum* is. The child who answers, "It must be some kind of fruit," has clearly used context to reach this conclusion. Since *zum* is a pseudoword, context is the only source of knowledge available. Of course, other logical possibilities exist, and a good teacher is alert to creative responses.

Multiple-Meaning Words

An important use of context involves deciding which of two or more meanings a word has in a particular instance. Providing children with pairs of sentences, such as the following, could be helpful in assessing their ability to make these decisions:

> The box was open.
> The store was open.

Asking what the word *open* means in each sentence elicits one of the most important applications of context awareness.

STRUCTURAL ANALYSIS

Structural analysis, also known as *morphemic analysis*, refers to the act of breaking down words into units of meaning (e.g., prefixes, suffixes, root words, etc.). Children are required to use structural analysis from an early age, as when they differentiate singular from plural forms or past and present tenses of verbs. As the material they read becomes more complex, a greater array of affixes confronts them. The ability to take apart an unfamiliar word in order to get a clue to its meaning is of increasing importance. Even familiar words containing prefixes and/or suffixes are usually recognized by noting the affixes. This means that structural analysis is useful with both familiar and unfamiliar words.

Assessing Affix Knowledge

Assessing a child's proficiency in this area can be problematic. A simplistic approach would be to assess prefixes and suffixes as we assess vocabulary words. That is, if the child understands that the prefix *un-* means *not,*" then that knowledge can be tested the way we might test other vocabulary knowledge. For example, a teacher could simply inventory a child's ability to supply the meanings of familiar affixes. The problem with this approach, however, is that it does not, in any way, guarantee that the child could apply this knowledge of affixes to the words encountered in real reading.

Real Words

Another way might be to show the child a sentence containing a word that is subject to structural analysis (that is, a word that can be structurally analyzed). For example, let's say the child is shown this sentence:

The hot sun made the man uncomfortable.

The teacher asks the child what the word *uncomfortable* means, or perhaps how the man felt. If the child responds by saying that the man felt bad, or words to that effect, would the teacher be justified in assuming that the child used structural analysis? Perhaps, but the word *uncomfortable* is so common that it might well have already been a sight word for that particular child.

Coined Words

An alternative method of assessment would be to coin a few words and present them to children in sentence form. Consider the following sentences, for example:

The mailman likes our street because it is dogless.
The woman wore the dress because of its blueness.

The teacher then asks a child why the mailman likes this street and hopes to hear a response such as, "Because there are no dogs on it." When asked why the woman wore that particular dress, a child who has used structural analysis may well respond, "Because it was blue." These words cannot be sight words because the teacher has coined them. (As English users, we are permitted to coin words so long as we follow a few simple rules.) By the same token, context is of little use because of the nature of the sentences. It is only by using structural analysis that a child can respond appropriately.

Composing a few age-appropriate sentences containing coined words is easy to do, and it can provide a rapid method of monitoring the development of structural analysis ability.

Common prefixes and their meaning

un-	not	ir-	not	ex-	out
in-	not	il-	not	ante-	before
im-	not	a-	not	anti-	against
sub-	below	kilo-	1000	de-	away
super-	above	mega-	large	dis-	apart from
mono-	one	micro-	small	dis-	opposite
uni-	one	multi-	many	extra-	beyond
bi-	two	over-	above	fore-	in front of

di-	two	poly-	many	mal-	bad
tri-	three	prim-	first	magni-	large
quad-	four	proto-	first	medi-	middle
tetra-	four	sol-	along	mid-	middle
quint-	five	tele-	far	mis-	wrong
penta-	five	under-	below	neo-	new
hexa-	six	ab-	away from	omni-	all
septa-	seven	ad-	to	post-	after
oct-	eight	auto-	self	pre-	before
deca-	ten	bene-	good	pro-	forward
cent-	hundred	circ-	around	re-	again
ambi-	both	con-	with	trans-	across
semi-	half	com-	with	ultra-	beyond
hyper-	over	con-	against		

Common suffixes and their meaning

-less	without	-ness	state of	-ment	state
-er	more	-ous	like	-itis	disease
-est	most	-ish	like	-phobe	one who fears
-ette	small	-logy	study of		
-trix	woman	-ly	like		

Suffixes can be difficult to define. We recommend that suffixes be presented in words, rather than in isolation.

Essential Words

For older children, it is useful to know what they know about survival words. These are words that children (and adults) need to know to survive in the real world. For a young person, perhaps the most important words to know, to avoid embarrassment in public restrooms, are *Men* and *Women* (or *Gentlemen* and *Ladies*). We present a list of "Essential Words" not as a prescriptive but as a beginning. The first part of this list (Table 6.1) contains an older set of words; the next part (Table 6.2) is an updated version by Davis and McDaniel (1998). There may be others that are important in your town or for particular children. Use our list as a starting point.

PHONICS

Phonics refers to the ability to use letter–sound correspondences to derive the pronunciation of words. Good phonics assessments are nearly always individually administered, because the application of phonics skills requires that students produce pronunciations. Teachers obviously cannot monitor pronunciations in a group setting. Three phonics assessments are reviewed in this chapter.

TABLE 6.1. The Original Essential Vocabulary

adults only	flammable	noxious
antidote	found	nurse
beware	fragile	office
beware of the dog	gasoline	open
bus station	gate	out
bus stop	gentlemen	out of order
caution	handle with care	pedestrians prohibited
closed	hands off	poison
combustible	help	poisonous
condemned	high voltage	police (station)
contaminated	inflammable	post no bills
deep water	information	post office
dentist	instructions	posted
do not cross, use tunnel	keep away	private
do not crowd	keep closed at all times	private property
do not enter	keep off (the grass)	pull
do not inhale fumes	keep out	push
do not push	ladies	safety first
do not refreeze	live wires	shallow water
do not shove	lost	shelter
do not stand up	men	smoking prohibited
do not use near heat	next (window) (gate)	step down (up)
do not use near open flame	no admittance	taxi stand
doctor (Dr.)	no checks cashed	terms cash
don't walk	no credit	thin ice
down	no diving	this end up
dynamite	no dogs allowed	this side up
elevator	no dumping	up
emergency exit	no fires	use before [date]
employees only	no fishing	use in open air
entrance	no hunting	use other door
exit	no loitering	violators will be prosecuted
exit only	no minors	walk
explosives	no smoking	wanted
external use only	no spitting	warning
fallout shelter	no swimming	watch your step
fire escape	no touching	wet paint
fire extinguisher	no trespassing	women
first aid	not for internal use	

Informal Phonics Survey

The Informal Phonics Survey (Form 6.3, pp. 138–142) provides a convenient means of monitoring specific skill acquisition. The first subtest (Beginning Consonants and Two-Letter Consonant Clusters) presents children with individual letters or two-letter combinations and asks that they provide pronunciations. Some educators may object to such a task on the grounds that individual consonants cannot be pronounced without attaching a vowel sound. This may be true, but it is of very little importance, and taking such an objection too seriously deprives us of a valid means of assessing phonics knowledge. When children see the letter *b*, for example, the teacher should expect them to say something like *buh.* Consonant clusters that occur only at the ends of words, such as *rt*, are not included in this inventory. It is likely that children who are capable of pronouncing the combinations *dr* and *tr* at the beginning of a word will have little difficulty pronouncing the combinations *rd* and *rt* at the end of a word.

TABLE 6.2. Updated List of Essential Words

10 items or less	falling rock	pay cashier before pumping
30 days same as cash	fasten seat belt	pay here
911	fax machine	pedestrian crossing
airbags	fire alarm	polluted area
alternate route	fire exit	prepare to stop
aluminum cans only	flagger ahead	quiet please
ambulance	flush	radiation hazard
asbestos hazard	for help dial	radioactive materials
automatic	form line here	radioactive waste
biohazard	handicapped parking	railroad crossing
biohazardous waste	hard hat area	read directions before using
blasting zone	harmful	recyclable
bomb threat	hazard	recycle
breakable	hazardous	refrigerate
bridge ices before road	hazardous area	restricted area
buckle up	hazardous chemicals	restrooms
bump	hazardous waste	resume safe speed
business route	help wanted	right of way
by-pass	hospital	right turn only
caffeine	ID required	road closed
cancerous	if swallowed, induce vomiting	school crossing
cash only	in case of fire	school zone
cellular phones prohibited	incinerate	service engine
chemicals	incinerator	self-service
children at play	infectious area	shake well
clearance	insert card (ATM)	shirt and shoes required
construction ahead	irritant	signature
consult physician before use	keep away from water	slippery when wet
danger	keep frozen	slow down
dangerous	keep out of reach of children	soft shoulders
deer crossing	keep refrigerated	speed limit
delay	kerosene	stairs (stairway)
deliveries	lifeguard on duty	stop ahead
detour	loading zone	subway
diesel fuel	makes wide turns	Surgeon General warning
directions	manager	take with food
dispose	may cause birth defects	teller machine
do not bend	may cause dizziness	through traffic
do not block intersection	may cause drowsiness	timecard
do not enter	microwave in use	time clock
do not get in eyes	microwave safe	tornado warning
do not ingest	minimum speed	tornado watch
do not mix	must be 21 years of age	tow away zone
do not take if allergic to . . .	no jet skis allowed	tow zone
do not take with milk	no left turn	toxic
do not use near water, fire, etc.	no littering	toxic waste
dosage	no outlet	turn off cellular phones
drive in	no pagers	turn signal
drive through	no parking	uneven shoulder
drive-up window	no pets	use only as directed
electrical hazard	no photographs permitted	ventilation required
Emergency Medical Services	no refunds	video camera in use
enter only	no returns	video monitor in use
escalator	no through traffic	watch for falling rocks
exact change (needed)	no turn on red	watch for trucks
exit only	no video cameras allowed	wear protective eye gear
expect delays	nonalcoholic	wear safety glasses
expiration	nontoxic	weight limit
expires (EXP)	nuclear waste	wide load
explosives	one way	wrong way
express line	order here	X-ray
evacuate	oxygen in use	yield

The vowel subtests use real words. On these subtests, children are scored correctly if they pronounce the vowel correctly, even if they do not correctly pronounce the consonants. For example, reading *sock* for *rock* on the short-vowel subtest is considered correct because the vowel was read correctly. It may be possible, although unlikely, that the child has mastered the vowels but needs work on consonants. The rule of silent *e* subtest is more difficult, since it seems to require that the child consciously apply the rule rather than simply read the words. Children who do not master this subtest, but can read vowel digraphs, often can often pick up the silent *e* rule quickly, since they have acquired the long-vowel concept.

Z-Test

A more advanced phonics assessment targets a child's ability to make analogies to known words based on familiar rimes. The Z-Test (Form 6.4, pp. 143–145) presents the child with the 34 most familiar rimes, using the same onset, in order to focus the child's attention on the rime itself. The result is a series of pseudowords, all beginning with the /z/ sound. Children who are familiar with the compare–contrast method of recognizing the spelling patterns that make up rimes will be able to pronounce most or all of these pseudowords. Students who are not proficient at making such comparisons will experience considerable difficulty. There are no norms or scoring criteria for interpreting the results of this test. Subjective judgment is required. On the other hand, pre- and postadministrations of this simple test will provide an enlightening indicator of improved decoding skills.

Test of Knowledge of Onsets

The Test of Knowledge of Onsets (Form 6.5, pp. 146–152) was developed by James W. Cunningham at the University of North Carolina and is one of the many public-domain instruments included in this book. It consists of two subtests; one targeting initial two-letter consonant blends, and one for consonant digraphs. In the first subtest, the student is shown two words for each item, such as *down* and *crown*. (See item 1.) The teacher pronounces the first word and asks the child to pronounce the second. The second word always begins with a two-letter consonant blend. By pronouncing the first word, the teacher has provided the child with the rime. It is up to the child to replace the onset of the word the teacher pronounces with the onset of the word the child must pronounce. A checkmark is placed in one of the three columns in the right-hand portion of the assessment form, depending on whether the child gives the whole word, just the onset, or just the rime correctly. If none of these is correct, no mark is made. The teacher is interested in those words for which the child has produced the correct onset and/or the entire word. Each of the two-letter blends is repeated three times throughout the assessment. You may wish to use the scoring grid to help identify which blends have been mastered and which will require additional work. For example, the blend *bl* occurs in items 11, 29, and 47. At the bottom of each column there is a fraction with a denominator of 3. The idea is to write in the numerator for each fraction—that is, the number of times the child correctly pronounced a specific blend (from 0 to 3).

The second subtest targets consonant digraphs. This is a shorter test because there are fewer digraphs to assess. Only five are targeted, and there are three words for each of them, as is the case in the first subtest. The administration is exactly the same. The chart at the end of this subtest is also used in the same way. Items 8, 9, and 10, for example, all contain the digraph *ch*.

The idea behind these instruments is not to produce a total score as an indicator of overall growth in this area. Rather, the usefulness of the assessment lies in its identification of specific blends and digraphs that the child has not yet mastered. The link between assessment and instruction is clear.

Developmental Test of Word Recognition

The Developmental Test of Word Recognition (Form 6.6, pp. 153–158) produces evidence in a variety of word-recognition developmental areas, including the child's concept of words and knowledge of initial and final consonant sounds, consonant blends, and vowel coding. The multiple-choice format is effective during individualized administration with youngsters, for the child need only point. The variety of subtests results in a useful profile for discerning deficit areas at an early point in development.

SPELLING

Since the pioneering work of Edmund Henderson (1981), Charles Read (1971), and Carol Chomsky (1979), educators have known that the invented spelling of young children follows a clear developmental pattern. As children learn about written words, their attempts at spelling reflect this growing sophistication of their knowledge of orthographic patterns. We will follow the stages outlined by Henderson as we examine this growth.

Emergent Spellings

Children's initial attempts at writing are generally nonalphabetic; sometimes these first attempts are pictures but are called "writing" by the child. Later attempts are scribbles, which, though illegible to an observer, can be "read" by the young writer. Harste, Burke, and Woodward (1982), working with children of different cultures in a university daycare center, found that their scribbles reflected the print to which they were exposed. Thus children from Arab families produce scribbles that resemble Arabic; children from Chinese families made scribbles that resembled Chinese, and so on. This correspondence suggests that scribbles represent an early understanding of the form of print.

When children learn letters, they incorporate those letters into their spelling. At first, these letter strings have nothing to do with the sounds in the word itself. So *bear* might be represented by *MSDF*.[*] The use of letters, rather than scribbles, suggests that

---

[*]We use all caps to note invented spelling, regardless of how a "word" was written.

(1) the child knows the convention that words must be made up of letters, and (2) knows at least some letters.

As children continue to learn letters and develop some phonological awareness, their spellings begin to reflect their emergent analysis of words. Children's spellings may consist only of a letter representing an initial or final sound, such as *J* for *jam* or *S* for *sun*. Sometimes a child at this stage may put down a letter representing a single sound and then add others, such as the girl we worked with who first put down an *f* for *fish* and then added additional letters—*FZTHSLT*—saying that "*f*-words were always long."

Children who can represent a sound in a word with a letter are developing rudimentary phonological awareness. Our research shows that such children nearly always use initial sounds to identify written words (Stahl & McKenna, 2001). Spelling development closely follows the development of word recognition (see Chapter 4) but lags a little behind, because spelling is a production task, and production tasks are more difficult than recognition tasks such as word recognition. This level, however, seems necessary for children to make sense out of the alphabetic system.

As children continue to analyze words in terms of phonological awareness as well as written word recognition, their spellings become increasingly complex. First they add final consonants, so that *bear* becomes *BR* or *hen* becomes *HN*. Often their spellings reflect the way they analyze the words as they are saying them. So blends such as *dr*, as in *dragon*, may be represented by *JR*, since that is how the child may hear it. Other blends may be represented by single consonants.

Letter-Name Spelling

Learning about vowels is the next large conceptual leap for children. Emergent spellings do not include vowels. The inclusion of vowel markers, whether correct or incorrect, represents the child's beginning knowledge of the alphabetic principle. In speech, spoken words fold consonants around the vowel, so that they are copronounced. A consonant is pronounced slightly differently with each vowel, but vowels are difficult to isolate within words. Children can be aware of consonants through sensitivity to articulatory gestures (Byrne, 1998); still, consonants are more difficult to isolate (Shankweiler & Liberman, 1972).

Children generally begin to include vowels in their spellings around grade 1. Whether this inclusion is due to instruction or experience with language is not clear, but the shift is an important one for children learning to read and spell. At this point, *bear* may be represented by *BAR*, with the child using the letter name to represent the long-vowel sound; similarly, *hen* may be spelled *HAN*.*

At the earlier points of this stage, children may use the letter name to represent a syllable—*GRL* and *LETR* are common—but most typical is the emergence of vowels. When a child consistently represents vowels in words, that child can be thought of as understanding the alphabetic principle.

---

*The substitution of *a* for short *e* may be due to a letter name. The sound of long *a* is really a diphthong of /ey/. When children want the short *e* sound, they find it in the sound of the letter name "a." Although this hypothesis seems to be a stretch, the substitution of short *a* for short *e*, and *i* for short *a* (/ay/), is common enough that it seems a plausible explanation.

Within-Word Pattern Spelling

The letter-name spelling stage represents acquisition of the alphabetic principle. The within-word pattern stage involves the learning of patterns that occur in written words. At this point, children (1) consistently spell words with short vowels correctly, (2) begin to show sensitivity to patterns in words, (3) make distinctions between long and short vowels, and (4) use long-vowel markers, although not always correctly. Thus *bake* might be *BAIK* but not *BAK*; *like* is spelled *LIKE*, not *LEIK*; *chart* is not spelled *CHRAT*. In addition, children use "ed" and "ing" endings and add preconsonantal nasals (i.e., the /n/ and /m/ in words such as *jump* and *hand*), which are the latest consonants to emerge.

This stage, which is usually achieved by the end of third or fourth grade, is characterized by a growing knowledge about spelling patterns and basic sound–symbol spelling conventions. Children's further growth in spelling moves from the purely sound–symbol level to the morphological level, as they master the basic orthographic patterns and move on to spelling–meaning relationships.

Syllable Juncture Spelling

The next stage represents children's knowledge of how syllables fit together. The most obvious marker is the consonant doubling rule; children during this stage develop consistency in spelling words that end with *ing* or *ed*, and in knowing when the consonants have to be doubled and when they do not (e.g., bat–batted vs. bait–baited). Children learn other conventions at this stage, such as the use if *y* or *le* at the end of words, but they may not consistently apply them.

This stage represents children's initial use of morphological knowledge to spell words. During this time period, children master *bound* morphemes, or morphemes that do not have their own meaning. The morphemes mastered also tend to function syntactic markers, such as tense or number (e.g., plural formed by adding *s* or *es*). Children usually go through this stage between grades 3 and 8.

Derivational Constancy Spelling

At this stage, the final one in Henderson's list, children learn to use semantic relationships between words, even words that are pronounced differently. Thus a child may use knowledge that words come from a common root to spell them conventionally. For example, children may use the relationships between words like *fantasy* and *fantastic* or *fantasize* or *inspire* and *inspiration* to help spell them conventionally.

We have included three spelling lists. The first one, the Elementary Qualitative Spelling Inventory (Bear et al., 2000; Form 6.7, pp. 159–162), is a developmental spelling list to capture children's growth from one stage to the next. A more finely grained analysis can be found in Ganske (2000). (The Qualitative Spelling Checklist [Form 6.8, p. 163] can be used interpret the results of the Elementary Qualitative Spelling Inventory. It can also be used to interpret the results of other spelling inventories as well as children's free writing samples, as discussed below.) The second scale, the Spelling

Skills Test (Form 6.9, p. 164), can be used to compare children's knowledge of phonics elements in spelling to their use of phonics elements in word recognition. The third list, the Morris–McCall Spelling List (Form 6.10, pp. 165–166), provides grade-level norms. All three instruments can be used to track growth over the year, though from somewhat different measurement perspectives.

Using the Qualitative Spelling Checklist to Observe Children's Writing

The Qualitative Spelling Checklist can be used as a general guide for observing children's writing, as well as used to evaluate a spelling inventory. Consider the pieces of children's early writing presented in Figure 6.1. (The first piece was written by Max Stahl; the remainder were taken from Chomsky, 1979.)

Max's writing, a caption to a drawing which reads "Danger! Bear! Help, please!," is an example of early letter-name writing. He is marking only the initial and final consonant sounds in his spelling. He would be at Stage 3 on the Qualitative Spelling Checklist. His writing is not using the left–right convention of English; instead, he is writing his words in vertical columns.

DR HP
BR PL
(Caption on Max's drawing)

TARWAN SWASALITLGRLE
AN DSHEWOTIDAFRE
      ND
OANDAY ALITLBOY
  KAMEBIHIIWOTAFREN
  UALIWOTIDAFENDTO
UALLESSBEFENDSOKY
(Story from first grader)

IV I CUD WISH ENEASING IT WOD BE TO MC
EVEREBODE LIV FOREVER
(First grader)

THIS IS A ROCKIT. THE LOONER MOJRAL IS ON THE
THERD DECK. IT'S A PEAS OF SIYINTIFIC EQUIPMENT.
THE NEXT PEAS OF SIYINTIFIC EQUIPMENT IS THE CMAND MOJRAL
(First grader)

FIGURE 6.1. Example of children's early writing.

The second piece, from a first grader, uses vowels, although not in every word (LITL, GRLE) and not always correctly.* Consonant blends and digraphs are used inconsistently (TAR, FEND, but SHE, FREN). We would estimate that this child was at Stage 4 or 5 (letter-name).

Although the third piece seems more advanced because of the use of spacing and the more sophisticated words (EVERYBODE, ENEASING), it would only rate a Stage 6. Short vowels are spelled correctly (WISH, IV, LIV), but long vowels are not (MC for *make*). The child is attempting longer words and the attempts are reasonable. This text is easy to read.

The fourth text probably includes spellings that were given to the child (EQUIP-MENT), but shows the sophistication of ideas possible in invented spelling. This child is using but confusing long vowels (LOONER, PEAS, SIYINTIFIC) but generally getting short vowels correct. We would rate this at Stage 7. The ideas, however, go far beyond the child's ability to spell, which is a prime reason for using invented spelling—at least in the draft stages—in the first place.

This discussion is only preliminary, the interested reader is referred to the books by Bear et al. (2000) and Ganske (2000) for more in-depth discussions of how spelling analysis can be used for planning instructional programs.

Spelling by Skill

We have developed the Spelling Skills Test (Form 6.9, p. 164), which might be useful in correlating children's knowledge of phonics conventions in reading and spelling. It is a developmental list, similar to that of the Qualitative Spelling Inventory, but evaluated by phonics elements and it is thus comparable to the Informal Phonics Survey (Form 6.3). The Spelling Skills Test is presented in the same way as other spelling inventories: first the teacher reads the word, then an example sentence, and repeats the word. The test can be administered either individually or in small groups. It is intended for children in grades K–2, but may be given to older struggling readers. As with the Informal Phonics Survey, mastery is considered 80% correct, review indicated to be 60–79%, with below 60% to indicate the need for systematic instruction.

This instrument provides another measure of phonics knowledge. We find that children use phonics knowledge in spelling after they are able to use it in word recognition, especially for long vowels which are more difficult to spell correctly because of the different possible variations (BOTE, DRIEV). The test also might be used as a screening for phonics knowledge. If a child can use an element such as short vowels in his or her spelling, it can be assumed that the child can use it in word recognition. If a child cannot use it in spelling, though, he or she may or may not be able to use it in reading words and further screening is needed.

---

*The text reads "There once was a little girl / And she wanted a friend / One day a little boy / Came by. Hi I want a friend / Well, I want a friend, too. / Well, let's be friends, Okay?"

TEACHING WORD RECOGNITION AND SPELLING

There could literally be a book written on techniques for teaching children to recognize words (and several of them have been written, such as those by Bear et al., 2000; Cunningham, 1999; Ganske, 2000). In this section, we highlight a few techniques that we use often in the clinic.

The first rule of clinical practice is to "find out what has been done before, and don't do it." This is truer in the area of word recognition than in any other area. A child with whom one of us worked as a teacher had come from another school and read at a preprimer level. He had worked very diligently and had reached a point where he was ready to use a particular phonics workbook for additional practice. In his then-current development, this would have been an easy review, for he had already mastered the material. However, because he had used that particular book in his previous school and had failed miserably with it, he recoiled and would not touch it. Perhaps this is an extreme example, but the principle holds. Do not use an approach that has failed in the past, whether or not it is appropriate, because it will not work now.

Numerous different approaches to teaching word recognition are currently available. Stahl, Duffy-Hester, and Stahl (1998) divide phonics instruction into traditional, constructivist-based, and spelling-based approaches. Hence, we briefly review synthetic phonics (a traditional approach), compare–contrast (a constructivist approach), and making words (Cunningham & Cunningham, 1992) and word sorts (Bear et al., 2000) (spelling-based approaches). We also describe "Three Strikes and You're Out," a method of building sight vocabulary.

Synthetic Phonics

The basic synthetic phonics approach begins with direct instruction of individual letter–sound correspondences. These then are practiced by reading words, first in lists and then in texts, often decodable texts. The hallmark of synthetic phonics is that children are taught to *blend* sounds together to make words, thus the instruction is *synthetic*. An example:

1. If the letter *e*, representing the short sound of *e*, is to be taught, the teacher might present the letter *e* on the blackboard or on a note card. The teacher might say, "This is the letter *e*. It says /e/."
2. Next, the teacher might write the word *pet* on the board or present three note cards with the letters *p e*, and *t* on them. (The use of note cards allows one to physically demonstrate blending.) The teacher would demonstrate the blending of the letters to make the word *pet* by running his or her finger under the letters (if the blackboard is used) or pushing the cards together.
3. Students would practice blending the word *pet* as a group.
4. The teacher would write or show a list of words, such as:

pen	bet	deck	mesh	then	peck	let
send	less	yet	fed	bent	shed	tell

The students would blend the words together, at first as a group and then individually.

5. Next the students would read a decodable text that contains words with the short sound of *e*.

6. We find that an especially effective follow-up, either later in the lesson or immediately following the reading of the decodable text, is to have children write short *e* words from dictation.

7. Following this lesson, the teacher might further follow up on the short sound of *e* by using a compare–contrast approach, practice on short *e* words with a partner, or practice with a computer program that provides practice on short *e* words.

Synthetic phonics is used in a number of commercial programs, but the basic lesson can be done quite easily. This foundational approach can be used to introduce patterns that the child has missed on the Informal Phonics Survey or on one of the other measures presented in this chapter.

Compare–Contrast Approaches to Phonics

In the compare–contrast approach, we are trying to teach children to compare new words to already known words. This method is used at the Benchmark School in Media, Pennsylvania (Gaskins et al., 1988; Gaskins, Ehri, Cress, O'Hara, & Donnelly, 1996). In synthetic phonics, teachers help children learn to sound out words; in the compare–contrast system, teachers help children learn how to use analogies to decode unknown words. Since adult learners use both types of knowledge, these approaches, in our view, are not mutually exclusive. Instead, we feel that, once children have acquired some sound–symbol knowledge, possibly through synthetic phonics instruction, they should learn to compare new words to already known words. Compare–contrast approaches are especially useful for decoding polysyllabic words, since that is where we use analogies the most.

The basic compare–contrast lesson consists of a dialogue aimed at helping the child internalize the process of identifying words by (1) identifying known words that resemble an unknown word, (2) seeing what is similar between the two, (3) using what is similar to make a tentative identification of the word, and (4) checking to make sure that the identified word makes sense in context. A simple version of a compare–contrast lesson follows:

1. Give students six slips of paper each. Have them print the following six words on the paper so that you can see them. These words become the students' key words.

black   hold   kind   play   rain   run

Now display words from the following group. Have each child find the word that looks most like the presented word. At a signal from you, have all the students display their "lookalike" word. Students should respond to questions such as, "Where are the two words alike? Where are they different?" Ask a volunteer to pronounce both words.

mind	crack	blind	hind	fold	lack	runt
pain	smack	hay	main	blast	slack	stack
gold	rind	bind	mold	tack	bay	bun
gain	gray	plain	raid	pray		

2. On the following day (or when you feel the students are ready), add three words to their key word list: *man, less, her*. Match these nine words to the following group.

clay	per	ban	lent	fan	bless	pan
led	press	sun	sold	sack	stain	

You can make up other words (with or without students' help) to add to any of these matching lists.

3. On the following day (or when you feel the students are ready), add six more words to their key word list: *be, sit, take, ten, will*. Students now have 15 words to match with word groups like the following:

flit	rut	scold	cop	crop	wit	span
bit	pop	top	train	lend	pack	hen
flake	plan	brain	spill	wig	bake	Ted
wake	Jill	stun	track	grain		

Optional evaluation procedure: Write the following 10 words on the board. Have students copy the words, and next to each word write the key word that looks most like each from their group of 15.

rack	gay	slit	sin	snake
grill	tan	mast	sip	crop

4. Students should have their 15 words on slips of paper, as previously described: *black, hold, kind, play, rain, run, man, less, her, be, sit, stop, take, ten, will*. The teacher now writes one of the words from the following word group on the board. Students copy the word from the board onto their papers, then try to think of which of their 15 words looks most like the presented word and write it under the word. Students should look through their store of 15 words only if they cannot first think of the word.

mud	rake	clack	ill	gun	grit	van
lay	rib	pit	lake	tend	fit	jack
cake	test	mask	pay	hit	hop	fake
tent	dill	drain	den	gill	herd	dress
slay	bran	drake	pen	hill	clop	Bess
mat	sake	Ben	kill	ray	clan	sway
slop	mill	sill	mop	rust	spun	flop
kit	sift	plain				

Optional evaluation procedure: See above. Students should not refer to their 15 words to do this.

spit	rug	grind	drill	tray	snack
tray	rail	mess	map	brake	

5. As in the previous lesson, proceed to write words on the board and have students think of a word that looks like the presented word. This time, however, they are *not* limited to the 15 words in their key word collections. Instead, they may think of any word they know. Several children may think of several different words, and they should be encouraged to use several of these words to figure out the unknown word.

gland	chin	con	spat	scat	stall	clan
clam	jot	shot	clot	clog	bout	spout
worm	worth	spike	dike	free	spree	rim
trim	prim	brim	dim	disk	rid	Sid
lid	frown	crown	clown	strong	throng	spades
glade	grade	trade	rig	brig	sway	clay
spend	sent	rent	tent	lent	few	screw
shrew	lame	flame	fair	stair	ground	pink
rink	stink	blink	skin	slink	shell	well
spell	such	stray	gold	scold	bold	fold
yelp	face	lace	ace	blouse	trust	bust
rust	smart	raw	claw	flaw	twine	spine
blast	mend	bleat	cleat	frill	freight	

Optional evaluation procedure: See above.

spun	wing	fry	prove	dish
card	floor	flight	moon	dell

The same procedure can be used with words in context. Whether or not you use the technique with words in context, you should make a significant effort to help students see the relationship between what they do during the exercises and how they can use the new skills during their normal reading.

The compare–contrast approach might be used with the phonograms in the Z-Test, described earlier in this chapter. For words that are not known, a key word can be taught, using the same procedures as above.

Making Words

Making words is a spelling-based decoding activity. In this activity, children learn to think about letters in words by manipulating letters in a spelling task. For example:

1. the teacher might take 1-inch-square index cards containing the following letters:

   a   i   o   d   n   s   r   u

2. The teacher announces, "I want you to make a two-letter word [signals with two

fingers]—'an.' " As children move letters to make the word, the teacher checks their efforts and offers praise.

3. After all children have spelled the word, the teacher writes the word on a word card and puts the card in a pocket chart.

4. The teacher proceeds through other two-letter words (e.g., *do, is, in*), three-letter words (e.g., *run, sad, rid, nod*), four-letter words (e.g., *said, rods, rind*), five-letter words (e.g., *sound, round*), and up to an eight-letter word (e.g., *dinosaur*).

Patricia Cunningham and Dorothy Hall have four books (and counting) with lesson plans for "making words" (short words, appropriate for students through second grade) and "making big words" (appropriate for students in third to sixth grade). These books are available from Good Apple.

Word Sorts

Word sorts are another spelling-based approach to teaching children how to decode. With this method, children are given lists of words and asked to sort them. In *closed sorts*, children are given categories; in *open sorts*, children are asked to come up with their own categories. Open sorts can be difficult for children who have reading problems. We recommend beginning with closed sorts, introducing open sorts only after children have had ample practice with the easier task. When introducing open sorts, the teacher needs to provide needed modeling to the group.

A list of words like the following word group might be used for children who are learning to contrast *sh* and *st*.

rest	stand	last	mush	list	shop
fist	fast	step	just	shut	stamp
fish	shall	shed	rash	past	mist
trash					

In a closed sort these words might be sorted as words with *sh*, as in *she*, and words with *st* as in *stop*. Or they might be sorted as having *st* and *sh* at the beginning or at the end. Bear et al. (2000) and Ganske (2000) have many ideas for word sorting that are tied to children's spelling and decoding knowledge.

"Three Strikes and You're Out"

Words missed or causing trouble during oral reading should be used to develop a word bank or as an informational source for planning additional instruction. Words can be put on 3 × 5 index cards and used for practice. Children can practice words from each other's word banks during individual reading time. We have used a "Three Strikes and You're Out" procedure; Words correctly identified by the child on three different occasions are retired from the word bank. A growing number of "retired" words is highly motivating.

FORM 6.1. Fry Sight-Word Inventory.

This instrument surveys a child's ability to recognize 300 frequently occurring words, as selected by Edward B. Fry (1980). The words are grouped into three sets of 100 by relative difficulty, and each group of 100 words is, in turn, grouped into sets of 25.

Directions for Administration

Place the student version of the First 100 Words in front of the child. Position the teacher's version so that you can make notations on it. There are three blanks for each word, for repeated administrations. You may want to record the date at the top of each column of blanks. Explain that you will be showing the child some words and that you want the child to say them aloud. Use the window card below to reveal the words one at a time, or make your own from a 3 x 5-inch index card with an X-Acto knife. A window card screens the other words and helps the child focus.

For each word, write a plus (+) in the blank next to it if the child correctly pronounces it in less than 1 second (informally timed). If the child takes more time but eventually pronounces the word accurately, write D, for *decoded*. That is to say, the word was not identified automatically and is therefore not yet a sight word. If the child mispronounces the word, try to spell the response phonetically. If there is no response, write NR. Move the window card to each word in succession while, with your other hand, you record the response. Proceed through each of the five columns.

Repeat these steps with the Second 100 and the Third 100. Discontinue testing if, in your judgment, the words become too difficult.

If you readminister the inventory, return only to those words not automatically recognized during previous testing.

Scoring and Interpretation

There is no cumulative score. Each word is actually a separate "skill," which means that there is a very direct link between testing and teaching. Any word that is not pronounceable automatically simply requires more practice!

(continued)

First 100 Words

the	or	will	number
of	one	up	no
and	had	other	way
a	by	about	could
to	word	out	people
in	but	many	my
is	not	then	than
you	what	them	first
that	all	these	water
it	were	so	been
he	we	some	call
was	when	her	who
for	your	would	oil
on	can	make	now
are	said	like	find
as	there	him	long
with	use	into	down
his	an	time	day
they	each	has	did
I	which	look	get
at	she	two	come
be	do	more	made
this	how	write	may
have	their	go	part
from	if	see	over

(continued)

First 100 Words

the	_____	or	_____	will	_____	number	_____
of	_____	one	_____	up	_____	no	_____
and	_____	had	_____	other	_____	way	_____
a	_____	by	_____	about	_____	could	_____
to	_____	word	_____	out	_____	people	_____
in	_____	but	_____	many	_____	my	_____
is	_____	not	_____	then	_____	than	_____
you	_____	what	_____	them	_____	first	_____
that	_____	all	_____	these	_____	water	_____
it	_____	were	_____	so	_____	been	_____
he	_____	we	_____	some	_____	call	_____
was	_____	when	_____	her	_____	who	_____
for	_____	your	_____	would	_____	oil	_____
on	_____	can	_____	make	_____	now	_____
are	_____	said	_____	like	_____	find	_____
as	_____	there	_____	him	_____	long	_____
with	_____	use	_____	into	_____	down	_____
his	_____	an	_____	time	_____	day	_____
they	_____	each	_____	has	_____	did	_____
I	_____	which	_____	look	_____	get	_____
at	_____	she	_____	two	_____	come	_____
be	_____	do	_____	more	_____	made	_____
this	_____	how	_____	write	_____	may	_____
have	_____	their	_____	go	_____	part	_____
from	_____	if	_____	see	_____	over	_____

(continued)

Second 100 Words

new	great	put	kind
sound	where	end	hand
take	help	does	picture
only	through	another	again
little	much	well	change
work	before	large	off
know	line	must	play
place	right	big	spell
year	too	even	air
live	mean	such	away
me	old	because	animal
back	any	turn	house
give	same	here	point
most	tell	why	page
very	boy	ask	letter
after	follow	went	mother
thing	came	men	answer
our	went	read	found
just	show	need	study
name	also	land	still
good	around	different	learn
sentence	form	home	should
man	three	us	America
think	small	move	world
say	set	try	high

(continued)

133

Second 100 Words

new _____	great _____	put _____	kind _____
sound _____	where _____	end _____	hand _____
take _____	help _____	does _____	picture _____
only _____	through _____	another _____	again _____
little _____	much _____	well _____	change _____
work _____	before _____	large _____	off _____
know _____	line _____	must _____	play _____
place _____	right _____	big _____	spell _____
year _____	too _____	even _____	air _____
live _____	mean _____	such _____	away _____
me _____	old _____	because _____	animal _____
back _____	any _____	turn _____	house _____
give _____	same _____	here _____	point _____
most _____	tell _____	why _____	page _____
very _____	boy _____	ask _____	letter _____
after _____	follow _____	went _____	mother _____
thing _____	came _____	men _____	answer _____
our _____	went _____	read _____	found _____
just _____	show _____	need _____	study _____
name _____	also _____	land _____	still _____
good _____	around _____	different _____	learn _____
sentence _____	form _____	home _____	should _____
man _____	three _____	us _____	America _____
think _____	small _____	move _____	world _____
say _____	set _____	try _____	high _____

(continued)

Third 100 Words

every	left	until	idea
near	don't	children	enough
add	few	side	eat
food	while	feet	face
between	along	car	watch
own	might	mile	far
below	close	night	Indian
country	something	walk	real
plant	seem	while	almost
last	next	sea	let
school	hard	began	above
father	open	grow	girl
keep	example	took	sometimes
tree	begin	river	mountain
never	life	four	cut
start	always	carry	young
city	those	state	talk
earth	both	once	soon
eye	paper	book	list
light	together	hear	song
thought	got	stop	leave
head	group	without	family
under	often	second	body
story	run	late	music
saw	important	miss	color

(continued)

135

Third 100 Words

every _____	left _____	until _____	idea _____
near _____	don't _____	children _____	enough _____
add _____	few _____	side _____	eat _____
food _____	while _____	feet _____	face _____
between _____	along _____	car _____	watch _____
own _____	might _____	mile _____	far _____
below _____	close _____	night _____	Indian _____
country _____	something _____	walk _____	real _____
plant _____	seem _____	while _____	almost _____
last _____	next _____	sea _____	let _____
school _____	hard _____	began _____	above _____
father _____	open _____	grow _____	girl _____
keep _____	example _____	took _____	sometimes _____
tree _____	begin _____	river _____	mountain _____
never _____	life _____	four _____	cut _____
start _____	always _____	carry _____	young _____
city _____	those _____	state _____	talk _____
earth _____	both _____	once _____	soon _____
eye _____	paper _____	book _____	list _____
light _____	together _____	hear _____	song _____
thought _____	got _____	stop _____	leave _____
head _____	group _____	without _____	family _____
under _____	often _____	second _____	body _____
story _____	run _____	late _____	music _____
saw _____	important _____	miss _____	color _____

FORM 6.2. Dolch words organized by level.

Preprimer	Primer	First reader	Second grade	Third grade
a	all	after	always	about
and	am	again	around	better
away	are	an	because	bring
big	at	any	been	carry
blue	ate	as	before	clean
can	be	ask	best	cut
come	black	by	both	done
down	brown	could	buy	draw
find	but	every	call	drink
for	came	fly	cold	eight
funny	did	from	does	fall
go	do	give	don't	far
help	eat	going	fast	full
here	four	had	first	got
I	get	had	five	grow
in	good	her	found	hold
is	have	him	gave	hot
it	he	his	goes	hurt
jump	into	how	green	if
little	like	just	its	keep
look	must	know	made	kind
make	new	let	many	laugh
me	no	live	off	light
my	now	may	or	long
not	on	of	pull	much
one	our	old	read	myself
play	out	once	right	never
red	please	open	sing	only
run	pretty	over	sit	own
said	ran	put	sleep	pick
see	ride	round	tell	seven
the	saw	some	their	shall
three	say	stop	these	sow
to	she	take	those	six
two	so	thank	upon	small
up	soon	them	us	start
we	that	then	use	ten
where	there	think	very	today
yellow	they	walk	wash	together
you	this	were	which	try
	too	when	why	warm
	under		wish	
	want		work	
	was		would	
	well		write	
	went		your	
	white			
	who			
	will			
	with			
	yes			

FORM 6.3. Informal Phonics Survey.

Directions for Administration

Consonant Sounds

Point to **S**. Say, **What sound does this letter say?** Go from left to right, repeating this instruction. It is fine if child reads across without prompting. For **C** and **G**, have child give both sounds.

Consonant Digraphs

Point to **Th**. Say, **What sound does this letter say?** Go from left to right, repeating this instruction. It is fine if child reads across without prompting.

Consonant Digraphs in Short-Vowel Words

Point to **ick**. Say, **If this says *ick*, what does this say?** Point to **brick** as you say second part of sentence. Go across the line and repeat for each word and each line.

The Rule of Silent E

Point to **cap**. Say, **If this is *cap*, what is this?** Point to **cape** as you say second part of sentence. Go across the row.

Vowel Digraphs, Vowel Diphthongs, Short Vowels, and R-Controlled Vowels and AL

Have children read each word across the line, going from left to right.

Alphabet

This subject is only given if the child cannot pass the first test or if you are interested in observing the child's knowledge of the alphabet. You can give this subtest two ways; Ask the child to identify each letter by name, or ask the child to give the name and a word that begins with that letter.

A response is considered correct if the tested element is correct. For example, saying *beast* for *beat* in the vowel digraph subtest is correct since the child pronounced the digraph correctly. Answering *bat,* would be incorrect. This is an informal instrument designed to see how well children can decode words in isolation. It should not be viewed as a general measure of reading and should be used only to assess children's instructional needs. Remember, you are trying to find out what the child knows. You can give general prompts, such as "Try sounding it out," and you should allow as much time as it appears the child needs. Do note excessive amounts of time taken, though.

(continued)

Scoring

For all subtests and the total test:

Mastery   80%+

Needs Improvement   60–79%

Needs Systematic Instruction   Below 60%

The following number of correct answers corresponds roughly to these levels.

Subtest	Total	Mastery	Review	Systematic Instruction
Consonant Sounds	23	18–23	14–17	0–13
Consonant Digraphs	3	2	2	0–1
Short Vowels in CVC Words	10	8–10	6–7	0–5
Consonant Blends in Short-Vowel Words	12	10–12	7–9	0–7
The Rule of Silent *E*	4	3	2	0–2
Vowel Digraphs	6	5–6	4	0–3
Vowel Diphthongs	6	5–6	4	0–3
R-Controlled Vowels and *AL*	6	5–6	4	0–3
Total	70	56–70	43–55	0–42

(continued)

Informal Phonics Survey

Child's Name _____

Consonant Sounds

S	D	F	G	H	J
K	L	Z	X	C	V
B	N	M	Qu	W	R
T	Y	P			

Consonant Digraphs

Th   Sh   Ch

Consonant Blends in Short-Vowel Words

ick	brick	slick	trick
op	drop	crop	prop
ash	flash	stash	trash
in	grin	spin	twin

Short Vowels in CVC Words

bit	led	nut	lap	hug
rock	tin	rag	hen	job

The Rule of Silent *W*

cap	tot	cut	kit
cape	tote	cute	kite

Vowel Digraphs

loaf	beat	sail	need	way
gain	feet	coal	leaf	sue

Vowel Diphthongs

town   loud   boy   threw   oil   law

R-Controlled Vowels and *AL*

tar   hall   sir   port   hurt   fern

(continued)

140

Alphabet

A	S	D	F	C	B	E
R	G	T	Y	U	H	J
M	Z	P	K	V	Q	W
N	O	I	X	L		

a	s	d	f	c	b	e
r	g	t	y	u	h	j
m	z	p	k	v	q	w
n	o	i	x	l	a	g

(continued)

Child's Name _____

	Real Words
Consonant Sounds	____/23
Consonant Digraphs	____/3
Short Vowels in CVC Words	____/10
Consonant Digraphs in Short-Vowel Words	____/12
The Rule of Silent *e*	____/4
Vowel Digraphs	____/10
Vowel Diphthongs	____/6
R-Controlled Vowels and *AL*	____/6
Total	____/74
Alphabet	____/54

FORM 6.4. Z-Test.

Name _____   Teacher/Clinician _____

Directions. Tell the student you are going to show him/her some pretend words and that you would like for him/her to pronounce each one. Say that all of the words begin with "/z/, like *zebra*." Then expose the words on the student form, one a time. Place a check in the blank under the date of testing if the child pronounces a pseudoword accurately.

Date of Testing	___	___	___	___
zit	___	___	___	___
zay	___	___	___	___
zin	___	___	___	___
zap	___	___	___	___
zan	___	___	___	___
zill	___	___	___	___
zack	___	___	___	___
zing	___	___	___	___
zip	___	___	___	___
zat	___	___	___	___
zore	___	___	___	___
zug	___	___	___	___
zell	___	___	___	___
zink	___	___	___	___
zump	___	___	___	___
zash	___	___	___	___
zank	___	___	___	___
zice	___	___	___	___
zoke	___	___	___	___
zick	___	___	___	___
zock	___	___	___	___
zunk	___	___	___	___

(continued)

zake   ___ ___ ___ ___

zame   ___ ___ ___ ___

zaw   ___ ___ ___ ___

zide   ___ ___ ___ ___

zeat   ___ ___ ___ ___

zop   ___ ___ ___ ___

zot   ___ ___ ___ ___

zuck   ___ ___ ___ ___

zight   ___ ___ ___ ___

zale   ___ ___ ___ ___

zail   ___ ___ ___ ___

zest   ___ ___ ___ ___

zain   ___ ___ ___ ___

zate   ___ ___ ___ ___

These words are arranged in order of increasing difficulty, as determined empirically. See J. W. Cunningham et al. (1999).

(continued)

zit	zell	zaw
zay	zink	zide
zin	zump	zeat
zap	zash	zop
zan	zank	zot
zill	zice	zuck
zack	zoke	zight
zing	zick	zale
zip	zock	zail
zat	zunk	zest
zore	zake	zain
zug	zame	zate

FORM 6.5. Test of Knowledge of Onsets.

Subtest for Initial Consonant Blends (2-letter)

Format: "This word is *(say word from first column)*. What is this word: *(point to word from second column)*?

Examples:			WHOLE WORD CORRECT	ONSET CORRECT	RIME CORRECT
	back	black			
	way	play			
	way	stay			
1.	down	crown			
2.	look	brook			
3.	did	grid			
4.	tell	swell			
5.	did	slid			
6.	not	trot			
7.	will	spill			
8.	just	crust			
9.	can	clan			
10.	him	skim			
11.	made	blade			
12.	more	snore			
13.	my	spy			
14.	ball	stall			
15.	way	pray			
16.	best	crest			
17.	rain	brain			
18.	back	track			
19.	sing	swing			
20.	make	flake			
21.	time	slime			
22.	make	brake			
23.	did	skid			
24.	way	tray			
25.	back	smack			
26.	set	fret			
27.	down	drown			
28.	cat	flat			

(continued)

			WHOLE WORD CORRECT	ONSET CORRECT	RIME CORRECT
29.	best	blest			
30.	down	frown			
31.	way	clay			
32.	my	dry			
33.	will	drill			
34.	way	sway			
35.	now	plow			
36.	hat	scat			
37.	made	glade			
38.	make	snake			
39.	made	grade			
40.	not	slot			
41.	will	grill			
42.	not	plot			
43.	see	free			
44.	rain	plain			
45.	had	glad			
46.	will	skill			
47.	find	blind			
48.	top	prop			
49.	like	spike			
50.	man	scan			
51.	back	snack			
52.	more	score			
53.	tell	smell			
54.	good	stood			
55.	same	flame			
56.	ride	glide			
57.	not	clot			
58.	time	prime			
59.	part	smart			
60.	back	stack			

(continued)

Scoring Grid

bl	br	cl	cr	dr	fl	fr	gl	gr	pl	pr	sc	sk	sl	sm	sn	sp	st	sw	tr
			1																
	2									3									4
												5							6
																7			
			8																
	9											10							
11																12	13	14	
			16							15									
	17																		
																			18
																		19	
					20								21						
	22											23							24
														25					
					26														
				27	28														
29						30													
		31		32															
				33															34	
								35			36								
						37										38			
							39						40						
							41	42											
					43			44											
						45						46							
47										48						49			
											50				51				
											52			53				54	
				55		56													
		57								58				59			60		
$\overline{3}$	$\overline{3}$	$\overline{3}$	$\overline{3}$	$\overline{3}$	$\overline{3}$	$\overline{3}$	$\overline{3}$	$\overline{3}$	$\overline{3}$	$\overline{3}$	$\overline{3}$	$\overline{3}$	$\overline{3}$	$\overline{3}$	$\overline{3}$	$\overline{3}$	$\overline{3}$	$\overline{3}$	$\overline{3}$

(continued)

Subtest for Initial Consonant Digraphs

Examples:	me cat	she that	WHOLE WORD CORRECT	ONSET CORRECT	RIME CORRECT
1.	feel	wheel			
2.	tell	shell			
3.	meat	wheat			
4.	saw	thaw			
5.	more	shore			
6.	tale	whale			
7.	bone	phone			
8.	best	chest			
9.	rain	chain			
10.	more	chore			
11.	see	thee			
12.	bird	third			
13.	make	shake			
14.	bony	phony			
15.	gooey	phooey			

Scoring Grid

ch	ph	sh	th	wh
				1
		2		
				3
			4	
		5		
				6
	7			
8				
9				
10			11	
			12	
		13		
	14			
	15			
3	3	3	3	3

(continued)

Subtest for Single Initial Consonants

Format: "This word is *(say word from first column)*. What is this word: *(point to word from second column)*?"

			WHOLE WORD CORRECT	ONSET CORRECT	RIME CORRECT
Examples:	ball way go	call day no			
1.	down	gown			
2.	look	nook			
3.	did	bid			
4.	tell	yell			
5.	did	rid			
6.	not	cot			
7.	will	mill			
8.	just	dust			
9.	can	van			
10.	him	dim			
11.	made	fade			
12.	more	core			
13.	like	hike			
14.	ball	mall			
15.	way	nay			
16.	best	vest			
17.	rain	vain			
18.	back	sack			
19.	sing	zing			
20.	make	wake			
21.	time	lime			
22.	make	fake			
23.	did	lid			
24.	way	gay			
25.	back	lack			
26.	set	yet			
27.	seen	keen			
28.	did	kid			
29.	best	nest			
30.	did	hid			
31.	way	bay			
32.	big	jig			
33.	will	sill			*(continued)*

150

			WHOLE WORD CORRECT	ONSET CORRECT	RIME CORRECT
34.	way	jay			
35.	now	wow			
36.	can	tan			
37.	best	zest			
38.	make	sake			
39.	too	zoo			
40.	not	rot			
41.	will	kill			
42.	not	jot			
43.	see	fee			
44.	make	rake			
45.	had	pad			
46.	will	dill			
47.	find	mind			
48.	but	cut			
49.	like	pike			
50.	will	pill			
51.	back	tack			
52.	more	bore			
53.	will	gill			
54.	hard	yard			
55.	look	hook			
56.	big	wig			
57.	not	tot			

(continued)

Scoring Grid

Test of Knowledge of Onsets (page 7 of 7)

b	c	d	f	g	h	j	k	l	m	n	p	r	s	t	v	w	y	z
				1						2								
3																	4	
												5						
	6								7									
		8													9			
		10	11															
	12				13			14	15						16			
															17			
													18					19
																20		
							21											
		22					23											
				24			25										26	
						27												
						28				29								
					30													
31							32						33					
							34									35		
														36				37
													38					39
											40							
							41											
						42												
			43									44						
											45							
			46						47									
	48										49							
											50			51				
52					53												54	
						55										56		
														57				
$\overline{3}$	$\overline{3}$	$\overline{3}$	$\overline{3}$	$\overline{3}$	$\overline{3}$	$\overline{3}$	$\overline{3}$	$\overline{3}$	$\overline{3}$	$\overline{3}$	$\overline{3}$	$\overline{3}$	$\overline{3}$	$\overline{3}$	$\overline{3}$	$\overline{3}$	$\overline{3}$	$\overline{3}$

FORM 6.6. Developmental Test of Word Recognition.

Directions for Administration and Scoring

Word Concept

Present words to child. <u>Do not</u> read words aloud. Put a card under each line and ask the question on the right.

1.	mow	motorcycle	man	mop	Which word is *motorcycle*? Why?
2.	baseball	bat	ball	base	Which word is *baseball*? Why?
3.	cat	cap	cot	caterpillar	Which word is *caterpillar*? Why?
4.	pumpkin	pump	pup	pin	Which word is *pumpkin*? Why?
5.	bat	but	butterfly	fly	Which word is *butterfly*? Why?

Partial Alphabetic Coding–Initial Sounds

Explain that these are going to be nonsense words, or words the child has never heard before. Then present, as above.

1.	mag	bag	pag	cag
2.	nin	yin	hin	min
3.	gop	sop	bop	lop
4.	pez	fex	bez	kez
5.	fub	wub	lub	dub
6.	tass	rass	jass	nass
7.	sug	lug	pug	cug
8.	fack	gack	mack	dack
9.	ging	ming	ping	ling
10.	rell	kell	mell	vell

Partial Alphabetic Coding–Final Sounds

1.	rim	rip	rib	rid
2.	man	mat	map	mad
3.	him	hip	hit	hick
4.	mug	muss	mum	mud
5.	gap	gag	gab	gas
6.	pot	pop	posh	pock
7.	met	men	meg	mew
8.	log	lot	lop	lock
9.	cat	can	cab	cap
10.	sum	sup	sun	sub

Fully Alphabetic Phase–Short Vowel Coding

1.	ron	ran	rin	run
2.	mat	mit	mut	met
3.	top	tap	tip	tup
4.	sun	san	sin	sen
5.	pen	pin	pan	pun
6.	hat	het	hot	hit
7.	fan	fun	fen	fin
8.	bet	bat	but	bit
9.	jot	jet	jat	jit
10.	wag	weg	wig	wug

(continued)

Fully Alphabetic Phase–Consonant Blends

1.	stack	slack	sack
2.	thin	twin	tin
3.	chick	kick	click
4.	grad	gad	glad
5.	sell	smell	spell
6.	stink	sink	shrink
7.	spit	split	sit
8.	shell	sell	swell
9.	bloom	broom	boom	Which word is *broom*? Why?
10.	pay	pray	play	Which word is *pray*? Why?

Fully Alphabetic Phase–Long-Vowel Coding

1.	tap	tape
2.	man	main
3.	rain	ran
4.	bit	bite
5.	bat	boat
6.	tote	tot
7.	made	mad
8.	pal	pail
9.	mean	men
10.	cute	cut

Polysyallabic Words

1.	anywhere	anyway	another	Which word is *anywhere*? Why?
2.	become	became	because	
3.	partner	panther	patter	
4.	contract	context	contact	
5.	baking	backing	bucking	
6.	propose	purpose	papoose	Which word is *purpose*? Why?
7.	father	farther	feather	
8.	butter	better	batter	
9.	staking	stalking	stacking	
10.	begging	begin	beginning	

Scoring

	Number correct	Explanations
Word Concepts	__/5	__/5
Initial Sounds	__/10	__/10
Final Sounds	__/10	__/10
Vowel Coding	__/10	__/10
Consonant Blends	__/10	__/10
Long-Vowel Coding	__/10	__/10
Polysyllabic Words	__/10	__/10

(continued)

Developmental Test of Word Recognition

mow	motorcycle	man	mop
baseball	bat	ball	base
cat	cap	cot	caterpillar
pumpkin	pump	pup	pin
bat	but	butterfly	fly

mag	bag	pag	cag
nin	yin	hin	min
gop	sop	bop	lop
pez	fex	bez	kez
fub	wub	lub	dub
tass	rass	jass	nass
sug	lug	pug	cug
fack	gack	mack	dack
ging	ming	ping	ling
rell	kell	mell	vell

(continued)

rim	rip	rib	rid
man	mat	map	mad
him	hip	hit	hick
mug	muss	mum	mud
gap	gag	gab	gas
pot	pop	posh	pock
met	men	meg	mew
log	lot	lop	lock
cat	can	cab	cap
sum	sup	sun	sub

ron	ran	rin	run
mat	mit	mut	met
top	tap	tip	tup
sun	san	sin	sen
pen	pin	pan	pun
hat	het	hot	hit
fan	fun	fen	fin
bet	bat	but	bit
jot	jet	jat	jit
wag	weg	wig	wug

(continued)

stack	slack	sack
thin	twin	tin
chick	kick	click
grad	gad	glad
sell	smell	spell
stink	sink	shrink
spit	split	sit
shell	sell	swell
bloom	broom	boom
pay	pray	play

tap	tape
man	main
rain	ran
bit	bite
bat	boat
tote	tot
made	mad
pal	pail
mean	men
cute	cut

(continued)

anywhere	anyway	another
become	became	because
partner	panther	patter
contract	context	contact
baking	backing	bucking
propose	purpose	papoose
father	farther	feather
butter	better	batter
staking	stalking	stacking
begging	begin	beginning

FORM 6.7. Elementary Qualitative Spelling Inventory: Spelling-by-stage assessment.

This is a short spelling inventory to assess the word knowledge students bring to their reading and spelling. You can administer this same list of words three times: in September, January and May to measure students' progress.

Let students know that you are administering this inventory to learn about how they spell. Let them know that this is not a test, but that they can help you plan your teaching if they do their best. Students are not to study this inventory beforehand.

Possible script: "I am going to ask you to spell some words. Spell them the best you can. Some of the words will be easy to spell; some may be difficult. When you do not know how to spell a word, spell it the best you can; write down all the sounds you feel and hear."

Say the word once, read the sentence if the meaning is unclear, and then say the word again. Work with groups of 5 words. You may want to stop testing when students miss 3 out of 5 words. Have students check their papers for their names and the date. See Chapter 2 for further instructions on administration and interpretation. Copy a Feature or Error Guide for each student. Do not count reversed letters as errors. Staple the student's paper to the Feature or Error Guide.

Directions for using the Feature Guide. For each word, check the features that are noted in the columns at the top of the feature guide. Add an additional point in the "correct" column if the word is spelled correctly. Do not count reversed letters as errors but note them in the boxes.

Total the number of points under each feature and across each word; this is a way to check your addition. The total score can be compared over time but the most useful information will be the feature analysis. Look down each feature column to determine the needs of individual students. For example, a student who spells 5 of 6 long vowels correctly is knowledgeable about long vowels although some review work might be in order. A student who spells only 2 or 3 of the 6 long vowels needs to be involved in word study around this feature. If a student did not get any points for a feature, then the feature is beyond the student's instructional range and earlier features need to be studied first.

Arrange students' papers in order from highest total points to lowest total points before transferring the numbers across the bottom row of each student's feature guide to the Class Composite. For a sense of your groups' needs and to form groups for instruction, *highlight* students who make *two or more errors* on a particular feature. If you call out less than the total list *adjust the totals* on the Class Composite.

Directions for using the Error Guide. Using the Error Guide on page 162, circle each error or write in the student's spelling by the error that is most similar. When a word is spelled correctly, circle the spelling at the end of the string of errors. After all words have been scored, determine where most circled words lie and look at the top row of the table for the developmental spelling level for this student. Total the words spelled correctly and note where the student is within the stage: *early* in the stage, in the *middle* or *late* in the stage.

Set One

1. bed   I hopped out of *bed* this morning.   *bed*
2. ship   The *ship* sailed around the island.   *ship*
3. when   *When* will you come back?   *when*

(continued)

4. lump   He had a *lump* on his head after he fell.   *lump*

5. float   I can *float* on the water with my new raft.   *float*

Set Two

6. train   I rode the *train* to the next town.   *train*

7. place   I found a new *place* to put my books.   *place*

8. drive   I learned to *drive* a car.   *drive*

9. bright   The light is very *bright*.   *bright*

10. throat   She had a sore *throat*.   *throat*

Set Three

11. spoil   The food will *spoil* if it is not keep cool.   *spoil*

12. serving   The restaurant is *serving* dinner tonight.   *serving*

13. chewed   The dog *chewed* up my favorite sweater yesterday.   *chewed*

14. carries   She *carries* apples in her basket.   *carries*

15. marched   We *marched* in the parade.   *marched*

Set Four

16. shower   The *shower* in the bathroom was very hot.   *shower*

17. cattle   The cowboy rounded up the *cattle*.   *cattle*

18. favor   He did his brother a *favor* by taking out the trash.   *favor*

19. ripen   The fruit will *ripen* over the next few days.   *ripen*

20. cellar   I went down to the *cellar* for the can of paint.   *cellar*

Set Five

21. pleasure   It was a *pleasure* to listen to the choir sing.   *pleasure*

22. fortunate   It was *fortunate* that the driver had snow tires during the snowstorm.   *fortunate*

23. confident   I am *confident* that we can win the game.   *confident*

24. civilize   They had the idea that they could *civilize* the forest people.   *civilize*

25. opposition   The coach said the *opposition* would give us a tough game.   *opposition*

(continued)

Feature Guide for Elementary Qualitative Spelling Inventory

Student's Name _____ Teacher _____ Grade _____ Date _____

Features →	Consonants Beginning	Final	Short Vowels	Digraphs & Blends	Long Vowel Patterns	Other Vowel Patterns	Syllable Junctures and Easy Prefixes and Suffixes	Harder Prefixes and Suffixes, & Unaccented Final Syllables	Reduced and Altered Vowels, Bases, Roots, & Derivatives	Feature Points	Words Spelled Correctly
LATE EMERGENT–LETTER NAME-ALPHABETIC											
1 bed	b	d	e								
2 ship		p	i	sh							
3 when		n	e	wh							
4 lump	l		u	mp							
WITHIN WORD PATTERN											
5 float				fl	oa						
6 train		n		tr	ai						
7 place					a-e						
8 drive		v		dr	i-e						
9 bright					igh						
10 throat					oa						
11 spoil						oi					
SYLLABLES AND AFFIXES											
12 serving						er	ing				
13 chewed				ch		ew	ed				
14 carries							rr ies				
15 marched				ch		ar	ed				
16 shower						ow	er				
17 bottle							tt	le			
18 favor								or			
19 ripen							en				
20 cellar							ll	ar			
MIDDLE SYLLABLES AND AFFIXES-MIDDLE DERIVATIONAL RELATIONS											
21 pleasure								ure	pleas		
22 fortunate						or		ate	fortun		
23 confident								ent	confid		
24 civilize								ize	civil		
25 opposition								op	position		
Totals →	(2)	(5)	(4)	(8)	(6)	(6)	(9)	(8)	(5)	(53)	(25)

- EMERGENT LATE — LETTER NAME – ALPHABETIC (EARLY · MIDDLE · LATE): Consonants Beginning / Final, Short Vowels, Digraphs & Blends
- WITHIN WORD PATTERN (EARLY · MIDDLE · LATE): Long Vowel Patterns, Other Vowel Patterns
- SYLLABLES & AFFIXES (EARLY · MIDDLE): Syllable Junctures and Easy Prefixes and Suffixes, Harder Prefixes and Suffixes & Unaccented Final Syllables
- DERIVATIONAL RELATIONS (LATE · EARLY · MIDDLE): Reduced and Altered Vowels, Bases, Roots, & Derivatives

SPELLING STAGES:
☐ EARLY ☐ MIDDLE ☐ LATE
☐ LETTER-NAME-ALPHABETIC
☐ WITHIN WORD PATTERN
☐ SYLLABLES & AFFIXES
☐ DERIVATIONAL RELATIONS

Chapters in WTW:
5
6
7
8

Words Spelled Correctly: _____ / 25
Feature Points: _____ / 53
Total: _____ / 78

Error Guide for Elementary Qualitative Spelling Inventory—1

Student's Name _____ Teacher _____ Grade _____ Date _____

Features	Consonants Beginning Final	Short Vowels	Digraphs & Blends	Long Vowel Patterns	Other Vowel Patterns	Syllable Junctures, and Easy Prefixes and Suffixes	Harder Prefixes and Suffixes, & Unaccented Final Syllables	Reduced and Altered Vowels, Bases, Roots, & Derivatives
SPELLING STAGES →	EMERGENT LATE — LETTER NAME–ALPHABETIC EARLY	LETTER NAME–ALPHABETIC MIDDLE	LATE	WITHIN WORD PATTERN EARLY — MIDDLE	LATE	SYLLABLES & AFFIXES EARLY — MIDDLE — LATE	DERIVATIONAL RELATIONS EARLY	DERIVATIONAL RELATIONS MIDDLE

LATE EMERGENT–LETTER NAME–ALPHABETIC

#	Word	Consonants (EARLY)	Short Vowels (MIDDLE)	Digraphs & Blends (LATE)
1	bed	b bd	bad	_bed_
2	ship	s sp shp	sep shep	_ship_
3	when	w yn wn	wan whan	_when_
4	lump	l lp lmp	lop lomp	_lump_

WITHIN WORD PATTERN

#	Word	Consonants (EARLY)	Short Vowels (MIDDLE)	Digraphs & Blends (LATE)	Long Vowel EARLY	Long Vowel MIDDLE	Other Vowel LATE
5	float	f ft vt flt	fot	flot	flott flowt floaut	flote	_float_
6	train	j t trn	jran chran tan	tran teran	traen trane	_train_	
7	place	p ps pls	pas pas palac	plas plac	plase pase	plais	_place_
8	drive	d j jrv drf	griv jriv griv jiv	driv	jrive drieve draive	_drive_	
9	bright	b bt brt	bit brit brit		bite brite	briete	_bright_
10	throat		trot	throt throt	throte	_throat_	
11	spoil		spol	sole	sool spoyle spole spoal	_spoil_	

SYLLABLES AND AFFIXES

#	Word	Syllable Junctures (EARLY — MIDDLE — LATE)
12	serving	sefng srvng srbving sering serfing surving serving _serving_
13	chewed	cud chud cooed chood cuwed c(h)ued chewd choud chewd _chewed_
14	carries	keres cares carise carys cairies carrys _carries_
15	marched	much march marchet marchd marcht _marched_
16	shower	shewr shour shuor shoer shower _shower_
17	bottle	badl badol batel batle bottel _bottle_
18	favor	favr faver favir _favor_
19	ripen	ribn ripn ripun ripan ripon _ripen_
20	cellar	salr selr celr sellar cellar seller _cellar_

LATE SYLLABLES AND AFFIXES–MIDDLE DERIVATIONAL RELATIONS

#	Word	Harder Prefixes (DERIVATIONAL RELATIONS EARLY)	Reduced & Altered Vowels (DERIVATIONAL RELATIONS MIDDLE)
21	pleasure	plasr plager plejer pleser plesher plesour plesure fortunet	_pleasure_ _fortunate_
22	fortunate	forhnat frehnit foohinit forchenut fochininte fortunet	_fortunate_
23	confident	confa(e)de(i)nt confia(e)dent confodent	_confident_
24	civilize	sivils sevelies sivilicse cifillazas sivelize civa(i)liz(s)e	_civilize_
25	opposition	opasishan opasion opozcison opasitian oppisition opasition oppisition oposit(s)ion	_opposition_

SPELLING STAGES: Chapters
☐ EARLY ☐ MIDDLE ☐ LATE in WTW:
  ☐ LETTER-NAME-ALPHABETIC   5
  ☐ WITHIN WORD PATTERN   6
  ☐ SYLLABLES & AFFIXES   7
  ☐ DERIVATIONAL RELATIONS   8

Words Spelled Correctly: _____ / 25

162

FORM 6.8. Qualitative Spelling Checklist.

Student _____   Date _____

Consider the following progression, and note when certain features are observed in students' spelling and writing. When a feature is always present, check "Yes." The last place where you check "Often" is the stage of spelling development to report. The numbers refer to the scale on the Spelling-by-Stage Assessment.

Preliterate

1 Marks on the page.   Yes ___ Often ___ No ___
    Scribbling followed the conventional direction.   Yes ___ Often ___ No ___
    Symbols or known letters represented in pretend writing.   Yes ___ Often ___ No ___

Early Letter-Name

2 Syllabic writing. Key sounds are spelled (*p* for *stop*).   Yes ___ Often ___ No ___
3 Beginning. Check "Yes" if ending sounds are included.   Yes ___ Often ___ No ___

Letter-Name

4 A vowel in every word.   Yes ___ Often ___ No ___
5 Consonant blends and digraphs in SHIP, DRIVE,   Yes ___ Often ___ No ___
    and WHEN, TRAIN, CHASE, and FLOAT.
6 Short vowels spelled correctly [BED, SHIP, WHEN].   Yes ___ Often ___ No ___
    Includes preconsonantal nasals [BUMP].

Within-Word Pattern

7 Uses but confuses long vowels   Yes ___ Often ___ No ___
    [DRIEV, TRIAN, FLOTE, BEECHES].
8 Spells many single-syllable long vowels correctly   Yes ___ Often ___ No ___
    but not consistently.
    Spells most consonant blends and digraphs correctly.
9 Spells long vowels, consonant blends, and digraphs   Yes ___ Often ___ No ___
    correctly, including low frequency consonant blends
    and digraphs [CAUGHT].

Syllable Juncture

10 Consonant doubling [POPPING, CATTLE, SQUIRREL, CELLAR].   Yes ___ Often ___ No ___
11 Plurals and other endings [BEACHES, POPPING, PREAPRING].   Yes ___ Often ___ No ___
12 Less frequent affixes, suffixes [PUNCTURE, CELLAR,   Yes ___ Often ___ No ___
    PLEASURE, CONFIDENT, CIVILIZE, FLEXIBLE].
    Prefixes [PREPARING, CONFIDENT, OPPOSITION].

Derivational Constancy

13 Knowledge of derived spellings [PLEASURE, FORTUNATE].   Yes ___ Often ___ No ___
14 Knowledge of derived spellings [CONFIDE, CIVILIZE].   Yes ___ Often ___ No ___
15 Knowledge of derived spellings [OPPOSITION, EMPHASIZE].   Yes ___ Often ___ No ___

FORM 6.9. Spelling Skills Test.

Name: _____

Directions for Scoring: Place a check in the column if the child spelled that feature correctly. Place a check in the "Correct Word" box if the child spelled the ENTIRE word correctly.

	Initial consonant	Final consonant	Blends and digraphs	Short vowel	Long vowel	Correct word
1. **Mop**	M	P		O		1.
2. **Wig**	W	G		I		2.
3. **Net**	N	T		E		3.
4. **Far**	F	R		A		4.
5. **Chin**		N	CH	I		5.
6. **Went**	W	T		E		6.
7. **This**		S	TH	I		7.
8. **Dump**	D	P		U		8.
9. **Trap**		P	TR	A		9.
10. **Hunt**	H	T		U		10.
11. **Wish**	W		SH	I		11.
12. **Slide**		D	SL		I_E	12.
13. **Brave**		V	BR		A_E	13.
14. **Sink**	S	K		I		14.
15. **Drive**		V	DR		I_E	15.
16. **Shade**		D	SH		A_E	16.
	Beg. sounds ___ / 9	Final sounds ___ / 15	Blends and digraphs ___ / 8	Short vowel ___ / 12	Long vowel ___ / 4	Total words correct ___ / 16
Mastery	7+	12+	6+	10+	3+	12+

FORM 6.10. Morris–McCall Spelling List (Grades 2–9).

Directions: "I am going to say some words that I want you to spell for me. Some of the words will be easy to spell, and some will be more difficult. When you don't know how to spell a word, just do the best you can. Each time, I will say the word, then use it in a sentence, and then I will say the word again." Start at the beginning of the list and continue testing until child makes five consecutive errors.

1.	run	The boy can *run*.
2.	top	The *top* will spin.
3.	red	My apple is *red*.
4.	book	I lost my *book*.
5.	sea	The *sea* is rough.
6.	play	I will *play* with you.
7.	lay	*Lay* the book down.
8.	led	He *led* the horses to the town.
9.	add	*Add* those numbers.
10.	alike	These books are *alike*.
11.	mine	That bicycle is *mine*.
12.	with	Mary will go *with* you.
13.	easy	Our lessons are not *easy*.
14.	shut	Please *shut* the door.
15.	done	Has he *done* the work?
16.	body	The chest is part of the *body*.
17.	anyway	I will go *anyway*.
18.	omit	Please *omit* the next verse.
19.	fifth	This is my *fifth* trip.
20.	reason	Give me a *reason* for being late.
21.	perfect	This is a *perfect* day.
22.	friend	She is my *friend*.
23.	getting	I am *getting* tired.
24.	nearly	*Nearly* all the candy is gone.
25.	desire	I have no *desire* to go.
26.	arrange	Please *arrange* a meeting for me.
27.	written	I have *written* four letters.
28.	search	*Search* for your book.
29.	popular	He is a *popular* boy.
30.	interest	Show some *interest* in your work.

(continued)

31. pleasant   She is very *pleasant*.
32. therefore   *Therefore*, I cannot go.
33. folks   My *folks* have gone away.
34. celebration   There will be a *celebration* today.
35. minute   Wait a *minute*.
36. divide   *Divide* this number by ten.
37. necessary   It is *necessary* for you to study.
38. height   What is your *height*?
39. reference   He made *reference* to the lesson.
40. career   The future holds a bright *career* for you.
41. character   He has a good *character*.
42. separate   *Separate* these papers.
43. committee   The *committee* is small.
44. annual   This is the *annual* meeting.
45. principle   The theory is wrong in *principle*.
46. immense   The man is carrying an *immense* load.
47. judgment   The teacher's *judgment* is good.
48. acquaintance   He is an *acquaintance* of mine.
49. discipline   The army *discipline* is strict.
50. lieutenant   He is a *lieutenant* in the Army.

Grade norms are based on of the average number of words spelled correctly. Use these as guides.

Grade	No. of Words
2	11
3	18
4	24
5	30
6	35
7	39
8	42
9	44

7

Comprehension

There has always been an intense interest in reading comprehension assessment. After all, comprehension could be called the "bottom line" of reading. Measuring it provides an indicator of how well all of the subprocesses of reading are working together. Comprehension assessment is a somewhat controversial topic, in that no general agreement exists on how best to do it. An extreme point of view was voiced by Frank Smith (1988) in the fourth edition of his book *Understanding Reading*. In it he says, "Comprehension cannot be measured at all . . . because it is not a quantity of anything" (p. 53). Most reading experts would certainly acknowledge that comprehension assessment raises important issues, but most would also agree that useful estimates can be reached of (1) a child's overall ability to comprehend, and (2) how well a child has comprehended a particular selection.

APPROACHES TO COMPREHENSION ASSESSMENT

Let's consider the major approaches to assessing comprehension and examine the strengths and limitations of each.

Questions

The most traditional method of testing reading comprehension is by asking questions. The use of questions offers great administrative flexibility, ranging from formal testing situations to class discussions. Questions allow teachers to focus on particular facts, conclusions, and judgments in which the teachers have an interest. By posing questions at various levels of thinking, a teacher can get a glimpse of how the child has processed a reading selection.

Types of Questions

There are many ways of categorizing questions. Bloom's (1969) taxonomy is sometimes used, for example. A far simpler approach is to think of questions in terms of levels of comprehension. We conventionally speak of three levels.

1. *Literal questions* require a student to recall a specific fact that has been explicitly stated in the reading selection. Such questions are easy to ask and answer, but they may reflect a very superficial understanding of content. Edgar Dale (1946), an eminent reading authority during the first half of the 20th century, once referred to literal comprehension as "reading the lines" (p. 1).

2. *Inferential questions*, like literal questions, have factual answers. However, the answers cannot be located in the selection. Instead the reader must make logical connections among facts in order to arrive at an answer. The answer to a question calling for a prediction, for example, is always inferential in nature even though we are uncertain of the answer, for the reader must nevertheless use available facts in an effort to arrive at a fact that is not stated.

Answers to inferential questions are sometimes beyond dispute and sometimes quite speculative. Let's say that a class has just read a selection on New Zealand. They have read that New Zealand is south of the equator and was colonized by Great Britain. If a teacher were to ask whether Auckland, New Zealand's capital, is south of the equator, the answer would require inferential thinking. There is no dispute about the answer, but the selection does not specifically mention Auckland, and the students must infer its location in relation to the equator.

On the other hand, were the teacher to ask the students if English is spoken in New Zealand, the answer would be inferential as well as speculative. The mere fact that Britain colonized New Zealand does not guarantee that English is spoken there today. For all inferential questions, the reader must use facts that are stated to reach a conclusion about a fact that is not stated. For this reason, Dale (1946) described inferential comprehension as "reading between the lines" (p. 1).

3. *Critical questions* call upon students to form value judgments about the selection. Such judgments can never be characterized as right or wrong, accurate or inaccurate because these types of answers are not facts. They are evaluations arrived at on the basis of an individual's value system. Critical questions might target whether the selection is well written, whether certain topics should have been included, whether the arguments an author makes are valid, and whether the writing is biased or objective. Understandably, Dale (1946) equated critical comprehension with "reading beyond the lines" (p. 1). (Hint: A short-cut to asking a critical-level question is to insert the word *should*. Doing so always elevates the question to the critical level. Of course, there are other ways to pose critical questions, but this method is surefire).

A teacher's judgment of how well a child comprehends may depend, in part, on the types of questions asked. Thus the choice of question type can affect a child's performance during a postreading assessment. A student may well do better if asked questions that are entirely literal than if asked questions at a variety of levels. The issue of which type(s) of questions to include in any postreading assessment is therefore an important one. Perhaps the best advice is to ask the type(s) of questions that you would expect a child to be able to answer during the course of day-to-day classroom instruction.

A final issue concerning types of comprehension questions is whether to subdivide each of the three levels into specific skills. For example, the literal level is often seen as comprised of skills involving sequences, cause-and-effect relationships, comparisons, character traits, and the like. Does it make sense to ask questions corresponding to each of these skills? Yes, as long as very little is made of the results. Skill-related questions can assure us that a range of comprehension skills is being developed, but when we attempt to compute scores for each skill, we often run into trouble. The problem is twofold. First, there are seldom enough questions for reliable measurement. Second, scores on specific skill tests tend to be almost perfectly correlated, suggesting that the skills are difficult to separate for assessment. In other words, a student who scores high on a test of literal sequences almost always scores high on a test of literal cause-and-effect relationships. It's hardly worth the effort to splinter comprehension to this extent.

Questions Based on Reading Dependency

Reading dependency (also called *passage dependency*) is the need to have read a selection in order to answer a particular comprehension question. Consider an example. The children have just read a story about a girl who brings a frog to school for Show and Tell. The frog jumps out of her hands and causes merry havoc in the classroom. The teacher then asks two comprehension questions:

1. "What did the girl bring to Show and Tell?"
2. "What color was the frog?"

These two questions are both literal. That is, they both require the students to respond with facts explicitly stated in the story. They differ considerably, however, in terms of their reading dependency. Even children with extensive experience participating in Show and Tell would be unlikely to predict the answer to the first question simply on the basis of experience. In short, it is necessary to have read the story in order to answer the question. The second question is another matter. Most children know that nearly all American frogs are green, and the children would not need to have read the passage in order to respond correctly. On the other hand, if the girl had brought some rare South American species that was, say, red and yellow, the same question would have been reading-dependent.

Which of these two questions tells the teacher more about whether the students comprehended the text? Clearly, questions that can be answered without having adequately comprehended a selection fail to assess reading comprehension. They may well be justified in the interest of conducting a worthwhile discussion, but teachers should not be misled into assuming that such questions would help them monitor their students' comprehension.

We have noted that even the questions in commercial test instruments tend to have problems regarding reading dependency. Many studies (e.g., Tuinman, 1971) have shown that when given only the questions and *not* the selections on which they are based, students do far better than chance would have predicted. This outcome implies that they are using prior knowledge to correctly answer some of the questions. The challenge in devising assessment instruments, or even informal approaches, is that it is difficult to determine what children are likely to know before they read a selection. This problem is especially troublesome with nonfiction text because of its factual content. Children already familiar with the content may find themselves with an unintended advantage in responding to postreading questions.

To better understand the concept of reading dependency, read the simple nonfiction example, "Crows," in Figure 7.1. The four comprehension questions that follow the passage represent four basic possibilities in regard to the degree of reading dependence reflected in the question. For most adults, the answer to question 1 lies not only in the passage but in their prior knowledge. This means that the question is not reading-dependent and is not a good indicator of reading comprehension. The answer to question 2, on the other hand, lies entirely within the adult's prior knowledge (in this case, prior experience) but not within the passage. The answer to question 3 lies in the passage but not in a typical adult's prior knowledge. This makes question 3 a reading-dependent one—and a much better indicator of comprehension. Finally, the answer to question 4 lies neither in prior knowledge (typically) nor in the passage. The issue of reading dependence boils down to a single guideline: If your intent is to assess reading comprehension, then your comprehension questions should target information that lies within the passage but that is not likely to lie within the student's prior knowledge. The Venn diagram used in Figure 7.1 may help conceptualize the four types of questions in relation to effective comprehension assessment.

Crows

Crows are large black birds that pose a threat to farmers. They belong to the genus *Corvus*.

1. What color are crows?
2. Have you ever had a pet crow?
3. To what genus do crows belong?
4. How long do crows usually live?

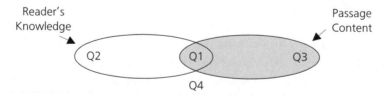

FIGURE 7.1. Examples of reading dependency.

Keep in mind that reading dependence is related to how much the reader knows in advance. What if question 3 were addressed to an ornithologist? Because an expert on birds could probably answer the question without needing to read the passage, the very same question is no longer a reading-dependent one. It all depends on whom you're asking. This is why the problem of reading dependence sometimes gets the better of commercial test developers. It's hard to predict what students, in general, may or may not know!

Readability of Questions

A third aspect of reading comprehension questions involves their readability. It is possible for the question itself to be harder to comprehend than the selection on which it is based. Written questions should be kept as simple as possible. Their difficulty level should certainly be no higher than that of the selections on which they are based, and ideally it should be simpler. Consider, in particular, the vocabulary you use in framing a question and also the complexity of your sentence structures. The KISS method (Keep It Simple, Stupid!) has much to recommend it when formulating comprehension questions.

Cloze Assessment

Cloze testing involves deleting words from a prose selection and asking students to replace them on the basis of the remaining context. The ability to provide logical replacement words is thought to indicate the extent to which a student is able to comprehend the material. Cloze testing has two important advantages. First, it can be administered in a group setting, once students have been introduced to its rather unusual format. Second, it does not require comprehension questions. This means that issues such as reading dependence and question readability do not arise. Third, cloze scores correlate highly with more conventional methods of assessing comprehension, such as asking questions.

On the other hand, cloze testing has significant limitations. Its strange format can confuse some students. Spelling and fine motor limitations can prevent students from displaying what they actually comprehended. (In fact, cloze testing is rarely administered below fourth grade for this reason.) Finally, research indicates that cloze assessments, as unusual as the format may appear, tend to assess comprehension at only a very low level. A student's ability to integrate information across sentences and paragraphs is not readily tapped by cloze items.

Figure 7.2 provides streamlined suggestions for constructing, administering, and scoring a cloze test. The sample cloze test in Form 7.1 (p. 183) serves as a model of what a cloze test should look like in its conventional format. You might try your hand at taking this test and then scoring it using the answer key in Figure 7.3. In scoring the test, make sure to give yourself credit for only verbatim responses—that is, for the exact word that was deleted in each case. You may be tempted to award credit for synonyms and other

Construction

- Start with a passage of about 300 words. Shorter passages may be used, but reliability could be jeopardized.
- Choose any word as the first to be deleted, but leave a sentence or so intact at the beginning of the test.
- Thereafter, mark every fifth word, until there are 50 in all.
- Word process the test so that the words you've marked are replaced by blanks.
- The blanks must be of equal length.
- For younger students, leave blanks of around 15 spaces to give them room to write.
- For older students, you may wish to number the blanks so that students can write their answers on a separate sheet.

Administration

- It is generally unwise to administer cloze tests prior to grade 4.
- Make certain students know that each blank represents only one word.
- Explain that this is more like a guessing game than a test. Even the best readers will not be able to guess many of the words.
- Encourage them to try to guess the word that was actually there—the word the author used.
- There is no time limit.

Scoring and Interpretation

- Give credit for verbatim answers only. Synonyms and other semantically acceptable responses are considered incorrect.
- Minor misspellings are counted as correct. However, spellings that indicate that the child might have been thinking of another word are counted as incorrect. Examples:

Original word	Child's answer	Scoring
Mississippi	Missisippi	Correct
scarlet	crimson	Incorrect

- Compute the percentage of correct answers and use the following scoring guide:

  Independent level: above 60%
  Instructional level: 40-60%
  Frustration level: below 40%

FIGURE 7.2. Guidelines for cloze testing.

reasonable responses, but this is a temptation that must be resisted. There are four reasons for accepting only verbatim replacements:

1. Verbatim scoring is more objective than the policy of awarding credit for synonyms. Otherwise, different scorers would tend to produce different scores.
2. Verbatim scoring leads to tests that are far easier to grade. Imagine how long it would take if you had to stop and carefully consider the semantic acceptability of every wrong answer.
3. Research has shown convincingly that verbatim scoring correlates very highly with scores based on accepting synonyms and other reasonable responses. The

From **The Telltale Heart**
Edgar Allan Poe

True!-nervous-very, very dreadfully nervous I had been and am; but why *will* you say that I am mad? The disease had sharpened my senses-not destroyed, not dulled them. Above ___all___ was the sense of __*hearing*__ acute. I heard all __*things*__ in the heaven and __*in*__ the earth. I heard __*many*__ things in hell. How, __*then*__, am I mad? Hearken! __*and*__ observe how healthily, how __*calmly*__ I can tell you __*the*__ whole story.

It is *impossible* to say how first __*the*__ idea entered my brain; __*but*__ once conceived, it haunted __*me*__ day and night. Object __*there*__ was none. Passion there __*was*__ none. I loved the __*old*__ man. He had never *wronged* me. He had never __*given*__ me insult. For his __*gold*__ I had no desire. __*I*__ think it was his __*eye*__! Yes, it was this! __*He*__ had the eye of __*a*__ vulture-a pale blue __*eye*__, with a film over __*it*__. Whenever it fell upon __*me*__, my blood ran cold; __*and*__ so by degrees-very *gradually* + made up my __*mind*__ to take the life __*of*__ the old man, and __*thus*__ rid myself of the __*eye*__ forever.

Now this is __*the*__ point. You fancy me __*mad*__. Madmen know nothing. But __*you*__ should have seen *me*. __*You*__ should have seen how __*wisely*__ I proceeded-with what __*caution*__, with what foresight, with __*what*__ dissimulation I went to __*work*__! I was never kinder __*to*__ the old man than __*during*__ the whole week before __*I*__ killed him. And every __*night*__, about midnight, I turned __*the*__ latch of his door __*and*__ opened it-oh, so __*gently*__! And then, when I __*had*__ made an opening sufficient __*for*__ my head, I put __*in*__ a dark lantern, all closed, closed, so that no light shone out, and then I thrust in my head. Oh, you would have laughed to see how cunningly I thrust it in! I moved it slowly-very, very slowly, so that I might not disturb the old man's sleep. It took me an hour to place my whole head within the opening so far that I could see him as he lay upon his bed. Ha!-would a madman have been so wise as this?

FIGURE 7.3. Answers to sample cloze test.

only thing accomplished by awarding credit for synonyms is to inflate scores. The rank ordering of students in a classroom is not likely to be changed.

4. Scoring criteria are based on verbatim scoring. If you give credit for synonyms and other logical responses, it will be nearly impossible to interpret the results. This reason alone is sufficient to justify giving credit for verbatim replacements only. The multitude of studies establishing the scoring criteria given in Figure 7.2 has assessed a variety of populations, including elementary students, middle and secondary students, college students, vocational–technical students, and even various special-education categories. If your score on the sample cloze test was 60% or higher, it is reasonable to conclude that the passage is at your independent reading level.

Oral Retellings

Comprehension is sometimes assessed by asking a student to retell orally the content of the reading selection. The degree of detail provided and the general coherence of the retelling are used to gauge comprehension. A checklist of details is used to record which points the student includes in the retelling. That is, when the student mentions a particular detail, a check is placed next to it for later reference by the teacher. Facts that go unmentioned in a student's retelling may be assessed by probe questions that are posed following the retelling. Retellings have the advantage of (1) being naturalistic, (2) avoiding many of the pitfalls of questioning, and (3) gauging how well the child internalized the content of a selection. But retellings have major limitations as well. They rely very heavily on the student's oral expressive ability, and a deficiency in this area could lead to an inaccurate judgment about how well the student has understood the selection.

Other Assessment Formats

Questions, cloze, and retellings are the three most popular approaches to comprehension assessments. These three by no means exhaust the possibilities, however. Other comprehension assessment formats include:

- ◆ Graded word lists
- ◆ Written responses to a selection
- ◆ Oral miscue analysis
- ◆ Maze formats
- ◆ Student-generated questions
- ◆ Performance tasks based on the selection

You may have used still other formats for assessing your students' comprehension. The relative merits of the various formats used to assess reading comprehension vary considerably in their advantages and drawbacks. The debate over which is best is not likely to be resolved in the near future.

TWO REASONS TO ASSESS COMPREHENSION

There are two principal reasons for assessing comprehension. One is to estimate general level of proficiency. The result of this kind of assessment might be an estimate of the instructional reading level by means of an informal reading inventory or a normative judgment by means of an achievement test. Mastery tests of specific comprehension skills also correspond to this purpose. The second reason for assessing reading comprehension is to gauge the degree to which a student has comprehended a particular selection. Chapter tests and other postreading assessments serve this second function.

WORD LISTS
FOR GENERAL COMPREHENSION ASSESSMENT

A shortcut to assessing general comprehension ability is to examine a student's ability to pronounce words, presented in the form of graded lists. Scoring criteria are then used to estimate a student's instructional level, based on how far the student can progress through these lists of increasing difficulty. Offsetting the obvious efficiency of this approach to comprehension assessment lies an important challenge to validity: It seems dubious to estimate a child's instructional reading level through an assessment that involves no actual reading and no measure of comprehension. On the other hand, research indicates that the correlation between word-list performance and more conventional approaches to reading comprehension assessment is high. Graded word lists are probably best thought of as a shortcut to estimating a child's overall proficiency as a reader. They are, however, no substitute for the "real thing."

One of the most popular graded word lists in the public domain is the San Diego Quick Assessment (SDQA). Form 7.2 (pp. 184–189) presents the SDQA in its entirety, including the student version of the word cards. You are free to reproduce the SDQA, if you feel this particular test meets your needs. The scoring protocol will help you organize all of the results of a single testing. The protocol might be included in a student's portfolio and updated through subsequent testing from time to time.

ASSESSING THE READABILITY OF MATERIALS

If we know the level of difficulty of the materials we ask our students to read, we are in a better position to foresee problems. The term *readability* refers to the difficulty level of prose, expressed as a grade level. It can be estimated by several means. You might, for instance,

- ◆ Use your subjective judgment,
- ◆ Create a short test out of the selection and see how well your students do, or
- ◆ Apply a readability formula.

Readability formulas are quantitative procedures that yield an estimated grade level based on surface features of text. These features are typically limited to the length of sentences and words, though some computerized formulas are much more sophisticated and tap other characteristics as well. Two of the most common formulas, developed by Edward Fry (1977) and Alton Raygor (1977), respectively, appear in Figures 7.4 and 7.5. Try applying them to the following passage, which we used in Chapter 3 (Forms 3.1 and 3.2). (In this case, ignore the direction to sample three passages from the beginning, middle, and end of a book.) Before you apply the formulas, read the passage and make your own best estimate of its readability! Then compare your estimate with those produced by the two formulas and the results of the two formulas with each other.

Togo

Togo is a small country in Africa, just north of the Equator. In area, it is about the same size as West Virginia. The people who live there produce coffee, cocoa, cotton, and other crops. The capital of Togo is called Lomé, a city of about a half million.

Togo has three neighbors. To the east is the country of Benin, to the west is Ghana, and to the north is Burkina Faso. Togo's fourth border is the Atlantic Ocean.

The main language of Togo is French, but four African languages are also spoken. Most of the people in Togo belong to one of 37 tribes. Togo is an interesting place, filled with variety and life.

ADDRESSING COMPREHENSION DIFFICULTIES

It is not enough to determine that a child has a problem with comprehension. It is essential to ask why. The answer to this question will help us sharpen our instructional response. We suggest three questions that can help clarify the issue.

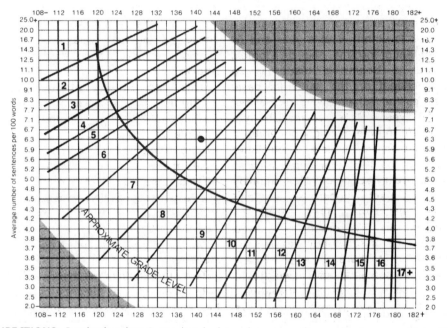

DIRECTIONS: Randomly select 3 one hundred word passages from a book or an article. Plot average number of syllables and average number of sentences per 100 words on graph to determine the grade level of the material. Choose more passages per book if great variability is observed and conclude that the book has uneven readability. Few books will fall in gray area but when they do grade level scores are invalid.

Count proper nouns, numerals, and initializations as words. Count a syllable for each symbol. For example, "1945" is 1 word and 4 syllables and "IRA" is 1 word and 3 syllables.

EXAMPLE:

	SYLLABLES	SENTENCES
1st Hundred Words	124	6.6
2nd Hundred Words	141	5.5
3rd Hundred Words	158	6.8
AVERAGE	141	6.3

READABILITY 7th GRADE (see dot plotted on graph)

FIGURE 7.4. Graph for Estimating Readability—Extended, by Edward Fry, Rutgers University Reading Center, New Brunswick, NJ 08904. Reprinted by permission of Dr. Edward Fry.

Chapter 7 pg. 174-178 Report to Class:
1. Two reasons for assessing Comprehension:
   (1) Estimate general level of proficiency - done by informal reading inventory
   (2) Gauge degree a student understands a particular selection - done by chapter test + other postreading assessments.
2. Word list - student read by pronouncing words, score estimates instructional level. Question of how valid a list is with no actual reading, but research show a correlation between list + reading comprehension is high. Popular word list is the SDQA San Diego Quick Assessment (found in this book pg 184-189).
3. Leveling Readability - the difficulty level of prose, expressed as a grade level.
Readability formulas - grade level based on text.
Two common formulas - Fry + Raygor (pg 176-177).
Compare 7.4 + 7.5 with 3.1 + 3.2
4. Children have problems with comprehension - should ask why?
   (1) Is it due to poor decoding? If child has to spend time + mental energy figuring out words it takes away from comprehension. If they improve when being read to - then they have a decoding problem. Can't assume if they can decode, comp will be okay, may have a problem in both.
   (2) Is Comprehension Hindered By Limited Prior Knowledge + Vocabulary? Yes →

*Need to build knowledge & vocab - long-term goal
comprehension ability will be gradual & cumulative.
Begins with background-building activities.
*For children who need more help - use the
listen - read - discuss technique.

5. Listen - read - discuss (for students with little or no
   background for nonfiction).
   Teacher covers the content of the selection. Teacher
   presents everything the student will read about.
   Such as lecture, discussion, demonstration.
   Then their reading will be greatly facilitated.
6. (#4) Finally, is comprehension hindered by
   poorly developed strategies?
   * Next presenter.

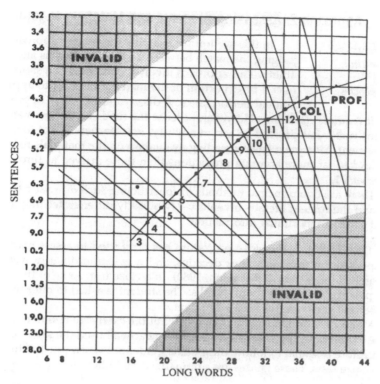

DIRECTIONS: Count out three 100-word passages at the beginning, middle, and end of a selection or book. Count out proper nouns, but not numerals.

1.   Count sentences in each passage, estimating to nearest tenth.
2.   Count words with six or more letters.
3.   Average the sentence length and word length over the three samples and plot the average on the graph.

EXAMPLE:

	Sentences	6+ Words
A	6.0	15
B	6.8	19
C	6.4	17
Total	19.2	51
Average	6.4	17

FIGURE 7.5. The Raygor Readability Estimate, by Alton L. Raygor, University of Minnesota. From Raygor (1977). Reprinted by permission of the National Reading Conference.

Is Comprehension Hindered by Poor Decoding?

Students who spend too much time and mental energy figuring out words have little of either to devote to comprehension. If comprehension improves when the child listens as a selection is read aloud, this improvement would be evidence of inadequate decoding ability as the fundamental problem. However, it is easy to be deceived into a belief that if we improve decoding, comprehension will automatically improve. Often the child may need instruction in *both* decoding and comprehension strategies.

Is Comprehension Hindered by Limited Prior Knowledge and Vocabulary?

We have mentioned the strong relationship between one's knowledge base, including knowledge of word meanings, and one's ability to comprehend. Building knowledge and vocabulary are long-term school goals, of course, and their effects on comprehension ability will be gradual and cumulative. Teachers can facilitate comprehension of particular selections, however, by providing thorough background information in advance, including preteaching key vocabulary. A conventional way of doing so is the directed reading activity, which begins with background-building activities. This lesson format is useful for students whose prior knowledge is not greatly deficient, but what about children who need more help before they can begin to comprehend what they read? A promising alternative is the listen–read–discuss technique.

Listen–Read–Discuss

Manzo and Casale (1985) introduced a technique doe improving comprehension that assumes little or no background for a nonfiction reading selection. Rather than creating a foundation of knowledge that will be useful for comprehending the additional knowledge presented in the selection, the teacher actually *covers* the content of the selection. That is, the teacher presents, in advance, everything the students will read about, almost as if there were no reading to be done. There is no guesswork or preassessment about what information the students may already know. The teacher assumes they know little or nothing.

The question many teachers raise when they learn about the listen–read–discuss method is, Why then bother to read? If the teacher presents—via lecture, discussion, demonstration, and the like—the entire contents of the selection, then what is the point of asking students to read it? The answer is that their reading will be greatly facilitated. Listen–read–discuss may not be the most exciting technique ever devised, but it permits children of limited knowledge to experience proficient comprehension, often for the first time. The studies conducted by Manzo and Casale (1985) and later by Watkins, McKenna, Manzo, and Manzo (1994) have established the listen–read–discuss procedure as a viable approach to the problem of limited knowledge and vocabulary.

Is Comprehension Hindered by Poorly Developed Strategies?

We use the word *strategies* to refer to methods proficient readers employ to assure their own comprehension. Such strategies include summarizing, self-questioning, forming mental images, and others. Our experience is that struggling readers almost invariably profit from strategy instruction. Not surprisingly, a number of evidence-based approaches has been introduced in recent years. We summarize a few of these in the following pages.

Think-Alouds

In a think-aloud, the teacher models how to handle a comprehension problem that may arise during reading. Proficient readers continually find themselves in minor comprehension predicaments. What distinguishes them from struggling readers, however, is the fact that good readers can apply strategies for "fixing" such problems. These "fix-up" strategies include (McKenna, 2002):

1. Reading ahead to see if the problem can be resolved.
2. Rereading to see if something has been misunderstood.
3. Reflecting on what has been read to see if some alternative explanation can be inferred.
4. Seeking information beyond the text (from an individual or a second print source) in order to resolve the dilemma.

In a think-aloud, a teacher models this "fix-up" process by articulating it. In the words of Scott Paris, the teacher "makes thinking public" so that students are privy to how a proficient reader contends with problem situations. For example, suppose a teacher is reading the following sentence aloud in science class:

Of the more than 26,000 types of spiders in the world, all are poisonous.

The teacher pauses at this point and says aloud to the students, "Wait a minute. How can there be so many poisonous spiders? Did I read that wrong? I'd better go back and check." The teacher then rereads the sentence. "Yeah, that's what it says. I thought there were only a few poisonous spiders. Maybe it'll explain if we keep reading." Sure enough, the passage continues:

However, very few spiders are dangerous to humans.

"I think I get it now," the teacher observes. "The dangerous ones are the ones I was thinking of. I didn't think the others were poisonous at all, but I guess they are."

Reciprocal Questioning (ReQuest)

One way to encourage self-questioning is to place students in the position of asking questions rather than merely answering them. Manzo's (1969) technique of reciprocal questioning (ReQuest) has been effectively used for more than three decades. It involves students actively in asking questions of the teacher (or one another) during a discussion. The basic idea is that in order to ask good questions, a reader must understand the content reasonably well. If a student reads with the aim of asking questions, then comprehension is apt to be good. In the years following its introduction, research has continually validated ReQuest, and many variations of the technique have been developed.

In one approach, the teacher introduces the reading selection and asks the students to begin reading. At a predesignated point, the students stop reading and one student is called on to ask questions of the teacher. The teacher must answer as many questions as the student can think to ask. When the student can think of no more questions, the teacher asks the student additional questions. Another student is called on for the next segment of the reading selection.

An alternative technique is for the teacher to call on a student, at random, after the selection has been completed. The student asks the teacher one question and the teacher asks the student a question. The teacher then calls on another student, and so forth.

In still another variation, the teacher begins the postreading discussion by calling on a student. The student asks a question but instead of answering it, the teacher reflects it to another student, who must try to answer. This second student may then ask a question, which the teacher reflects to a third student, and so forth. The teacher may use his or her knowledge of students' abilities to decide which questions to reflect to which students.

Summary Writing

Studies have clearly shown that writing summaries improves comprehension of the material that has been read and enhances comprehension ability generally (see Pressley & Woloshyn, 1995). These are impressive claims! One reason summary writing is so effective is that it compels students to transform content into their own words and expressions; doing so requires active thought. Another reason is that students must make repeated judgments about the relative importance of ideas. They must separate main ideas from details and string the main ideas together into a coherent account. We briefly describe two evidence-based, step-by-step approaches to summary writing.

Barbara Taylor (1986) developed a five-steps method of assisting middle schoolers in writing coherent hierarchical summaries:

1. Read only the subheadings of a chapter.
2. List the subheadings on paper.
3. Read the material.
4. Convert each subheading into a main-idea sentence.
5. For each main-idea sentence, add from one to three sentences containing supporting details.

Contrast her approach with that of Jack Hayes (1989), who developed an effective group strategy for teaching summary writing. He called it the guided reading and summarizing procedure (GRASP). GRASP also has five steps:

1. After the students have read a section of text, ask them to turn their books face down. Ask them to recall whatever they can from the material. Record their input in a list on the board or on a transparency.
2. Allow the students to return to the text and to locate more information and to make corrections.
3. With student participation, rearrange the information into categories.
4. Help the students write a topic sentence for each category and detail sentences that support it.
5. Engage the students in revising the summary to make it more coherent.

Reading Guides

A reading guide is "a list of questions and other tasks to which a child must respond while reading" (McKenna, 2002, p. 132). Reading guides focus a child's attention on the key ideas of the reading selection, and in so doing, model the process of strategic reading. Reading guides are not the same as postreading questions because students complete the guides *while* they read, not afterward.

Each guide is unique in that a teacher must first decide what is important for students to grasp and then construct tasks for helping them do so. These tasks might include (McKenna, 2002):

- ◆ Questions to be answered
- ◆ Charts to be completed
- ◆ Diagrams to be constructed
- ◆ Pictures to be drawn
- ◆ Responses to be written

There is really no limit to the ways such tasks can be created and interwoven, and there is certainly an element of creativity in constructing a good reading guide! The following steps might be helpful:

- ◆ Read the selection carefully.
- ◆ Decide which ideas and facts are important to know.
- ◆ Create tasks that help students attain this knowledge.
- ◆ Include a variety of tasks, not just questions.
- ◆ Aim for simple wording.
- ◆ Leave plenty of space for children to write.
- ◆ Arrange the tasks sequentially.
- ◆ Include page numbers and/or subheads.
- ◆ Where appropriate, include comprehension aids.

Using reading guides can be effective, but only with adequate preparation. Teachers sometimes balk at the work involved in developing a good guide, but since they are to be completed in class, as the teacher circulates and assists, there is no need to create a conventional lesson. If you teach students at grade 3 or higher, we urge you to try reading guides.

Reciprocal Teaching

An overarching teaching approach that encompasses several effective strategies is that of reciprocal teaching. Modeled after ReQuest, this approach was introduced by Palincsar and Brown in 1984. According to Duke (2002), reciprocal teaching is among the most thoroughly validated of comprehension strategies, and it deserves careful consideration.

Students work in small groups, applying comprehension strategies to a new reading selection. These strategies include predicting, clarifying, questioning, and summarizing. In order for reciprocal teaching to work, the teacher must spend some time explaining these four strategies so that the students can apply them to new material. Research suggests that this is time well spent. Let's briefly examine each of them.

The students begin by examining the reading selection and *predicting* the topic it seems likely to cover. To do so they consider subtitles, pictures, bold-face terminology, and graphic aids. Some students may not be used to predicting, so that starting with simple examples, such as pictures and picture books, may be necessary.

New content material may well contain concepts and ideas that are not entirely clear while students are reading. In *clarifying*, they focus on words, ideas, and even pronunciations that may require further explanation. Others in the group may be able to help, as can the teacher. The important point is that they realize where their problems lie.

Students are asked to engage in *questioning* once they have read each portion of a selection. They are encouraged to ask questions at a variety of comprehension levels. Other members of the group attempt to answer these questions, as they are asked.

Once the students are finished asking and answering their own questions, they begin *summarizing* what they have read and discussed. One option is to have students co-author a written summary; other possibilities include producing an informal outline of new material, creating a semantic map, or simply identifying the most important ideas and terminology introduced in the selection.

These four strategies are used by proficient readers whenever they encounter new content material. Such readers form predictions about what the text will be about, though these predictions may not always be formally worded. Then, as they read, they attempt to clarify the meanings of new terms and reflect on difficult ideas before continuing with the passage. They often form questions and do their best to answer them as they read. When they finish a selection, they consider its major points and overall significance. For the proficient reader, all of these strategies are applied internally and independently. The strategies form a kind of dialogue through which good readers attempt to monitor their own comprehension in order to ensure understanding. Struggling readers frequently lack this internal "conversation," and their comprehension suffers as a result. Reciprocal teaching is a means of fostering these healthy mental habits.

We believe reciprocal teaching can be employed effectively at grades 4 and higher, though with modifications it might work with younger students. For more on specific steps for implementing this important technique, see McKenna (2002).

FORM 7.1. Sample cloze test.

From **The Telltale Heart**
Edgar Allan Poe

True!-nervous-very, very dreadfully nervous I had been and am; but why *will* you say that I am mad? The disease had sharpened my senses-not destroyed, not dulled them. Above _____ was the sense of _____ acute. I heard all _____ in the heaven and _____ the earth. I heard _____ things in hell. How, _____, am I mad? Hearken! _____ observe how healthily, how _____ I can tell you _____ whole story.

It is _____ to say how first _____ idea entered my brain; _____ once conceived, it haunted _____ day and night. Object _____ was none. Passion there _____ none. I loved the _____ man. He had never _____ me. He had never _____ me insult. For his _____ I had no desire. _____ think it was his _____! Yes, it was this! _____ had the eye of _____ vulture-a pale blue _____, with a film over _____. Whenever it fell upon _____, my blood ran cold; _____ so by degrees-very _____+ made up my _____ to take the life _____ the old man, and _____ rid myself of the _____ forever.

Now this is _____ point. You fancy me _____. Madmen know nothing. But _____ should have seen me. _____ should have seen how _____ I proceeded-with what _____, with what foresight, with _____ dissimulation I went to _____! I was never kinder _____ the old man than _____ the whole week before _____ killed him. And every _____, about midnight, I turned _____ latch of his door _____ opened it-oh, so _____! And then, when I _____ made an opening sufficient _____ my head, I put _____ a dark lantern, all closed, closed, so that no light shone out, and then I thrust in my head. Oh, you would have laughed to see how cunningly I thrust it in! I moved it slowly-very, very slowly, so that I might not disturb the old man's sleep. It took me an hour to place my whole head within the opening so far that I could see him as he lay upon his bed. Ha!-would a madman have been so wise as this?

FORM 7.2. San Diego Quick Assessment, Form I.

Description: Beginning with the three readiness levels (RR–1, RR–2, RR–3) of recognizing letters as similar, saying letter names, and matching sounds to letters, this test proceeds to recognition of words. Level 1 is representative of PP, Level 2–Primer, Level 3–Grade 1, and to Level 13, which is representative of Grade 11.

Appropriate for: Students at the end of summer vacation or new students entering the classroom without recent or detailed records.

Ages: 5–16, or older students with learning disabilities.

Testing Time: 2 minutes.

Directions for Use: *Preparation:* For this test you will need copies of the 13 SDQA assessment cards. Sequence the cards in ascending order of difficulty.

You will also need copies of the attached SDQA record sheet.

Administration: Administer each form of the SDQA individually, as follows:

1. Begin with a card that is at least two years below the student's grade-level assignment.
2. Ask the student to read the words aloud to you. If he or she misreads any on the list, drop to easier lists until the student makes no errors. This indicates the base level.
3. Place a checkmark (FIXME) at the appropriate entry on the record sheet for each correct response. This indicates the base leveli.
4. Direct the child as follows:

   RR^1: "Which letters are alike?"
   RR^2: "Name these letters."
   RR^3: "Circle the letter you think this word begins with."
   1–13: "Read as many of the words on this list as you can."
   "Try to sound out words that are new to you."
   "Don't be afraid to tell me ANY part of a word that you recognize."
   1–13: "Each list gets harder. You won't be able to recognize all of the words,
   but do the best you can."

5. Encourage the student to read words he or she does not know so that you can identify the techniques the student uses for word identification.

Scoring: The list in which a student misses no more than one of the 10 words is the level at which he or she can read independently. Two errors indicate his or her instructional level. Three or more errors identify the level at which reading material will be too difficult for the student.

The type of errors noted in the word substitutions dictates the remediation to be used. For example, students who consistently miss words by starting the word incorrectly:

toad for *road*
give for *live*
digger for *bigger*
right for *night*

need exercises stressing initial consonants. This is equally true of medial and final errors.

(continued)

B	B	
A	C	
M	M	
C	C	
S	Q	
J	J	
T	T	
H	H	
D	L	
W	M	I-RR [1]

B
A
M
C
S
J
T
H
D
W

I-RR [2]

D	B	A
A	E	K
L	F	M
B	C	G
O	S	P
A	B	J
D	G	T
A	H	B
D	I	M
W	G	J

I-RR [3]

see
play
me
at
run
go
and
look
can
here

I-1

(continued)

you		road	
come		live	
not		thank	
with		when	
jump		bigger	
help		how	
is		always	
work		night	
are		spring	
this	I-2	today	I-3
our		city	
please		middle	
myself		moment	
town		frightened	
early		exclaimed	
send		several	
wide		lonely	
believe		drew	
quietly		since	
carefully	I-4	straight	I-5

(continued)

decided	scanty
served	business
amazed	develop
silent	considered
wrecked	discussed
improve	behaved
certainly	splendid
entered	acquainted
realized	escape
interrupted I-6	grim I-7
bridge	amber
commercial	dominion
abolish	sundry
trucker	capillary
apparatus	impetuous
elementary	blight
comment	wrest
necessity	enumerate
gallery	daunted
relativity I-8	condescend I-9

(continued)

capacious limitations pretext intrigue delusions immaculate ascent acrid binoculars embankment I–10	conscientious isolation molecule ritual momentous vulnerable kinship conservatism jaunty inventive I–11
zany jerkin nausea gratuitous linear inept legality aspen amnesty barometer I–12	galore rotunda capitalism prevaricate risible exonerate superannuate luxuriate piebald crunch I–13

(continued)

SAN DIEGO QUICK ASSESSMENT   Student _____

I–1 (Preprimer)	I–2 (Primer)	I–3 (1st Reader)	I–4 (Grade 2)
____ see	____ you	____ road	____ our
____ play	____ come	____ live	____ please
____ me	____ not	____ thank	____ myself
____ at	____ with	____ when	____ town
____ run	____ jump	____ bigger	____ early
____ go	____ help	____ how	____ send
____ and	____ is	____ always	____ wide
____ look	____ work	____ night	____ believe
____ can	____ are	____ spring	____ quietly
____ here	____ this	____ today	____ carefully

I–5 (Grade 3)	I–6 (Grade 4)	I–7 (Grade 5)	I–8 (Grade 6)
____ city	____ decided	____ scanty	____ bridge
____ middle	____ served	____ business	____ commercial
____ moment	____ amazed	____ develop	____ abolish
____ frightened	____ silent	____ considered	____ trucker
____ exclaimed	____ wrecked	____ discussed	____ apparatus
____ several	____ improve	____ behaved	____ elementary
____ lonely	____ certainly	____ splendid	____ comment
____ drew	____ entered	____ acquainted	____ necessity
____ since	____ realized	____ escape	____ gallery
____ straight	____ interrupted	____ grim	____ relativity

I–9 (Grade 7)	I–10 (Grade 8)	I–11 (Grade 9)	I–12 (Grade 10)
____ amber	____ capacious	____ conscientious	____ zany
____ dominion	____ limitations	____ isolation	____ jerkin
____ sundry	____ pretext	____ molecule	____ nausea
____ capillary	____ intrigue	____ ritual	____ gratuitous
____ impetuous	____ delusions	____ momentous	____ linear
____ blight	____ immaculate	____ vulnerable	____ inept
____ wrest	____ ascent	____ kinship	____ leaglity
____ enumerate	____ acrid	____ conservatism	____ aspen
____ daunted	____ binoculars	____ jaunty	____ amnesty
____ condescend	____ embankment	____ inventive	____ barometer

I–13 (Grade 11)
____ galore
____ rotunda
____ capitalism
____ prevaricate
____ risible
____ exonerate
____ superannuate
____ luxuriate
____ piebald
____ crunch

DATE: _____

ESTIMATED READING LEVELS:

INDEPENDENT   ____

INSTRUCTIONAL   ____

FRUSTRATION   ____

8

Strategic Knowledge

When you picked this book up, you had a purpose. You knew what you wanted to get out of it and had some tentative strategies that you intended to use to achieve your purpose. If you intended to use this book to find measures that you might use for an individual assessment of a child with reading difficulties, then you have probably skipped over this introduction, since it did not match your purpose. If you are reading this for a course, then you might spend a little more time, possibly taking notes. Odds are good that you are in a chair or a place that you ordinarily use for studying. Some people like quiet when they study; others like music. You are probably in an environment of your choice. You might be using a highlighter or note cards. Again, different people prefer to use different study techniques. Chances are that you will flip through the material to find out how long it is and how difficult you think it will be. You will compare that time to the amount of time that you have before dinner or bed or some other point in the future. You are also likely to be asking yourself what information the teacher will think is important, as well as what information you feel that you need to get out of the reading. If you are reading this textbook for a course, you will want to get as good a grade as possible, which requires figuring out what the teacher will want you to know and making sure you know it.

A second situation is reading a book for pleasure. Here you will sit in a comfortable chair, on a couch, or even lie in bed. You might read before you go to sleep, or outdoors on a sunny weekend. You will not be concerned with how much you remember or what a teacher would ask, nor would you plan to use cards, a highlighter, or any study aids.

These two situations differ in terms of the text used and the purpose for reading, leading to the use of different strategies while reading. As an accomplished reader, you have knowledge of a broad range of strategies that you can apply to a number of different purposes and texts. In addition, if you are not achieving your purpose during reading, because the text is more difficult than you thought or for some other reason, you can adjust your strategies so that you do achieve those purposes. You would probably allocate different amounts of time for different purposes, according more time for reading a text in detail, for example, in the knowledge that you might be tested.

In the work we have done with children who have reading problems, we find that they often have no idea how to deploy different strategies to achieve different purposes. Often, they are even unaware of their purpose for reading. Children with reading problems tend to be focused on the basic decoding of a text, rather than on what they need to get out of it—even after they become competent at decoding and word recognition.

Consider one child from our clinic. When one of us (Stahl) asked him how he would study a textbook, he said that he would "start at the beginning and read through to the end." Since he had previously said that he read very slowly, I asked whether he often got to the end. He said that he didn't. When I asked him whether he paid any special notice to bold-faced words or any features of the text, like a summary or headings, he said that he did not. Finally, I asked him what kind of grades he got reading in this way, and he replied, "D's and F's." It was unclear from this interview whether he knew that his system of studying was not working, or, if he did, whether he felt there was any other way of doing it.

Given the paucity of strategy instruction in schools, it is likely that no one taught you to be as flexible in your strategy use as we are assuming that you are. Instead, you developed these abilities through trial and error, in high school and college. Research has found that teaching children strategies can improve their reading and studying abilities (Pressley & Woloshyn, 1995). This instruction can help diminish some of the differences between proficient and struggling readers.

We have found that interviews or self-reports are the best way of ascertaining how strategic children are in their reading . An alternative is to have children think aloud during reading or studying. If children are comfortable with thinking aloud, this approach can supply a very valuable form of data. But most children are not comfortable thinking aloud, so if you do not get useful information, it could be because the child is not able to think about reading strategies, or it could simply be that the child does not know how to handle thinking aloud. The textbook interview is a structured way of having children demonstrate their thinking during reading, which might suffice for this purpose.

GENERAL PURPOSES FOR READING

Proficient and struggling readers differ in their knowledge of general reading purposes. If I asked a proficient reader, in fifth grade or above, a question such as "What makes someone a good reader?" or "If I gave you something to read, how would you know you were reading it well?" the answer would probably focus on comprehension. For example, the student might reply that good readers understand what they read, or that people are reading well if they understand what they read, if they get the main ideas from their reading, and so on. Struggling readers, even into the middle-school grades, tend to focus on decoding. To a struggling reader, good readers are those who say the words correctly, and people who are reading well pronounce all the words correctly in a story. For a question such as "What makes something difficult to read?" proficient readers tend to focus on the ideas or the difficult vocabulary, whereas struggling readers cite "big words."

These differences are likely to be significant; after all, if one does not know the desired end of reading instruction, it is difficult to get there. Differences in the instruction given to children of different reading abilities certainly affect the way they view reading. Allington (1983), reviewing a number of observational studies, identified the following differences:

♦ Proficient readers tend to have a greater focus on comprehension in their lessons; struggling readers are focused more on word recognition.

♦ When they miss a word during reading, proficient readers are more likely to be given meaning cues than struggling readers, who tend to receive more decoding cues.

♦ Proficient readers are interrupted fewer times during their lessons than struggling readers. (In other words, teachers sanction more interruptions from better readers, since it is the proficient readers who are interrupting the struggling readers' work time.)

♦ Proficient readers are more likely to read a whole story during a reading period; struggling readers are more likely to read a portion of a story.

♦ Proficient readers are more likely to read silently; struggling readers are more likely to read orally.

♦ Proficient readers cover more material in the course of the school year than struggling readers (Allington, 1984). Moreover, since practice in reading is related to progress, the gap between struggling and proficient readers appears to widen as children move through school (Stanovich, 1986).

The different cues that readers receive, the different focus in instruction, whether students read a story as a whole or not, and how much they are interrupted during reading all seem to lead to different orientations toward reading. These orientations can be turned around relatively easily through comprehension-oriented reading instruction. Even if one's immediate instructional goals are decoding and fluency, a teacher should make sure that the child understands that the purpose of reading is comprehension.

We include two interviews: in this chapter: the Burke Reading Interview (Burke, 1993; Form 8.1, p. 194) and the Awareness of Purposes of Reading Interview (Garner & Kraus, 1981; Form 8.2, p. 195). The Burke Reading Interview is especially suited to younger children, in grades 1 and 2. The Awareness of Purposes Reading Interview can be used with older children.

SPECIFIC PURPOSES AND STRATEGY KNOWLEDGE

As we noted earlier, proficient readers can differentiate between different purposes for reading and can adapt their strategies to meet those differences. Two interviews that can help you ascertain how children adapt their reading for different purposes are provided: the Index of Reading Awareness (Jacobs & Paris, 1987; Form 8.3, pp. 196–201) and a Textbook Interview (Form 8.4, pp. 202–203).

We find that for older children, including the college students we see occasionally, an interview is the most useful means for helping us understand how they approach text and how to change that approach. Older children are very aware of their deficiencies, even if they do not act upon that awareness. A dialogue around a textbook can be useful not only for the examiner but also for the child. This dialogue can include discussion of study strategies, so that the child can learn as much as the examiner.

After you have conducted the Burke Reading Interview, note that questions 2 and 4 set up the questions that follow. Questions 3, 5, 6, and 7 elicit the child's orientation toward reading. Note whether the orientation is toward meaning, decoding, or something else. Look for a pattern across these questions. Question 1 elicits the strategies that the child might use during reading. Note whether the child uses one strategy or can provide multiple strategies. We find that struggling readers tend to say they would "sound words out" but cannot give any other strategy. It is important to look for evidence of flexible strategy use even with young children.

As you interpret the Awareness of Purposes of Reading Interview, note first that questions 1 and 5 are set-up questions. Ignore them. Questions 2, 3, and 4 elicit the child's orientation toward reading. Evaluate them, as in the Burke Reading Interview. Question 6 elicits strategies. Again, you are interested in whether a child can list multiple strategies. You are also interested in any independent strategies. Children often say they would "ask my teacher" or "ask my mother." There is nothing wrong with this as a response, but you would prefer the child to suggest some independent strategies.

FORM 8.1. Burke Reading Interview.

Name _____ Class _____

Date _____ Interviewer _____

1. When you are reading and you come to something you don't know, what do you do?

   Do you ever do anything else?

2. Who is a good reader that you know?

3. What makes him/her a good reader?

4. Do you think that she/he ever comes to something she/he doesn't know when she's/he's reading?

5.   (If yes)   When she/he does come to something she/he doesn't know, what do you think she/he does about it?

      (If no)   *Pretend* that she/he does come to something that she/he doesn't know. What do you think she/he does about it?

6. If you knew that someone was having difficulty reading, how would you help them?

7. What would your teacher do to help that person?

8. How did you learn to read?

   What do (they/you) do to help you learn?

9. What would you like to do better as a reader?

10. Do you think that you are a good reader? Why?

FORM 8.2. Awareness of Purposes of Reading Interview.

Name _____   Date of Interview _____

1. What kind of reader are you?

2. What makes someone a good reader?

3. If I gave you something to read right now, how would you know you were reading it well?

4. What makes something hard to read?

5. Do you understand everything you read?

6. What do you do if you don't understand something?

FORM 8.3. Index of Reading Awareness.

Administration and Scoring

Because of its multiple-choice format, the Index of Reading Awareness (Form 8.3) may be administered in a group setting. If significant decoding deficits are suspected, it may be wise to read each item aloud to the students (both stem and choices).

The instrument comprises four subtests of five items each. These are Evaluation, Planning, Regulation, and Conditional Knowledge. Each student earns a score for each of these subtests. No composite score is computed. The subtest scores are computed by using the following key. The response to each item receives 0, 1, or 2 points. The subtest score is simply the sum of these points for the five items of that subtest.

Once the subtest scores are determined, the following scale can be used to interpret them:

Subtest score	Interpretation
8–10	No significant weakness.
6–7	Some instructional support needed.
0–5	Serious need for instruction in this area.

Name _____

1. What is the hardest part about reading for you?

   a. Sounding out the hard words.

   b. When you don't understand the story.

   c. Nothing is hard about reading for you.

2. What would help you become a better reader?

   a. If more people would help you when you read.

   b. Reading easier books with shorter words.

   c. Checking to make sure you understand what you read.

3. What is special about the first sentence or two in a story?

   a. They always begin with "Once upon a time . . . "

   b. The first sentences are the most interesting.

   c. They often tell what the story is about.

4. How are the last sentences of a story special?

   a. They are the exciting action sentences.

   b. They tell you what happened.

   c. They are harder to read.

(continued)

5. How can you tell which sentences are the most important ones in a story?
    a. They're the ones that tell the most about the characters and what happens.
    b. They're the most interesting ones.
    c. All of them are important.

6. If you could only read some of the sentences in the story because you were in a hurry, which ones would you read?
    a. Read the sentences in the middle of the story.
    b. Read the sentences that tell you the most about the story.
    c. Read the interesting, exciting sentences.

7. When you tell other people about what you read, what do you tell them?
    a. What happened in the story.
    b. The number of pages in the book.
    c. Who the characters are.

8. If the teacher told you to read a story to remember the general meaning, what would you do?
    a. Skim through the story to find the main parts.
    b. Read all of the story and try to remember everything.
    c. Read the story and remember all of the words.

9. Before you start to read, what kind of plans do you make to help you read better?
    a. You don't make any plans. You just start reading.
    b. You choose a comfortable place.
    c. You think about why you are reading.

10. If you had to read very fast and could only read some words, which ones would you try to read?
    a. Read the new vocabulary words because they are important.
    b. Read the words that you could pronounce.
    c. Read the words that tell the most about the story.

11. What things do you read faster than others?
    a. Books that are easy to read.
    b. When you've read the story before.
    c. Books that have a lot of pictures.

12. Why do you go back and read things over again?
    a. Because it is good practice.
    b. Because you didn't understand it.
    c. Because you forgot some words.

(continued)

13. What do you do if you come to a word and you don't know what it means?

    a. Use the words around it to figure it out.

    b. Ask someone else.

    c. Go on to the next word.

14. What do you do if you don't know what a whole sentence means?

    a. Read it again.

    b. Sound out all the words.

    c. Think about the other sentences in the paragraph.

15. What parts of the story do you skip as you read?

    a. The hard words and parts you don't understand.

    b. The unimportant parts that don't mean anything for the story.

    c. You never skip anything.

16. If you are reading a story for fun, what would you do?

    a. Look at the pictures to get the meaning.

    b. Read the story as fast as you can.

    c. Imagine the story like a movie in your mind.

17. If you are reading for science or social studies, what would you do to remember the information?

    a. Ask yourself questions about the important ideas.

    b. Skip the parts you don't understand.

    c. Concentrate and try hard to remember it.

18. If you are reading for a test, which would help the most?

    a. Read the story as many times as possible.

    b. Talk about it with somebody to make sure you understand it.

    c. Say the sentences over and over.

19. If you are reading a library book to write a report, which would help you the most?

    a. Sound out words you don't know.

    b. Write it down in your own words.

    c. Skip the parts you don't understand.

20. Which of these is the best way to remember a story?

    a. Say every word over and over.

    b. Think about remembering it.

    c. Write it down in your own words.

(continued)

SCORING GUIDE

EVALUATION

1. What is the hardest part about reading for you?

1   a.   Sounding out the hard words.

2   b.   When you don't understand the story.

0   c.   Nothing is hard about reading for you.

2. What would help you become a better reader?

1   a.   If more people would help you when you read.

0   b.   Reading easier books with shorter words.

2   c.   Checking to make sure you understand what you read.

3. What is special about the first sentence or two in a story?

1   a.   They always begin with "Once upon a time . . . "

0   b.   The first sentences are the most interesting.

2   c.   They often tell what the story is about.

4. How are the last sentences of a story special?

1   a.   They are the exciting action sentences.

2   b.   They tell you what happened.

0   c.   They are harder to read.

5. How can you tell which sentences are the most important ones in a story?

2   a.   They're the ones that tell the most about the characters and what happens.

1   b.   They're the most interesting ones.

0   c.   All of them are important.

PLANNING

6. If you could only read some of the sentences in the story because you were in a hurry, which ones would you read?

0   a.   Read the sentences in the middle of the story.

2   b.   Read the sentences that tell you the most about the story.

1   c.   Read the interesting, exciting sentences.

(continued)

7. When you tell other people about what you read, what do you tell them?

2   a.   What happened in the story.

0   b.   The number of pages in the book.

1   c.   Who the characters are.

8. If the teacher told you to read a story to remember the general meaning, what would you do?

2   a.   Skim through the story to find the main parts.

1   b.   Read all of the story and try to remember everything.

0   c.   Read the story and remember all of the words.

9. Before you start to read, what kind of plans do you make to help you read better?

0   a.   You don't make any plans. You just start reading.

1   b.   You choose a comfortable place.

2   c.   You think about why you are reading.

10. If you had to read very fast and could only read some words, which ones would you try to read?

1   a.   Read the new vocabulary words because they are important.

0   b.   Read the words that you could pronounce.

2   c.   Read the words that tell the most about the story.

REGULATION

11. What things do you read faster than others?

1   a.   Books that are easy to read.

2   b.   When you've read the story before.

0   c.   Books that have a lot of pictures.

12. Why do you go back and read things over again?

1   a.   Because it is good practice.

2   b.   Because you didn't understand it.

0   c.   Because you forgot some words.

13. What do you do if you come to a word and you don't know what it means?

2   a.   Use the words around it to figure it out.

1   b.   Ask someone else.

0   c.   Go on to the next word.

(continued)

14. What do you do if you don't know what a whole sentence means?

1   a.   Read it again.

0   b.   Sound out all the words.

2   c.   Think about the other sentences in the paragraph.

15. What parts of the story do you skip as you read?

1   a.   The hard words and parts you don't understand.

2   b.   The unimportant parts that don't mean anything for the story.

0   c.   You never skip anything.

CONDITIONAL KNOWLEDGE

16. If you are reading a story for fun, what would you do?

1   a.   Look at the pictures to get the meaning.

0   b.   Read the story as fast as you can.

2   c.   Imagine the story like a movie in your mind.

17. If you are reading for science or social studies, what would you do to remember the information?

2   a.   Ask yourself questions about the important ideas.

0   b.   Skip the parts you don't understand.

1   c.   Concentrate and try hard to remember it.

18. If you are reading for a test, which would help the most?

1   a.   Read the story as many times as possible.

2   b.   Talk about it with somebody to make sure you understand it.

0   c.   Say the sentences over and over.

19. If you are reading a library book to write a report, which would help you the most?

1   a.   Sound out words you don't know.

2   b.   Write it down in your own words.

0   c.   Skip the parts you don't understand.

20. Which of these is the best way to remember a story?

0   a.   Say every word over and over.

1   b.   Think about remembering it.

2   c.   Write it down in your own words.

FORM 8.4. Textbook Interview.

Name _____   Date _____

Grade _____

Directions: For this section, use the student's classroom basal reader. If no basal is used in the classroom, select a piece of literature that is representative of classroom reading materials. Place the text in front of the student. As each question is asked, open the appropriate text in front of the student to help provide a point of reference for the question.

Basal Reader or Literature

Open to a story that the student has not yet read.

1. Why do we read this kind of book? [*Note*: Possible answers might be "to learn to read from" or "enjoyment."]

2. Why do you think your teacher wants you to read this book?

3. Describe how you might read this story in class?

4. Do you enjoy reading this type of material? [Probe for a fuller answer than "yes" or "no"]

5. What do you need to do to get a good grade in reading?

Directions: For this section, use a content area text, preferably the one the student uses in the classroom. Choose a text that has a great many features, such as bold-faced words, headings, a summary, etc. Place the text in front of the student. As each question is asked, open the appropriate text in front of the student to help provide a point of reference for the question. This is an informal interview. You can integrate questions 8–12 into a natural conversation.

6. Why do we read this kind of book? [*Note*: Possible answers might be "to learn from" or "to learn to read from."]

7. Why do you think your teacher wants you to read this book?

(continued)

8. [Open to a chapter somewhat beyond where the child has already covered.] Suppose you were to be given a text on this chapter. How would you read it? [Have the child model his or her reading, showing you the things that he or she would do.]

9. Would you pay attention to any particular parts of the text? [Possible answers: bold-faced words, chapter summary, headings, etc.]

10. [If not included in the answer to #8] Would you pay attention to these? [Point to bold-faced words.] What are these for?

11. [If not included in the answer to #8] Would you pay attention to these? [Point to headings.] What are these for?

12. [If not included in the answer to #8] Would you pay attention to this? [Point to summary at the end of the chapter.] What is this for?

13. [If not included in the answer to #8] Would you pay attention to these? [Point to questions at the end of the chapter.] What are these for?

14. Does the teacher do anything additional to help you study? [Probe for study guides, prequestioning, and so on.]

15. How well do you do on tests on this type of material?

16. What do you have to do to get a good grade in _____?

17. What do you think you need to do in order to do better?

18. Have you ever tried skimming before you read a chapter to get an idea of what it is about?

19. Have you ever tried summarizing or making notes to remember what you've read?

20. Have you ever tried asking yourself questions to remember what you've read?

9

Affective Factors

If you hope to influence students' attitudes toward reading in a truly substantial way, you must first know something about your children. How positive are their attitudes? What are their likes and dislikes? How do their friends and family feel about reading? A good starting point is to familiarize yourself with the basics concerning reading attitudes—how they're formed, the chief trends you can expect, and the interest areas on which you might be able to capitalize.

ORIGINS OF ATTITUDES

Attitudes are learned. They are not innate but develop over time as the result of cultural forces and our own day-to-day experiences with reading and books. The more positive these forces are, the more likely it is that a child will become a lifelong reader. We can summarize these forces quite simply. Our attitudes toward reading are shaped by:

1. Each and every reading experience;
2. Our beliefs about what will happen when we open a book; and
3. Our beliefs about how those we hold in high regard feel about reading.

All three of these forces are subject to teacher intervention—even the last! Effective attitude-building strategies such as those described here, target one or more of the factors.

WHAT DO WE KNOW ABOUT CHILDREN'S ATTITUDES?

Studies have led to several important conclusions that are useful in understanding what we, as teachers, can expect (McKenna, 2001; McKenna, Kear, & Ellsworth, 1995). Here, in brief, are the major findings of reading attitude research:

1. Reading attitudes tend to worsen over time.
2. Reading attitudes worsen more rapidly for poor readers.
3. Girls tend to possess more positive reading attitudes than boys.
4. Ethnic group membership is not, in itself, strongly related to reading attitudes.
5. Instructional methods can have a positive influence on attitudes.

WHAT DO WE KNOW ABOUT CHILDREN'S INTERESTS?

An interest area is really an attitude toward reading about a particular topic. In other words, we have a general attitude toward reading, and we have specific attitudes toward reading about certain subjects. For instance, you may love to read but hate the thought of reading science-fiction books. Knowing about children's interest areas arms teachers with the know-how they need to recommend books that match existing enthusiasms. Through these positive experiences, children come to realize that books afford a means of satisfying and furthering the interests they already have.

Studies of children's reading interests offer useful generalizations that may confirm your own instincts and classroom observations (e.g., McKenna, 1986, 2001). Here are some of the most important findings:

◆ The number of interests declines with age.
◆ The influence of gender increases with age.
◆ Girls are more likely to read "boys' books" than are boys to read "girls' books."
◆ Typical male interests include science, machines, sports, and action/adventure.
◆ Typical female interests include interpersonal relationships and romance.
◆ Three interest areas of strong appeal, regardless of gender or reading ability, are humor, animals, and the unusual.

ASSESSING ATTITUDES AND INTERESTS

It is vital to keep in mind that conclusions based on research are simply generalizations. Although they adequately describe large populations of children and can guide our thinking as we plan instruction and form broad expectations, the attitudes and interests of an individual child may differ sharply from the norm. This is why it is always important to assess children and not merely to assume that they conform to stereotypical patterns. Some useful ways of gathering information about your students include the following:

◆ Classroom observation
◆ Tracking entries in students' reading journals
◆ Asking open-ended questionnaires
◆ Administering interest inventories
◆ Administering attitude surveys

These activities complement each other nicely. The information offered by each is unique and contributes to a complete picture of the child as a developing reader. Let's look briefly at each.

Classroom Observation

Observing children as they take part in classroom activities can provide you with valuable information about their likes and dislikes. One way to systematize these observations is to jot them briefly into a log, which can be kept in a child's portfolio. Entries might include notations such as these:

9–25	Beth told me she really liked the Critter books.
10–14	Beth's mom said she wants to be a scientist.
11–2	Beth checked out two books about snakes.

Reading Journals

Another means of gathering data about students' attitudes and interests is by reading their entries in their reading journals. Some teachers require students to make regular entries in such journals. These typically include the title of each book they complete, the date, and a brief response to the material. Journals also might contain general commentaries about reading. An advantage of reading journals is that they compel students to do some introspecting about their feelings toward reading and about their emerging identity as readers. Journal entry keeping also encourages the formation of critical judgments about what was read and conveys the message that their opinions count. This significance becomes especially evident to students when teachers add written responses to their entries. Reading journals also offer a good opportunity for writing development and provide a meaningful context in which to apply writing skills.

An important cautionary note about reading journals: Do not allow them to turn into a series of book reports. You do not want to create an expectation in your students that every book they read for "pleasure" will inevitably be followed by a laborious writing exercise. Setting some guidelines at the beginning regarding your expectations— and making sure those expectations are modest—can prevent this undesirable shift from occurring.

Open-Ended Questionnaires

A good get-acquainted activity involves asking students to respond to incomplete sentences designed to elicit personal beliefs about reading as well as existing interests. These need not be long and involved—a few statements can go a long way. These statements can be used as a written activity in a group setting (in which case, they also reveal information about writing development) or individually as an interview guide, in which you provide each sentence starter orally and jot down the student's response. Try using the questionnaire in Form 9.1 (p. 212) as a starting point and modify it as appropriate.

Interest Inventories

An interest inventory is a list of topics used to identify those that hold high appeal for individual students. They're easy to make and simple to give, and the results can be very helpful in recommending books that are likely to engage students' interest. In other words, interest inventories can make you a better book broker! They can be given to your class as a group as long as you read the choices aloud, so that poor decoding does not prevent children from making informed choices.

Form 9.2 (p. 213) is a sample interest inventory that you are free to duplicate or modify. Or you can start from scratch. Whichever route you take, here are some guidelines that might help:

♦ Word process your inventory so that you can add or delete topics after you've used it a few times.
♦ Make sure you can deliver the goods—don't include topics for which you have no materials.
♦ Include a wide range of topics, including those typically of interest to boys and to girls.
♦ Include topics that might suggest nonfiction titles as well as fiction.
♦ Add a few blank lines at the end. An interest inventory is like a ballot, and a place for write-ins should be provided! (Trying to fully anticipate kids' interests in advance can be frustrating.)
♦ Don't mention reading when you give the directions. A negative attitude may lead to negative responses even for true interests.
♦ Make it easy to respond. Try asking kids to "grade" each topic, just as a teacher might, using whatever grading system they know (such as *A*, *B*, *C*, *D*, *F*). This method provides more detailed information than a checklist, because it indicates the *strength* of the interest.
♦ Keep completed inventories where you can find them, perhaps in portfolios.
♦ Use the topics that receive the highest "grades" to recommend books to individual students.

Attitude Surveys

Rating scales are available for assessing the general reading attitudes of your students. The results can be easily quantified and will provide an accurate barometer of how positive (or negative) attitudes may be. They also can be used on a pre–post basis to document progress over the course of a year.

Elementary Reading Attitude Survey

The ERAS (Form 9.3, pp. 214–222) is based on the cartoon character *Garfield*, together with directions for administering, scoring, and interpreting it (McKenna & Kear, 1990). Permission has been granted from cartoonist Jim Davis, codeveloper of the ERAS, to duplicate the survey for classroom use. You'll even find a table of percentile ranks, so you can see how your students compare to a national sample of more than 17,000 children. A one-page version is provided for older students.

Motivations for Reading Questionnaire

The MRQ (Form 9.4, pp. 223–229), designed by Gambrell et al. (1995), can be used in grades 3 and above to gauge a range of affective dimensions. This instrument was developed at the National Reading Research Center.

Reader Self-Perception Scale

This group instrument (Form 9.5, pp. 230–233), designed by Henk and Melnick (1995), provides a window on how students see themselves as readers. Its domain overlaps slightly with that of the MRQ.

Reading Activity Inventory

The RAI (Form 9.6, pp. 234–239) is an instrument developed by Guthrie, McGough, and Wigfield (1994) that is designed to reveal the amount and types of reading your students do. Like the ERAS and MRQ, it can be administered on a group basis.

Title Recognition Test

This clever group survey (Form 9.7, pp. 240–241) by Cunningham and Stanovich (1991) indirectly measures attitude by assessing students' knowledgeability of well-known titles—well known to literacy educators and well-read children, that is. In theory, the more reading students have done, the more titles they should be able to select from a list that includes fictitious distractors.

ADDRESSING NEGATIVE ATTITUDES

To make progress with children who are not predisposed to read, it is important to ask why they do not enjoy this crucial activity. Their answers are not always clear, but a few basic questions can help clarify the situation.

Is the Attitude Problem the Result of Poor Decoding?

No one voluntarily engages in an activity that is frustrating. Nonfluent reading, with all of its natural frustrations, can be a barrier to positive attitudes. Apart from fostering proficiency, teachers can initiate the following actions:

♦ *Read aloud to children.* Doing so relieves students of the burden of decoding, while acquainting them with interesting books and giving them a clearer vision of the benefits of proficient reading.

♦ *Make materials of appropriate difficulty available.* Sometimes called "hi–lo" books, these materials aim to interest older children but place few demands on their limited decoding and vocabulary. An excellent source of these books is Phelan (1996).

♦ *Use electronic supports.* E-books with pronunciation supports can make it possible for students to read independently, because they remove the decoding barrier without the need for constant teacher presence. Somewhat less desirable are audiotapes of books—though these can bring literature to life, they do little to further word recognition development.

Is the Attitude Problem the Result of Uninteresting Materials?

Teachers must become "brokers," using their knowledge of books, on the one hand, and children's interests, on the other, to recommend appropriate matches. This is why interest inventories can be so important. Teachers must still "deliver the goods," however. Specifically, we recommend the following possibilities:

♦ *Establish an extensive classroom library.* Don't worry about the condition of the materials—aim for quality and variety. Include back copies of magazines that you can get from the media specialist. Visit garage sales and flea markets. Don't forget the free books you can earn by having your children participate in book clubs. House the books in plastic tubs or baskets.

♦ *Don't forget nonfiction.* Teachers often forget that nonfiction can be just as appealing to children as literature. In fact, many find it more engaging. Moreover, the ability to read nonfiction is vital to eventual success in the workplace, so there is a powerful educational rationale for including nonfiction titles in your classroom library. Strive for an effective balance.

♦ *Note the Children's Choice Awards.* Research shows that award-winning books are not always popular with children, at least when the awards are decided on by adults. This conclusion makes sense when we stop to consider that children's sensibilities and worldviews differ substantially from ours and that it is often difficult to put ourselves in their place. Awards are frequently given to the kinds of books we, as teachers, would like to see our students reading rather than those they might prefer to read. The fact that a particular book attains critical appeal should not be regarded as unerring testimony about how well kids will like it. One means of contending with this dilemma is to rely on polls conducted among children and teens. Each year the International Reading Association conducts two such polls, one among children, ages 5–13, and the other among students in grades 7–12. The books evaluated in these polls are submitted by publishers and must meet certain criteria before they are distributed to classrooms around the country for rating. For example, each book submitted for consideration as a Young Adults' Choice must have received two positive published reviews. In reality, then, adults do have a say about which books qualify, but the final ratings are rendered by students—a vital difference.

♦ *Include series books.* These can be sequential books (e.g., the Laura Ingalls Wilder series) or books that simply reuse characters (e.g., *Curious George, Clifford,* etc.). One advantage of series books is that if a child becomes interested in one, then an entire line of additional books suddenly attains high appeal. A second advantage is that such books are easier to comprehend, because so much of the prior knowledge needed to understand them (information about characters, setting, and typical plot structures) is already present as a result of having read other books in the series.

♦ *Include illustrated books.* Research shows that older struggling readers often lack the ability to visualize the events about which they read. Illustrated books can support them by providing visual images. This support will lead to a greater willingness to read. The *Illustrated Classics*, for example, provide one drawing on every other page; they are "naturals" for coaxing reluctant readers into extended reading by providing them with the support they need.

What Instructional Techniques Are Effective in Fostering Positive Attitudes?

Although there is no magic bullet, some techniques and activities have yielded good results:

♦ *Bring in adult models.* Try inviting a variety of adults, over the course of a year, to speak to your class about their own reading. Individuals such as the principal, the custodian, the school nurse, etc., can convey the message that *everybody* reads; of course, outside visitors can bring the same message. Consider extending invitations to those who reflect the cultural backgrounds of your class.

♦ *Be a good model yourself.* If reading is worth doing, you must be seen doing it yourself. Children must observe that you, in fact, practice what you preach. Bring, and talk about, what you've read, whether it's a bestseller, a teacher resource book, or an article from a magazine or newspaper. You will be modeling not only the value of reading as a part of life outside school but the social process of sharing what we read with one another.

♦ *Provide time for recreational reading.* This protected block of time has been called Drop Everything and Read (DEAR), Uninterrupted Sustained Silent Reading (U.S.S.R.), and Self-Selected Reading (SSR). Regardless of the name, it is a method of scheduling time during the school day for recreational reading by providing the opportunity to explore books in a relaxed atmosphere, without the threat of accountability. It also affords students another means of becoming more proficient by reading in pleasant, authentic contexts.

♦ *Be cautious of incentive programs.* Outside incentive programs designed to increase the amount of reading children do are a matter of ongoing debate. The Accelerated Reader, Pizza Hut's Book-It program, Scholastic's Reading Counts, and various schoolwide goals (such as the principal or library media specialist kissing a pig, jumping into a tub of Jell-O™, etc.) are now commonplace in elementary and middle schools. There is no debate about the fact that these programs can increase the amount of reading children do. Whether they lead to lifelong reading habits is far less certain, though two facts argue that some children may indeed come to value reading more highly. First, the increased amount of reading undoubtedly makes some children more proficient, and having to contend with poor proficiency is a sure way *not* to become an avid reader. Second, by reading in quantity, children are inadvertently exposed to a variety of books, and their perspectives on what is available are broadened. One clever modification is to use *books* as an incentive!

◆ *Consider cross-age tutoring.* Placing older and younger children together for tutoring can bolster the attitudes of the older students, particularly if they themselves are experiencing problems. The logistics of coordinating your efforts with another teacher are worth the effort. The tutoring need not be technical and is perhaps best when limited to the sharing of books chosen by the older partner.

◆ *Employ literature circles.* Literature circles, also called *literature response groups* and *literature study groups*, are student discussion groups in which risk-free exchanges about mutually read books are invited. In these circles, students interact with other members of the same age and similar cultural background—which, research suggests, can lead to improved attitudes toward reading (e.g., Leal, 1993). The rationale of literature circles is persuasive. Literature groups offer one way to model the sort of behavior that teachers should seek to foster in children if they are to participate in a literate culture. Although reading is typically a solitary activity, it is also an inherently social act involving at least two individuals: reader and writer. In the case of published works, multiple readers afford the opportunity of introducing a second social dimension among readers of the same work. Exposure to peers with positive reading attitudes may improve a struggling reader's perception of reading. Moreover, discussion among readers has the potential to broaden children's critical perspectives on what is reading.

◆ *Try idea circles.* Literature groups typically bring students together to discuss the *fiction* book(s) they have all read. Guthrie and McCann (1996) discovered that using *nonfiction* as the basis of these discussions can be highly motivating as well. Best of all, kids need not have read the same selection. Rather, the common element is the topic. Guthrie and McCann define an idea circle as a "peer-led, small-group discussion of concepts fueled by multiple text sources" (p. 88). In an idea circle, everyone has something unique to contribute to the discussion by virtue of having read a different source. You can differentiate these assignments deftly, ensuring that abler readers undertake more challenging materials. You may need to take precautions, however, to guard against one or two students' taking over the discussion and eclipsing others. Spelling out some simple ground rules in advance can foster balanced discussions. For example, the discussion might begin with each student sharing one fact he or she discovered. A moderator also might be appointed, whose duty is to solicit input from all participants.

FORM 9.1. Here's How I Feel about Reading.

Name _____

1. I like to read about _____.

2. My friends think reading is _____.

3. My favorite book is _____.

4. At home, reading is _____.

5. On weekends, my favorite thing to do is _____.

6. When I get older, I'll read _____.

7. I like books about _____.

8. When we read library books at school, I _____.

9. The best thing about reading is _____.

10. The worst thing about reading is _____.

FORM 9.2. Tell Me What You Like!

Name _____

Which topics do you like the most? Pretend you're a teacher and give each one of these a grade. Give it an *A* if you really like it, a *B* if you like it pretty well, a *C* if it's just OK, a *D* if you don't like it, and an *F* if you can't stand it! If I've missed some topics you really like, please write them on the lines at the bottom of the page.

_____ sports	_____ monsters
_____ animals	_____ horses
_____ magic	_____ detectives
_____ jokes	_____ love
_____ exploring the unknown	_____ famous scientists
_____ sharks	_____ ghosts
_____ camping	_____ other countries
_____ UFOs	_____ dogs
_____ spiders	_____ cooking
_____ the jungle	_____ the ocean
_____ drawing, painting	_____ music
_____ riddles	_____ science fiction
_____ friendship	_____ cats
_____ snakes	_____ families
_____ the wilderness	_____ the desert
_____ fishing	_____ computers

What other topics do you really like? Write them here:

_____

_____

_____

FORM 9.3. Elementary Reading Attitude Survey.

Elementary Reading Attitude Survey
Directions for use

The Elementary Reading Attitude Survey provides a quick indication of student attitudes toward reading. It consists of 20 items and can be administered to an entire classroom in about 10 minutes. Each item presents a brief, simply-worded statement about reading, followed by four pictures of Garfield. Each pose is designed to depict a different emotional state, ranging from very positive to very negative.

Administration
Begin by telling students that you wish to find out how they feel about reading. Emphasize that this is *not* a test and that there are no "right" answers. Encourage sincerity.

Distribute the survey forms and, if you wish to monitor the attitudes of specific students, ask them to write their names in the space at the top. Hold up a copy of the survey so that the students can see the first page. Point to the picture of Garfield at the far left of the first item. Ask the students to look at this same picture on their own survey form. Discuss with them the mood Garfield seems to be in (very happy). Then move to the next picture and again discuss Garfield's mood (this time, a *little* happy). In the same way, move to the third and fourth pictures and talk about Garfield's moods—a little upset and very upset. It is helpful to point out the position of Garfield's *mouth*, especially in the middle two figures.

Explain that together you will read some statements about reading and that the students should think about how they feel about each statement. They should then circle the picture of Garfield that is closest to their own feelings. (Emphasize that the students should respond according to their own feelings, not as Garfield might respond!) Read each item aloud slowly and distinctly; then read it a second time while students are thinking. Be sure to read the item *number* and to remind students of page numbers when new pages are reached.

Scoring
To score the survey, count four points for each leftmost (happiest) Garfield circled, three for each slightly smiling Garfield, two for each mildly upset Garfield, and one point for each very upset (rightmost) Garfield. Three scores for each student can be obtained: the total for the first 10 items, the total for the second 10, and a composite total. The first half of the survey relates to attitude toward recreational reading; the second half relates to attitude toward academic aspects of reading.

Interpretation
You can interpret scores in two ways. One is to note informally where the score falls in regard to the four nodes of the scale. A total score of 50, for example, would fall about mid-way on the scale, between the slightly happy and slightly upset figures, therefore indicating a relatively indifferent overall attitude toward reading. The other approach is more formal. It involves converting the raw scores into percentile ranks by means of Table 1. Be sure to use the norms for the right grade level and to note the column headings (Rec = recreational reading, Aca = academic reading, Tot = total score). If you wish to determine the average percentile rank for your class, average the raw scores first; then use the table to locate the percentile rank corresponding to the raw score mean. Percentile ranks cannot be averaged directly.

(continued)

Mid-year percentile ranks by grade and scale

Raw Scr	Grade 1 Rec	Grade 1 Aca	Grade 1 Tot	Grade 2 Rec	Grade 2 Aca	Grade 2 Tot	Grade 3 Rec	Grade 3 Aca	Grade 3 Tot	Grade 4 Rec	Grade 4 Aca	Grade 4 Tot	Grade 5 Rec	Grade 5 Aca	Grade 5 Tot	Grade 6 Rec	Grade 6 Aca	Grade 6 Tot
80			99			99			99			99			99			99
79			95			96			98			99			99			99
78			93			95			97			98			99			99
77			92			94			97			98			99			99
76			90			93			96			97			98			99
75			88			92			95			96			98			99
74			86			90			94			95			97			99
73			84			88			92			94			97			98
72			82			86			91			93			96			98
71			80			84			89			91			95			97
70			78			82			86			89			94			96
69			75			79			84			88			92			95
68			72			77			81			86			91			93
67			69			74			79			83			89			92
66			66			71			76			80			87			90
65			62			69			73			78			84			88
64			59			66			70			75			82			86
63			55			63			67			72			79			84
62			52			60			64			69			76			82
61			49			57			61			66			73			79
60			46			54			58			62			70			76
59			43			51			55			59			67			73
58			40			47			51			56			64			69
57			37			45			48			53			61			66
56			34			41			44			48			57			62
55			31			38			41			45			53			58
54			28			35			38			41			50			55
53			25			32			34			38			46			52
52			22			29			31			35			42			48
51			20			26			28			32			39			44
50			18			23			25			28			36			40
49			15			20			23			26			33			37
48			13			18			20			23			29			33
47			12			15			17			20			26			30
46			10			13			15			18			23			27
45			8			11			13			16			20			25
44			7			9			11			13			17			22
43			6			8			9			12			15			20
42			5			7			8			10			13			17
41			5			6			7			9			12			15
40	99	99	4	99	99	5	99	99	6	99	99	7	99	99	10	99	99	13
39	92	91	3	94	94	4	96	97	5	97	98	6	98	99	9	98	99	12
38	89	88	3	92	92	3	94	95	4	95	97	5	96	98	8	97	99	10
37	86	85	2	88	89	2	90	93	3	92	95	4	94	98	7	95	99	8
36	81	79	2	84	85	2	87	91	2	88	93	3	91	96	6	92	98	7
35	77	75	1	79	81	1	81	88	2	84	90	3	87	95	4	88	97	6
34	72	69	1	74	78	1	75	83	2	78	87	2	82	93	4	83	95	5
33	65	63	1	68	73	1	69	79	1	72	83	2	77	90	3	79	93	4
32	58	58	1	62	67	1	63	74	1	66	79	1	71	86	3	74	91	3
31	52	53	1	56	62	1	57	69	0	60	75	1	65	82	2	69	87	2
30	44	49	1	50	57	0	51	63	0	54	70	1	59	77	1	63	82	2
29	38	44	0	44	51	0	45	58	0	47	64	1	53	71	1	58	78	1
28	32	39	0	37	46	0	38	52	0	41	58	1	48	66	1	51	73	1
27	26	34	0	31	41	0	33	47	0	35	52	1	42	60	1	46	67	1
26	21	30	0	25	37	0	26	41	0	29	46	0	36	54	0	39	60	1
25	17	25	0	20	32	0	21	36	0	23	40	0	30	49	0	34	54	0
24	12	21	0	15	27	0	17	31	0	19	35	0	25	42	0	29	49	0
23	9	18	0	11	23	0	13	26	0	14	29	0	20	37	0	24	42	0
22	7	14	0	8	18	0	9	22	0	11	25	0	16	31	0	19	36	0
21	5	11	0	6	15	0	6	18	0	9	20	0	13	26	0	15	30	0
20	4	9	0	4	11	0	5	14	0	6	16	0	10	21	0	12	24	0
19	2	7		2	8		3	11		5	13		7	17		10	20	
18	2	5		2	6		2	8		3	9		6	13		8	15	
17	1	4		1	5		1	5		2	7		4	9		6	11	
16	1	3		1	3		1	4		2	5		3	6		4	8	
15	0	2		0	2		0	3		1	3		2	4		3	6	
14	0	2		0	1		0	1		1	2		1	2		1	3	
13	0	1		0	1		0	1		0	1		1	2		1	2	
12	0	1		0	0		0	0		0	1		0	1		0	1	
11	0	0		0	0		0	0		0	0		0	0		0	0	
10	0	0		0	0		0	0		0	0		0	0		0	0	

(continued)

**Elementary Reading Attitude Survey
Scoring sheet**

Student name _____

Teacher _____

Grade _____ Administration date _____

```
┌─────────────────────────────────────────┐
│              Scoring guide                │
│                                           │
│   4   points    Happiest Garfield         │
│   3   points    Slightly smiling Garfield │
│   2   points    Mildly upset Garfield     │
│   1   point     Very upset Garfield       │
└─────────────────────────────────────────┘
```

Recreational reading   Academic reading

  1. ____   11. ____
  2. ____   12. ____
  3. ____   13. ____
  4. ____   14. ____
  5. ____   15. ____
  6. ____   16. ____
  7. ____   17. ____
  8. ____   18. ____
  9. ____   19. ____
10. ____   20. ____

Raw score: ____   Raw score: ____

Full scale raw score (Recreational + Academic): _____

Percentile ranks   Recreational   ┌──────┐
                                        │   │
                                        ├──────┤
                      Academic   │   │
                                        ├──────┤
                      Full scale   │   │
                                        └──────┘

(continued)

ELEMENTARY READING ATTITUDE SURVEY

School_____   Grade___   Name_____

1. How do you feel when you read a book on a rainy Saturday?

2. How do you feel when you read a book in school during free time?

3. How do you feel about reading for fun at home?

4. How do you feel about getting a book for a present?

(continued)

217

5. How do you feel about spending free time reading?

6. How do you feel about starting a new book?

7. How do you feel about reading during summer vacation?

8. How do you feel about reading instead of playing?

(continued)

9. How do you feel about going to a bookstore?

10. How do you feel about reading different kinds of books?

11. How do you feel when the teacher asks you questions about what you read?

12. How do you feel about doing reading workbook pages and worksheets?

(continued)

13. How do you feel about reading in school?

14. How do you feel about reading your school books?

15. How do you feel about learning from a book?

16. How do you feel when it's time for reading class?

(continued)

5

17. How do you feel about the stories you read in reading class?

18. How do you feel when you read out loud in class?

19. How do you feel about using a dictionary?

20. How do you feel about taking a reading test?

(continued)

Elementary Reading Attitude Survey

School _____ Grade _____ Name _____

1. How do you feel when you read a book on a rainy Saturday?

2. How do you feel when you read a book in school during free time?

3. How do you feel about reading for fun at home?

4. How do you feel about getting a book for a present?

5. How do you feel about spending free time reading?

6. How do you feel about starting a new book?

7. How do you feel about reading on summer vacation?

8. How do you feel about reading instead of playing?

9. How do you feel about going to a bookstore?

10. How do you feel about reading different kinds of books?

11. How do you feel when the teacher asks you questions about what you read?

12. How do you feel about doing reading workbook pages and worksheets?

13. How do you feel about reading in school?

14. How do you feel about reading your school books?

15. How do you feel about learning from a book?

16. How do you feel when it's time for reading class?

17. How do you feel about the stories you read in reading class?

18. How do you feel when you read out loud in class?

19. How do you feel about using a dictionary?

20. How do you feel about taking a reading test?

FORM 9.4. Motivations for Reading Questionnaire.

Administration and Scoring

The Motivations for Reading Questionnaire (MRQ) measures different dimensions or aspects of elementary school-age children's reading motivations. It can be used to discover the nature of children's motivations for reading, as well as some of the things about reading children do not find motivating. It consists of 54 items, and can be administered in 20–25 minutes. It can be used in conjunction with the Reading Activity Inventory developed by Guthrie et al. (1994).

The MRQ follows these instructions. It may be photocopied for use in the classroom.

Administration

Before you distribute the MRQ forms, tell students you are interested in finding out what they think and feel about reading as an activity. Assure the students that there are no right or wrong answers to the questions, and that children sitting near them might answer an item differently. Encourage the students to answer the questions honestly. The measure is designed to be given to a classroom-size group; it also can be given in smaller groups. Individual administration generally is not necessary.

For third- and fourth-grade children, it is recommended that the MRQ be read aloud (if all students in a fourth-grade class read well, then they could complete the questionnaire on their own). Fifth- and sixth-grade children can read the questions on their own, but the administrator should be prepared to answer any questions they have about some of the words contained in the different items.

A cover page can be added to the questionnaire to obtain demographic and other information, if that is desired. The first page of the questionnaire contains three sample questions to familiarize children with the 4-point answer scales used. The class should complete these sample items before answering the items on the questionnaire itself. The administrator should emphasize to children to use the full range of the 4-point scale.

Scoring

Each item is scored on a 4-point scale; higher scores mean stronger endorsement of the item. A total score can be derived by summing the scores of all the items (with the exception of the Work Avoidance items; these should *not* be included in a summary score). However, we strongly recommend deriving separate scores for each of the proposed dimensions of reading motivations. The scale scores provide much more information than does a total score. Specifically, they provide information about the pattern of children's responses and how children rate different aspects of their motivation for reading. These profiles could be quite useful for teachers and reading specialists interested in understanding what things children like about reading and what things they don't like about it.

(continued)

SPECIFIC STEPS FOR SCORING THE INSTRUMENT BY HAND

1. Check each questionnaire to be sure that each student completed each item. If some items are left blank, they should not be included in the scoring of the instrument. Each item that is completed should be scored from 1 to 4.
2. If a student circled more than one answer for an item and the answers are adjacent (e.g., circled both 1 and 2 or 3 and 4), take the number closer to the middle. However, if both 1 and 4 were circled, do not count that item.
3. If a student added numbers to the scale (e.g., the student wrote in numbers less than 1 or greater than 4), convert them to the scale. Numbers less than 1 can be scored as 1; numbers greater than 4 can be scored as 4.
4. To create scale scores, use the table (pp. 225–226) to identify the items in each scale. Add the students' responses to the items in each scale (e.g., in the case of the Reading Efficacy scale, add the scores from the four items shown under that heading on p. 225) and divide by the number of items completed (e.g., in the case of the Efficacy scale, divide by 4 if all the items were completed by the student). Dividing by the number of items on each scale means that all the scale scores also will have a range of 1 to 4, which makes them easier to compare.
5. For the Compliance scale, the first two items should be reversed before computing the score here. That is, a score of 1 should be converted to 4, a score of 2 converted to 3, a score of 3 converted to 2, and a score of 4 converted to 1.

SPECIFIC STEPS FOR SCORING THE INSTRUMENT BY COMPUTER

The scales also can be created using different statistical packages, such as SPSS.

1. Follow steps 1 through 3 above.
2. To create scale scores, use the table below to identify the items in each scale. Use your computer program to add the appropriate items for each scale, being sure to reverse the first two items on the Compliance scale.
3. The scale scores can be saved on the computer for later use and analysis.

Interpretation

The scores can be used in several ways. First, individual profiles of the students can be examined. Each profile gives an indication of the kinds of things by which a child is motivated. For instance, does he or she read primarily for curiosity, or to get good grades? Does he or she like to be challenged by reading assignments? These profiles could be used to tailor the curriculum to better match individual student needs, or perhaps to provide special activities for different students. For instance, children who strongly endorse the Reading Challenge items could be given some especially involved assignments. Children strongly endorsing the Reading Recognition items could be given the opportunity to receive some recognition for their work. Children strongly endorsing the Social Reasons for Reading items could be allowed to read more with their peers.

(continued)

Second, the scores also could be grouped and group differences examined to answer questions such as: Are the boys more positively motivated than the girls? Do boys and girls have different things that appear to motivate them most in their reading?

Third, the measure could be given twice or three times over a school year, and patterns of change in different children's motivations could be assessed.

Subscales On The Motivations For Reading Questionnaire

Reading Efficacy

I know that I will do well in reading next year.

I am a good reader.

I learn more from reading than most students in the class.

In comparison to my other school subjects, I am best at reading

Reading Challenge

I like hard, challenging books.

If the project is interesting, I can read difficult material.

I like it when the questions in books make me think.

I usually learn difficult things by reading.

If a book is interesting, I don't care how hard it is to read.

Reading Curiosity

If the teacher discusses something interesting, I might read more about it.

If I am reading about an interesting topic, I sometimes lose track of time.

I read to learn new information about topics that interest me.

I read about my hobbies to learn more about them.

I like to read about new things.

I enjoy reading books about people in different countries

Aesthetic Enjoyment of Reading

I read stories about fantasy and make-believe.

I like mysteries.

I make pictures in my mind when I read.

I feel like I make friends with people in good books.

I read a lot of adventure stories.

I enjoy a long, involved story or fiction book.

Importance of Reading

It is very important to me to be a good reader.

In comparison to other activities I do, it is very important to me to be a good reader.

Compliance

I do as little schoolwork as possible in reading.*

I read because I have to.*

I always do my reading work exactly as the teacher wants it.

Finishing every reading assignment is very important to me.

I always try to finish my reading on time.

* *Reverse the direction of these two items when scoring them.*

(continued)

Reading Recognition

I like having the teacher say I read well.

My friends sometimes tell me I am a good reader.

I like to get compliments for my reading.

I am happy when someone recognizes my reading.

My parents often tell me what a good job I am doing in reading.

Reading for Grades

Grades are a good way to see how well you are doing in reading.

I look forward to finding out my reading grade.

I read to improve my grades.

My parents ask me about my reading grade.

Social Reasons for Reading

I visit the library often with my family.

I often read to my brother or my sister.

My friends and I like to trade things to read.

I sometimes read to my parents.

I talk to my friends about what I am reading.

I like to help my friends with their schoolwork in reading.

I like to tell my family about what I am reading.

Reading Competition

I try to get more answers right than my friends.

I like being the best at reading.

I like to finish my reading before other students.

I like being the only one who knows an answer in something we read.

It is important for me to see my name on a list of good readers.

I am willing to work hard to read better than my friends.

Reading Work Avoidance

I don't like vocabulary questions.

Complicated stories are no fun to read.

I don't like reading something when the words are too difficult.

I don't like it when there are too many people in the story.

(continued)

MOTIVATIONS FOR READING QUESTIONNAIRE

Directions

We are interested in your reading.

The statements tell how some students feel about reading.

Read each statement and decide whether it talks about a person who is like you or different from you.

There are no right or wrong answers. We only want to know how you feel about reading.

Here are three examples.

If the statement is **very different from you**, circle a 1.

If the statement is **a little different from you**, circle a 2.

If the statement is **a little like you**, circle a 3.

If the statement is **a lot like you**, circle a 4.

CIRCLE ONE ANSWER FOR EACH QUESTION, USING THESE ANSWERS:	Very different from me	A little different from me	A little like me	A lot like me
1. I like ice cream.	1	2	3	4
2. I like to swim.	1	2	3	4
3. I like spinach.	1	2	3	4
1. I visit the library often with my family.	1	2	3	4
2. I like hard, challenging books.	1	2	3	4
3. I know that I will do well in reading next year.	1	2	3	4
4. I do as little schoolwork as possible in reading.	1	2	3	4
5. If the teacher discusses something interesting, I might read more about it.	1	2	3	4
6. I read because I have to.	1	2	3	4
7. I like it when the questions in books make me think.	1	2	3	4
8. I read about my hobbies to learn more about them.	1	2	3	4
9. I am a good reader.	1	2	3	4
10. I read stories about fantasy and make-believe.	1	2	3	4
11. I often read to my brother or sister.	1	2	3	4
12. I like being the only one who knows an answer in something we read.	1	2	3	4
13. I read to learn new information about topics that interest me.	1	2	3	4
14. My friends sometimes tell me I'm a good reader.	1	2	3	4
15. I learn more from reading than most students in my class.	1	2	3	4

(continued)

227

CIRCLE ONE ANSWER FOR EACH QUESTION, USING THESE ANSWERS:	Very different from me	A little different from me	A little like me	A lot like me
16. I like to read about new things.	1	2	3	4
17. I like hearing the teacher say I read well.	1	2	3	4
18. I like being the best at reading.	1	2	3	4
19. I look forward to finding out my reading grade.	1	2	3	4
20. I sometimes read to my parents.	1	2	3	4
21. My friends and I like to trade things to read.	1	2	3	4
22. It is important for me to see my name on a list of good readers.	1	2	3	4
23. I don't like reading something when the words are too difficult.	1	2	3	4
24. I make pictures in my mind when I read.	1	2	3	4
25. I always do my reading work exactly as the teacher wants it.	1	2	3	4
26. I usually learn difficult things by reading.	1	2	3	4
27. I don't like vocabulary questions.	1	2	3	4
28. Complicated stories are no fun to read.	1	2	3	4
29. I am happy when someone recognizes my reading.	1	2	3	4
30. I feel like I make friends with people in good books.	1	2	3	4
31. My parents often tell me what a good job I'm doing in reading.	1	2	3	4
32. Finishing every reading assignment is very important to me.	1	2	3	4
33. I like mysteries.	1	2	3	4
34. I talk to my friends about what I am reading.	1	2	3	4
35. If I am reading about an interesting topic, I sometimes lose track of time.	1	2	3	4
36. I like to get compliments for my reading.	1	2	3	4
37. Grades are a good way to see how I'm doing in reading.	1	2	3	4
38. I like to help my friends with their schoolwork in reading.	1	2	3	4
39. I read to improve my grades.	1	2	3	4
40. My parents ask me about my reading grade.	1	2	3	4
41. I enjoy a long, involved story or fiction book.	1	2	3	4
42. I like to tell my family about what I am reading.	1	2	3	4
43. I try to get more answers right than my friends.	1	2	3	4
44. If the project is interesting, I can read difficult material.	1	2	3	4
45. I enjoy reading books about people living in different countries.	1	2	3	4

(continued)

CIRCLE ONE ANSWER FOR EACH QUESTION, USING THESE ANSWERS:	Very different from me	A little different from me	A little like me	A lot like me
46. I read a lot of adventure stories.	1	2	3	4
47. I always try to finish my reading on time.	1	2	3	4
48. If a book is interesting, I don't care how hard it is to read.	1	2	3	4
49. I like to finish my reading before other students.	1	2	3	4
50. In comparison to my other school subjects, I am best at reading.	1	2	3	4
51. I am willing to work hard to read better than my friends.	1	2	3	4
52. I don't like it when there are too many people in the story.	1	2	3	4
53. It is very important to me to be a good reader.	1	2	3	4
54. In comparison to other activities I do, it is very important for me to be good at reading.	1	2	3	4

FORM 9.5. The Reader Self-Perception Scale.

The Reader Self-Perception Scale
Directions for administration, scoring, and interpretation

The Reader Self-Perception Scale (RSPS) is intended to provide an assessment of how children feel about themselves as readers. The scale consists of 33 items that assess self-perceptions along four dimensions of self-efficacy (Progress, Observational Comparison, Social Feedback, and Physiological States). Children are asked to indicate how strongly they agree or disagree with each statement on a 5-point scale (5 = Strongly Agree, 1 = Strongly Disagree). The information gained from this scale can be used to devise ways to enhance children's self-esteem in reading and, ideally, to increase their motivation to read. The following directions explain specifically what you are to do.

Administration

For the results to be of any use, the children must: (a) understand exactly what they are to do, (b) have sufficient time to complete all items, and (c) respond honestly and thoughtfully. Briefly explain to the children that they are being asked to complete a questionnaire about reading. Emphasize that this is not a *test* and that there are no *right* answers. Tell them that they should be as honest as possible because their responses will be confidential. Ask the children to fill in their names, grade levels, and classrooms as appropriate. Read the directions aloud and work through the example with the students as a group. Discuss the response options and make sure that all children understand the rating scale before moving on. It is important that children know that they may raise their hands to ask questions about any words or ideas they do not understand.

The children should then read each item and circle their response for the item. They should work at their own pace. Remind the children that they should be sure to respond to all items. When all items are completed, the children should stop, put their pencils down, and wait for further instructions. Care should be taken that children who work more slowly are not disturbed by children who have already finished.

Scoring

To score the RSPS, enter the following point values for each response on the RSPS scoring sheet (Strongly Agree = 5, Agree = 4, Undecided = 3, Disagree = 2, Strongly Disagree = 1) for each item number under the appropriate scale. Sum each column to obtain a raw score for each of the four specific scales.

Interpretation

Each scale is interpreted in relation to its total possible score. For example, because the RSPS uses a 5-point scale and the Progress scale consists of 9 items, the highest total score for Progress is 45 ($9 \times 5 = 45$). Therefore, a score that would fall approximately in the middle of the range (22–23) would indicate a child's somewhat indifferent perception of her or himself as a reader with respect to Progress. Note that each scale has a different possible total raw score (Progress = 45, Observational Comparison = 30, Social Feedback = 45, and Physiological States = 40) and should be interpreted accordingly.

As a further aid to interpretation, Table 2 presents the descriptive statistics by grade level for each scale. The raw score of a group or individual can be compared to that of the pilot study group at each grade level.

(continued)

The Reader Self-Perception Scale scoring sheet

Student name _____

Teacher _____

Grade _____ Date _____

Scoring key: 5 = Strongly Agree (SA)
4 = Agree (A)
3 = Undecided (U)
2 = Disagree (D)
1 = Strongly Disagree (SD)

Scales

General Perception	Progress	Observational Comparison	Social Feedback	Physiological States
1. ____	10. ____	4. ____	2. ____	5. ____
	13. ____	6. ____	3. ____	8. ____
	15. ____	11. ____	7. ____	16. ____
	18. ____	14. ____	9. ____	21. ____
	19. ____	20. ____	12. ____	25. ____
	23. ____	22. ____	17. ____	26. ____
	24. ____		30. ____	29. ____
	27. ____		31. ____	32. ____
	28. ____		33. ____	

Raw score	____ of 45	____ of 30	____ of 45	____ of 40

Score interpretation

High	44+	26+	38+	37+
Average	39	21	33	31
Low	34	16	27	25

(continued)

The Reader Self-Perception Scale

Listed below are statements about reading. Please read each statement carefully. Then circle the letters that show how much you agree or disagree with the statement. Use the following:

SA = Strongly Agree
A = Agree
U = Undecided
D = Disagree
SD = Strongly Disagree

Example: **I think pizza with pepperoni is the best.**   SA A U D SD

If you are *really positive* that pepperoni pizza is best, circle SA (Strongly Agree).
If you *think* that is good but maybe not great, circle A (Agree).
If you *can't decide* whether or not it is best, circle U (undecided).
If you *think* that pepperoni pizza is not all that good, circle D (Disagree).
If you are *really positive* that pepperoni pizza is not very good, circle SD (Strongly Disagree).

	1. I think I am a good reader.	SA	A	U	D	SD
[SF]	2. I can tell that my teacher likes to listen to me read.	SA	A	U	D	SD
[SF]	3. My teacher thinks that my reading is fine.	SA	A	U	D	SD
[OC]	4. I read faster than other kids.	SA	A	U	D	SD
[PS]	5. I like to read aloud.	SA	A	U	D	SD
[OC]	6. When I read, I can figure out words better than other kids.	SA	A	U	D	SD
[SF]	7. My classmates like to listen to me read.	SA	A	U	D	SD
[PS]	8. I feel good inside when I read.	SA	A	U	D	SD
[SF]	9. My classmates think that I read pretty well.	SA	A	U	D	SD
[PR]	10. When I read, I don't have to try as hard as I used to.	SA	A	U	D	SD
[OC]	11. I seem to know more words than other kids when I read.	SA	A	U	D	SD
[SF]	12. People in my family think I am a good reader.	SA	A	U	D	SD
[PR]	13. I am getting better at reading.	SA	A	U	D	SD
[OC]	14. I understand what I read as well as other kids do.	SA	A	U	D	SD
[PR]	15. When I read, I need less help than I used to.	SA	A	U	D	SD
[PS]	16. Reading makes me feel happy inside.	SA	A	U	D	SD
[SF]	17. My teacher thinks I am a good reader.	SA	A	U	D	SD
[PR]	18. Reading is easier for me than it used to be.	SA	A	U	D	SD
[PR]	19. I read faster than I could before.	SA	A	U	D	SD
[OC]	20. I read better than other kids in my class.	SA	A	U	D	SD

(continued)

232

The Reader Self-Perception Scale

[PS]	21. I feel calm when I read.	SA	A	U	D	SD
[OC]	22. I read more than other kids.	SA	A	U	D	SD
[PR]	23. I understand what I read better than I could before.	SA	A	U	D	SD
[PR]	24. I can figure out words better than I could before.	SA	A	U	D	SD
[PS]	25. I feel comfortable when I read.	SA	A	U	D	SD
[PS]	26. I think reading is relaxing.	SA	A	U	D	SD
[PR]	27. I read better now than I could before.	SA	A	U	D	SD
[PR]	28. When I read, I recognize more words than I used to.	SA	A	U	D	SD
[PS]	29. Reading makes me feel good.	SA	A	U	D	SD
[SF]	30. Other kids think I'm a good reader.	SA	A	U	D	SD
[SF]	31. People in my family think I read pretty well.	SA	A	U	D	SD
[PS]	32. I enjoy reading.	SA	A	U	D	SD
[SF]	33. People in my family like to listen to me read.	SA	A	U	D	SD

FORM 9.6. Reading Activity Inventory.

ADMINISTRATION AND SCORING

The Reading Activity Inventory (RAI) is a quick way to find out how frequently and how widely students read and about some of their other activities as well. It consists of 26 questions and can be administered to a class in 20 minutes or less.

Administration

As you distribute the RAI forms, tell students that you want to find out what they read in school and what they do when they are on their own. Explain that the RAI is not a test and that there are no "right" answers. Encourage them to be honest.

The RAI can be administered in two ways: (1) teachers may read the questionnaire aloud to the students, or (2) they may permit students to read and answer the questions silently. We recommend that teachers read a few of the questions aloud and allow students who may not be sure of the definitions of words such as *fiction*, *mystery*, and *biography*, to ask questions if they need to. Teachers can model answering the questions by thinking aloud about what they read in their spare time. This procedure might add a few minutes to the administration time but would probably improve the accuracy of the students' answers.

For those questions that request an author, title, or topic, explain that students only have to give one answer, but encourage them to give all three if they can remember.

Scoring

Activities. The Activities questions are coded according to frequency ("How often do you ?") on a scale of 1 to 4 and scored as follows: 1 = *Almost never*; 2 = *About once a month*; 3 = *About once a week*; 4 = *Almost every day*. The minimum score a student can receive is 5; the maximum score is 20.

School Reading. The School Reading questions are coded according to whether students' reading is consistent with what is being taught in the classroom. This section was developed to see how aware students are of what they are studying in school and how well they understand the format of the questionnaire.

If an answer is consistent, it receives 1 point. For example, assuming that science is being taught in the classroom at the time this survey is administered, the student should circle "yes" to the question "Did you read a science book or a science textbook for school last week?" This answer would receive 1 point. If the student wrote in the title, author, or topic of the science book, that answer would receive 1 point. A "no" answer would receive 0. If the student failed to write in a title, author, or topic, the answer would receive a 0.

Consistency is also examined by questions about frequency, such as "How often do you read a science book or science textbook for school?" Assuming again that science is being taught in the classroom, the student would receive a 1 for circling "About once a week" or "Almost every day." A student with the same instruction who circles "Almost never" or "About once a month" would receive 0.

The minimum score a student can receive is 0; the maximum score is 9.

(continued)

Reading for Personal Interest. Questions about books read for personal interest in the past week are scored: 0 = No; 1 = Yes, without a title given; 2 = Yes, with a title.

Questions about frequency are scored: 0 = circled 1 or 2 and wrote title; 0 = circled 3 or 4 and did not write title; 1 = circled 1 or 2 and did not write title; 2 = circled 3 or 4 and wrote title.

The minimum score a student can receive is 0; the maximum score is 30.

Interpretation

The results of the Reading Activity Inventory can be used to plan instruction for individual students and for whole classes. For example, a student who does not read outside of school but does go to the movies a lot might be motivated to read books that retell the plots of his or her favorite movies. Or, the RAI results show that students have little experience following written directions, a teacher might plan a project in which students do something like build a model town or record a videotape, for which they would follow printed instructions. They could then create a companion project in which they themselves write directions to be used by other students.

(continued)

READING ACTIVITY INVENTORY

Directions: We are interested in knowing about your activities and in finding out how often you do them. Circle the answers to some of the questions, and write the answers to the others.

Practice Questions

1. Do you have a first name? (Circle only one.)

   No   1

   Yes   2

If yes, write your first name.

First name: _____

2. How often do you tell another person your first name? (Circle only one number.)

Questions about Your Activities

	Almost never	About once a month	About once a week	Almost every day
1. How often do you listen to music?	1	2	3	4
2. How often do you watch television?	1	2	3	4
3. How often do you play outside?	1	2	3	4
4. How often do you go to the movies?	1	2	3	4
5. How often do you do chores at home?	1	2	3	4

Questions about School Reading

Directions: In this section, think about the reading you do for school and for homework. Include textbooks and other books in your answers.

6. Did you read a science book or science textbook for school last week?
   (Circle only one answer.)

   No   1

   Yes   2

If yes, write in the title, author, or specific topic that you read about.
Science book title/author/topic:

_____

	Almost never	About once a month	About once a week	Almost every day
7. How often do you read a science book or science textbook for school?	1	2	3	4

(continued)

8. Did you read a book of literature or fiction last week for school? (Circle only one number.)

   No   1

   Yes   2

If yes, write in the title, author, or specific topic that you read about.
Fiction book title/author/topic:

_____

	Almost never	About once a month	About once a week	Almost every day
9. How often do you read a literature or fiction book for school?	1	2	3	4

10. Did you read a book about history or a history textbook last week for school?
    (Circle only one number.)

    No   1

    Yes   2

If yes, write in the title, author, or specific topic that you read about.
History book title/author/topic:

_____

	Almost never	About once a month	About once a week	Almost every day
11. How often do you read a book about history or a history textbook for school?	1	2	3	4

Questions about Reading for Your Own Enjoyment

Directions: In this section, think about books that you read for your own interest that are not assigned for school or homework.

12. Did you read a fiction book, like a mystery or an adventure book, last week for your own interest? (Circle only one number.)

    No   1

    Yes   2

If yes, write in the title, author, or specific topic that you read about.
Book title/author/topic:

_____

	Almost never	About once a month	About once a week	Almost every day
13. How often do you read a fiction book, like a mystery or an adventure book, for your own interest? (Circle only one number.)	1	2	3	4

(continued)

237

14. Did you read a sports book last week for your own interest? (Circle only one number.)

    No   1

    Yes   2

If yes, write in the title, author, or specific topic that you read about.
Book title/author/topic:

_____

	Almost never	About once a month	About once a week	Almost every day
15. How often do you read a sports book for your own interest? (Circle only one number.)	1	2	3	4

16. Did you read a nature book last week for your own interest? (Circle only one number.)

    No   1

    Yes   2

If yes, write in the title, author, or specific topic that you read about.
Book title/author/topic:

_____

	Almost never	About once a month	About once a week	Almost every day
17. How often do you read a nature book for your own interest? (Circle only one number.)	1	2	3	4

18. Did you read a romance book last week for your own interest?
(Circle only one number.)

    No   1

    Yes   2

If yes, write in the title, author, or specific topic that you read about.
Book title/author/topic:

_____

	Almost never	About once a month	About once a week	Almost every day
17. How often do you read a romance book for your own interest? (Circle only one number.)	1	2	3	4

20. Did you read a biography last week for your own interest? (Circle only one number.)

    No   1

    Yes   2

If yes, write in the title, author, or specific topic that you read about.
Book title/author/topic:

_____

(continued)

	Almost never	About once a month	About once a week	Almost every day
21. How often do you read a biography for your own interest? (Circle only one number.)	1	2	3	4

22. Did you read a comic book or magazine last week for your own interest? (Circle only one number.)

No   1

Yes   2

If yes, write in the title, author, or specific topic that you read about.
Book title/author/topic:

_____

	Almost never	About once a month	About once a week	Almost every day
23. How often do you read a comic book or magazine for your own interest? (Circle only one number.)	1	2	3	4

24. Did you read any other kind of book last week for your own interest that was not mentioned? (Circle only one number.)

No   1

Yes   2

If yes, write in the title, author, or specific topic that you read about.
Book title/author/topic:

_____

	Almost never	About once a month	About once a week	Almost every day
25. How often do you read this kind of book? (Circle only one number.)	1	2	3	4
26. How often do you read written directions or instructions that tell you how to do something you enjoy, like for putting together a model airplane, or baking a cake, or some similar activity? (Circle only one number.)	1	2	3	4

FORM 9.7. Title Recognition Test.

Name _____

Some of these titles are the names of actual books and some are not. Read the names and put a checkmark next to the names of those you know are books. Do not guess, but only check those that you know are actual books. Remember, some of the titles are not those of popular books and can easily be detected.

____ A Light in the Attic

____ By the Shores of Silver Lake

____ Call of the Wild

____ Curious Jim

____ Dear Mr. Henshaw

____ Don't Go Away

____ Dr. Dolittle

____ Ethan Allen

____ Freedom Train

____ From the Mixed-up Files of Mrs. Basil E. Frankweiler

____ Harriet the Spy

____ Heidi

____ Henry and the Clubhouse

____ He's Your Little Brother

____ Homer Price

____ Hot Top

____ How to Eat Fried Worms

____ Iggie's House

____ Island of the Blue Dolphins

____ It's My Room

____ James and the Giant Peach

____ Joanne

____ Misty of Chincoteague

____ Ramona the Pest

____ Sadie Goes to Hollywood

____ Skateboard

____ Superfudge

____ Tales of a Fourth Grade Nothing

____ The Chosen

____ The Cybil War

____ The Great Brain

____ The Hideaway

____ The Indian in the Cupboard

____ The Lion, the Witch and the Wardrobe

____ The Lost Shoe

____ The Missing Letter

____ The Polar Express

____ The Rollaway

____ The Schoolhouse

(continued)

Scoring the Title Recognition Test

√	A Light in the Attic		It's My Room
√	By the Shores of Silver Lake	√	James and the Giant Peach
√	Call of the Wild		Joanne
	Curious Jim	√	Misty of Chincoteague
√	Dear Mr. Henshaw	√	Ramona the Pest
	Don't Go Away		Sadie Goes to Hollywood
√	Dr. Dolittle		Skateboard
	Ethan Allen	√	Superfudge
√	Freedom Train	√	Tales of a Fourth Grade Nothing
√	From the Mixed-up Files of Mrs. Basil E. Frankweiler	√	The Chosen
√	Harriet the Spy	√	The Cybil War
√	Heidi	√	The Great Brain
√	Henry and the Clubhouse		The Hideaway
	He's Your Little Brother	√	The Indian in the Cupboard
√	Homer Price	√	The Lion, the Witch and the Wardrobe
	Hot Top		The Lost Shoe
√	How to Eat Fried Worms		The Missing Letter
√	Iggie's House	√	The Polar Express
√	Island of the Blue Dolphins		The Rollaway
			The Schoolhouse

Checked items are actual titles.

_____ No. actual titles/25 _____ No. Foils / 14

Evaluation:

If a child recognizes six or fewer, they would be considered to have low literacy exposure, seven to 12 titles would be average literacy exposure, and 13 or more would be high literacy exposure.

10

Preparing a Reading Clinic Report

Reports fill a number of different functions; they can be nothing more than short notes to summarize an assessment for a staff meeting, or more elaborate, formal documents. The reports discussed in this chapter are the more formal kind; reports written about an assessment. Since all aspects of the issue being assessed are addressed, as much as possible, this type of report is also useful for communicating with parents, teachers, principals, and so on. The assumption made when formulating such a report is that you do not know who will be reading it, so you need to spell out exactly what actions you took in the assessment process.

Although most teachers will never write such a report, we include it here as an exercise. Writing a formal report requires that you think about the child and your procedures in a comprehensive manner. To write a thorough report, you need to ask yourself questions about the child's overall performance and how the different pieces of the assessment puzzle come together. You also need to think about how to communicate this information to a parent or another teacher, explaining what you did and what you found in a clear manner. This is why we require such report writing in our clinic. Here are some suggestions for writing a formal report.

PREPARATION

1. Spread out all the material from your testing—protocols, notes and so on—on the kitchen table. Ask yourself mentally the questions listed in Table 10.1 about the child's performance. Think about both the level of his or her performance on the various tasks and the quality of that performance (the processes used to produce that perfor-

242

TABLE 10.1. Guiding Questions for Interpreting a Reading Profile

Question	Source of information
Is the child able to read texts at his or her grade placement with automatic word recognition and adequate expression?	
• Does the child make use of context to monitor his or her reading?	Informal reading inventory; running records (Chapter 3)
• Is the child fluent?	Timed oral reading, fluency scale (Chapters 3–4)
• Does the child have adequate sight-word knowledge?	Sight-word list such as Dolch or Fry lists (Chapter 6); Informal reading inventory
• Does the child have adequate knowledge of decoding strategies?	Decoding inventories (Chapter 6)
• Does the child have adequate phonological awareness?	Comprehensive Test of Phonemic Awareness Processing (Chapter 5)
Is the child able to comprehend the language of the text?	
• Does the child have an adequate vocabulary for his or her age and grade?	Formal measures such as the Peabody Picture Vocabulary Test or the Receptive One-Word Vocabulary Test
• Does the child have the background knowledge necessary to understand the particular passage that he or she is reading?	Prereading questions, PreP (Chapter 7)
• Is the child able to use common text structures to aid in comprehension?	Recall; written recall with story map (Chapter 7)
Does the child have adequate knowledge of the purposes for reading and strategies available to achieve those purposes?	
• Does the child have a set of strategies that can be used to achieve different purposes in reading?	Textbook Interview, Index of Reading Awareness (Chapter 8)
• What does the child view as the goal of reading, in general?	Awareness of Purposes of Reading Inventory, Burke Reading Interview (Chapter 8)
• What concepts of print does the child have?	Concepts of print measure, concept of word measure (Chapter 5), observations

mance). You should have an answer to each of these questions before you begin to write your report. These questions will guide you in understanding the assessment materials in front of you.

BACKGROUND INFORMATION

2. Begin by describing the reason for referral. Couch the comments made by the teacher or parent in terms such as "The teacher reports . . ." and so on. Be careful about "dangerous statements," such as he or she is reported to be "hyperactive" or behaviorally disordered. Unless you are a qualified clinical psychologist who has conducted an ap-

propriate assessment and rendered the diagnosis, you cannot classify children in these ways. Similarly, you cannot classify someone as "speech-impaired" or "mentally retarded," unless you have appropriate training and have conducted appropriate assessments. Furthermore, do not report intimate family details (e.g., suspected abuse, difficulties experienced by siblings) that might prejudice a person meeting the child for the first time. *Remember that your report may be the first impression that someone gets about this child.* Do no prejudice that person about this child by making statements that go beyond what you yourself observe about this child. The statements in the background section should describe behaviors you have seen or reports that you have read.

3. Describe the setting in which the assessment was conducted. Was the child cooperative? Were any factors present that might invalidate some of the results? (Did the child respond poorly to interruptions? Was the child too shy to respond in an informative manner? etc.)

TESTS ADMINISTERED

4. List the tests administered, with the results. If the tests do not lend themselves to numerical results, just list them (perhaps for a principal who does not want to read an entire report but is interested in numbers)

OBSERVATIONS DURING TESTING

5. This section on your observations should be the longest of the report. For each area—Oral Reading, Silent Reading, Word Recognition, Decoding, Language, etc.—report *all* of the measures that have an impact on that area. If you administered two oral reading measures, list them both under "Oral Reading." You may use any set of categories or any order that makes sense in presenting your data. If you give a test (such as a phoneme awareness measure) because you noticed a weakness in another area (such as decoding), you might want to order your list so that the reader can follow the progression of your thinking.

6. For each area, do the following:
   a. Describe the tests given. Write descriptions in one or two sentences, if possible that are clear and understandable for parents.
   b. Present the quantitative results. At what level is the child? How well did the child score numerically?
   c. Present the qualitative analysis of these results—perhaps, for example, a miscue analysis of oral reading, an analysis of a word-recognition list describing patterns that you have seen, an analysis of spelling, and so on. What process is the child using during this activity? Make interpretations. For each interpretive statement, give examples, such as miscues, spellings, word readings, etc.

SUMMARY AND RECOMMENDATIONS

7. In the first paragraph, recapitulate the information in the previous sections of the report. *In a report, do not be afraid to be redundant.* Make sure this first paragraph contains a thorough summary of all the areas.

8. Compare the child's performance across the different areas. Look for strengths and weaknesses in his or her reading knowledge and ability. Interpret those strengths and weaknesses, if appropriate.

9. Finally, list and describe the major goals for tutoring; you should have somewhere between three and five goals. Describe each goal briefly and why it is important. Then describe sample activities that you plan to use to achieve those goals. You also may append longer descriptions of the activities to the report. These can be your own descriptions or photocopies of activity descriptions. Good sources for such descriptions include the following:

Tierney, R. J., & Readence, J. (2000). *Reading strategies and practices: A compendium* (5th ed.). Boston: Allyn & Bacon.

Harvey, S., & Goudvis, A. (2000). *Strategies that work*. York, ME: Stenhouse.

Opitz, M. F., Rasinski, T. V., & Bird, L. B. (1998). *Good-bye Round Robin: Twenty-five effective oral reading strategies*. Portsmouth, NH: Heinemann.

Shanker, J. L., & Ekwall, E. E. (2003). *Locating and correcting reading difficulties* (8th ed.). Upper Saddle River, NJ: Merrill/Prentice Hall.

OTHER POINTS

Be clear, concise, and avoid jargon. If you use a technical term, explain it. The audience is an intelligent layman (parent, teacher, and so on), not the instructor. Make sure you explain yourself clearly and unambiguously. Read through the report after it is done and try to misinterpret it—if someone can misinterpret what you say, they will. Redundancy is fine in a report, since many people do not read the report from beginning to end, but instead look for parts that answer their particular questions or concerns. Positioning information in several places (a list, the body of the report, a summary) increases the chance that a reader will come across that information.

The sample reports in the appendix contain boilerplate descriptions of the tests used. If you use the same assessments, do not worry about using these descriptions. Since these are the same (presumably), copying the descriptions is not plagiarism, simply a way to avoid wasting your time and creativity.

APPENDIX

Case Studies

BACKGROUND INFORMATION

Angela was brought to the clinic by her mother after having completed her first-grade year. Angela's mom is concerned about her daughter's reading problems and lack of confidence in reading. She reports that Angela looks at pictures more than words and that she tends to daydream while reading. Her main reason for referring Angela to the clinic is to help her to feel more comfortable with reading and sounding out words.

Her teacher reports that Angela has a good attitude and is usually well behaved. Prior to Christmas she was performing on grade level with only a slight degree of difficulty. During the second semester, however, her comprehension and decoding skills declined slightly below grade level. Her teacher reports that Angela appears to have difficulty applying phonetic skills and lacks self-confidence in the area of reading.

At the testing Angela was very friendly and outspoken. When interviewed concerning her feelings about reading, she expressed some frustration with her problems sounding out words. She does not feel that she is a good reader because sometimes "words don't come" to her and she "can't remember them." She enjoyed elaborating on the examiner's questions and telling stories about herself and her friends.

TESTS ADMINISTERED

Qualitative Reading Inventory
    Word Recognition   preprimer, instructional level
    Oral Reading   preprimer, instructional level

Fry Instant Word List   74/100 correct

Letter Identification   100% correct

Informal Phonics Survey

Consonants	19/23	mastery
Consonant digraphs	3/3	mastery
Short vowels	6/10	needs review
Consonant blends	4/12	needs systematic instruction
Silent *e*	0/4	needs systematic instruction
Vowel digraphs	2/10	needs systematic instruction
Vowel diphthongs	2/6	needs systematic instruction
r-controlled vowels and *al*	1/6	needs systematic instruction

Test of Phonemic Awareness
Blending	8/15	needs systematic instruction
Phoneme isolation	10/10	mastery
Deletion	0/20	needs systematic instruction

Qualitative Reading Inventory
    Letter-name pattern

Concepts about print test   18/24   5th stanine

OBSERVATIONS DURING TESTING

Word Recognition

The word recognition section of the Qualitative Reading Inventory (QRI) contains eight word lists consisting of 20 words each. The word lists begin with a primer readability level and end with a junior high readability level.

Angela was able to read 16/20 words on the preprimer list automatically or within 1 second. She misread four words. She read 9/20 words from the primer list correctly, putting her at her frustration level—that is, the level at which she would become frustrated if reading independently.

Most of Angela's errors consisted of guesses based on the first letter of a word. For example, she said "please" for *place*, "that" for *thing*, and "so" for *saw*. For *need*, she simply said the letter *n*. Some substitutions showed more awareness of the end of the word: "Oliver" for *other*, "chicken" for *children*, and "when" for *went*.

Oral Reading

The oral reading section of the QRI consists of 42 passages ranging in readability levels from preprimer, primer, and first-grade passages through junior high level. Grade scores are derived from the number of miscues (any deviations from the text) as well as the student's ability to answer comprehension questions. Some comprehension questions have answers that can be found directly in the text, and some have answers that require the student to infer information from the text.

Angela read the preprimer and primer passages. On the preprimer passage with pictures, she made two miscues and answered four out of the five comprehension questions correctly. This story was at her instructional level, meaning she could read and completely comprehend this story with help from a teacher. On the test at the primer level, Angela made 65 miscues. Of these, 43 changed the meaning of the text. She correctly answered three of the six comprehension questions. This story was at her frustration level, meaning that the material was too difficult for her even with assistance.

Because there was a big difference between the number of miscues in the preprimer and primer passages, the examiner gave Angela a preprimer story without pictures. It was thought that perhaps she had relied heavily on picture clues to decode words and answer comprehension questions for the first story. When given the preprimer passage without pictures, Angela made 21 miscues, 19 of which changed the meaning of the text. She answered one out of five comprehension questions correctly. This variance between scores on the two preprimer passages suggests that Angela relies heavily on picture clues to construct meaning when reading.

Before reading a passage, Angela was asked various concept questions about the story topic. She often answered these questions with a rambling, off-subject story related to herself.

EXAMINER: What is "doing something new"?

CHILD: If you're being picked on and you're doing your work and the teacher tells you to shut the door and people pick on you . . . (*continued*).

When asked to predict what a story would be about, she usually related it to herself and only occasionally to the concept questions or title. When asked to retell the story, she remembered between three and seven story details. She was unable to retell any details from the passage without pictures.

An analysis of Angela's miscues showed that she often made substitutions based on the first letter of the target word—a very similar pattern to the types of miscues she made on the word list. She also made mistakes that were syntactically correct, meaning that when she didn't know a group of words, she constructed a phrase that made structural sense (+ indicates word was read correctly):

> *Text:* He did that every day.
> *Child:* + + not see it.
> *Text:* His father said, "But pigs can't read!"
> *Child:* + + had big teeth + rock.

At this point in her development Angela understands that text carries meaning and that each word is a separate idea, but she often gets frustrated with decoding and then constructs her own meaning using picture clues. This strategy is especially evident in her frustration with the comprehension questions and retelling of the pictureless preprimer story. She knows that letters represent sounds, but she is uncomfortable with decoding individual words. She correctly reads sight words or words whose meaning is conveyed are indicated by the pictures.

Informal Phonics Survey

At this point, we wanted to determine if any of Angela's miscues could be due to her not knowing the sounds of written letters. She was therefore given an informal phonics survey, which is a criterion-referenced measure intended to assess the child's knowledge of letter sounds in isolation and in words. Angela knew the sounds of all consonants except the "hard" sounds of *c* and *g*. She was confident about the consonant digraphs and could read most short vowel words. She had greater trouble with consonant blends: "bick" for *brick*, "shick" for *slick*, "fash" for *flash*, and "pop" for *prop*. Vowel combinations, such as vowel digraphs, diphthongs, and silent *e* words were difficult for her as well. She misunderstands the role of silent *e*, evidenced by her comment that a silent *e* makes no difference in a word because *e* never makes a sound at the end of a word.

Prereading Knowledge and Abilities

In order to be a true reader, children need to have a secure knowledge of three basic concepts. They need to have a secure concept about print, including that words carry meaning, what print is used for, directionality, etc. They also need to have a comfortable knowledge of letters. Finally, they need to have an awareness of phonemes or sounds in spoken words. This awareness is needed so that a child can match written letters to individual sounds.

Angela was examined in each of these areas. She seemed to have a good idea about print concepts. She was aware of the correct place to start when reading and could follow along as the examiner read, matching word to word. She could identify the differences between letters and

251

words and knew the function of periods and commas. She did not notice changes in word order or incorrectly spelled words, but that is not overly surprising considering her age.

Angela was very confident identifying her letter names. She correctly named 54 out of 54 capital and lower-case letters, including irregular forms of *a* and *g*.

The third assessment, the test of phonemic awareness, was given orally to determine if Angela was aware of sounds in spoken words. Phoneme awareness is the ability to reflect on spoken words and identify the phonemes within those words. This skill is an important prerequisite for learning phonics. The child is assessed on blending sounds into words, identifying letters/sounds in words in isolation, and substituting letter sounds in words.

The first task is a blending activity in which the examiner slowly sounds out a word, and the student must combine the sounds to determine the target word. Angela correctly blended 8/15 words, or 53%. This rating indicates that she needs direct instruction on blending separate sounds into words. In the second task, however, when Angela was given a word and asked to identify the first or last letter of that word, she correctly identified 100% of the onsets and 90% of the rimes. The third task of the test required Angela to delete a sound from a particular word supplied by the examiner. For instance, when given the word *meat*, she was asked to repeat it without the *m*. Angela was unable to understand this task and so not complete this last section of the test.

These results confirm many of the conclusions made earlier from Angela's oral reading. It appears that she is confident pronouncing the initial sounds of words and can also distinguish final sounds. Her difficulty lies in blending sounds together and in separating sounds. In order to determine if this difficulty carries over to her writing, Angela was given two tests of her invented spelling.

Spelling

Angela was given a list of words to spell. This list was developed in order to evaluate the child's level of invented spelling. It has been found that children go through a developmental sequence in their invented spelling—from prephonemic, in which their writing does nit reflect sounds in words; to an early phonemic stage, in which they use an initial consonant to represent a word; to a letter-name stage, in which they use letter names to represent their sounds and often omit vowels; to a transitional stage, in which their spellings reflect all phonemic features.

Angela's spellings were as follows:

bed	bed	(correct)
shepe	ship	(letter-name stage)
grive	drive	(letter-name stage)
bupe	bump	(letter-name stage)
wen	when	(transitional stage)

Angela also was given a dictation test in which she was asked to write a sentence. The correctness of her spelling was not as important here as her ability to represent all the sounds of the words. Of the 37 sounds included in this sentence, Angela represented all 37, with only two reversals: she wrote "ti" for *it* and "no" for *on*.

Angela's spelling tells us several things. Most of her words were at the letter-name stage, meaning that she included a vowel in each syllable of the word; has progressed beyond using only initial consonants in her spelling. The fact that she could represent all the sounds she heard during the sentence dictation indicates that she can hear and synthesize these sounds.

SUMMARY AND RECOMMENDATIONS

Angela is an end-of-first-grade student having difficulty with reading. She was given the Qualitative Reading Inventory and found to be instructional at the preprimer level. Many of her miscues were guesses based on the first letter of the target word. Although Angela can identify letters and is comfortable with the sounds of consonants, she lacks knowledge about the sounds of vowels and has great difficulty blending sounds together when reading. It is interesting to note that Angela seems able to represent all sounds in her invented spelling when writing, indicating that she has no difficulty hearing the letter sounds. Her difficulty seems to lie in decoding sounds in existing words.

Angela appears to be knowledgeable about basic print concepts, such as directionality, letter identification, and the use of punctuation. She understands that the purpose of print is to convey meaning. However, her struggle with analyzing unknown words hinders her ability to create meaning from text. Her occasional lack of prior concepts and poor ability to predict story outcomes also greatly interferes with her comprehension.

We recommend the following goals and activities for Angela:

1. *Develop decoding ability.* Given that Angela understands many of the basic concepts about print and yet is reading below grade level with a high number of miscues, it appears that she needs direct instruction in decoding unknown words through the explicit teaching of vowel sounds and techniques for blending sounds together. Since she is able to put sounds together to create words in her writing, it seems advantageous to use her invented spellings to help her decode words. Activities with the "making words" approach would work well: having Angela build words with individual letter cards, decode words created by the tutor, sort words with similar characteristics, and explore some reliable rules of phonics (such as the silent *e* rule).

Angela also would benefit from comparing unknown words to words of similar structure that already are part of her sight vocabulary (such as comparing *black* and *sack*). To facilitate this learning, we will use a "compare and contrast" activity to encourage her to see the similarities between designated key words and new words in her reading.

Another way to help Angela develop word decoding strategies is to have her dictate stories in her own words to the tutor. These stories can then be read, cut apart, sequenced, and reread. Individual words that she dictates can be explored for patterns and phonemic regularity. These activities will help develop Angela's fluency, confidence and sight-word recognition.

2. *Increase comprehension of text.* Angela's comprehension will increase as her decoding improves. However, she would benefit from direct instruction on applying prediction strategies through reading predictable stories and using picture clues to predict vocabulary. Regularly retelling stories immediately after reading will reinforce comprehension and improve her awareness of story structure.

3. *Develop a sight vocabulary.* Angela already has a good beginning base of sight words, as evidenced by her knowledge of 74/100 words on the Fry list. Given that the fluency of sight-word recognition can greatly influence a student's comprehension, improving Angela's sight-word base will positively affect the other areas in which she needs added instruction. Activities for improving sight-word recognition include use of flashcards in a game called "Three Strikes and You're Out," and "racetrack spelling," in which she will need to correctly say each word, without hesitation, to reach the end of the "track."

4. *Develop oral reading.* Angela's oral reading will improve by asking her to read actual text. She can be taught to apply decoding strategies in context as well as practice her sight words and begin to develop fluency. Along with consistently reading new stories, we will work on improving Angela's oral reading through echo reading, repeated reading, and paired choral reading.

BACKGROUND INFORMATION

Mel was referred to the reading clinic by his foster mother in order to improve his reading skills and to read more proficiently. Mel attended the reading clinic during the summer of 1997, and Mel's foster mother felt that he would benefit again from one-on-one tutoring and intensive instruction in reading. Comparing his work from his clinic experience in 1997 to his entrance to the program this summer, it became apparent that Mel had made reading progress over this school year as a third-grade student in a self-contained special education class.

During the testing and the tutoring sessions, Mel was eager to try new tasks and agreeable to the demands placed on him. Although Mel was aware of the difficulty he experienced in reading, he diligently worked to complete any of the tasks placed before him. Throughout the 3 weeks of testing and tutoring, Mel was easily distracted and often had to be redirected to stay on task with assignments. Auditory distractions (such as noises in the hallway) or visual distractions (such as pictures hanging on the walls in the office) caused Mel to abruptly stop working and ask questions about them. Although he was frequently distracted, once redirected, Mel would amicably comply to the request to refocus on the task he needed to complete.

TESTS ADMINISTERED

Observational Survey
    Letter identification   53/54
    Word recognition   29/60
    Test of written vocabulary   22 words written in 10 minutes
    Test of dictation   24/37

Informal Phonics Survey
    Consonant sounds   19/23   mastery
    Consonant digraphs   0/3   systematic instruction indicated
    Consonant blends in short vowel words   1/12   systematic instruction indicated
    Short vowels in CVC words   10/10   mastery
    Rule of silent *e*   0/4   systematic instruction indicated
    Vowel digraphs   1/10   systematic instruction indicated
    Vowel diphthongs   0/6   systematic instruction indicated
    r-controlled vowels and *al*   0/6   systematic instruction indicated

Test of Phonemic Awareness
    Blending   11/15   review indicated
      Simple rime   5/5
      Cluster onset   3/5

Cluster rime	3/5
Phoneme isolation	16/20 mastery indicated
Onset rime	5/5
Cluster onset	5/5
Simple rime	1/5
Cluster rime	5/5
Deletion	11/20 systematic instruction indicated
Onset rime	5/5
Cluster onset	0/5
Simple rime	3/5
Cluster rime	3/5

Durrell Analysis of Reading Difficulty

Oral reading	preprimer
Silent reading	preprimer
Listening comprehension	grade 4

OBSERVATIONS DURING TESTING

Letter Identification

Mel identified by name 53 out of 54 upper- and lower-case letters of the alphabet. He had difficulty with lower case *b* and *d*; on the test, he named lower-case *b* as *d*, and when he got to the lower-case *d*, he paused for about 10 seconds before tentatively guessing it to be a *d*. Mel has mastered letter recognition and would benefit from an emphasis on identification of lower-case *b* and *d*.

Word Recognition

Mel was given the Ohio Word Test in order to assess the number of sight words that he could recognize automatically. This test contains three word lists consisting of 20 words each; these lists are comprised of high-frequency words from the Dolch Word List used in most basal reading series. Although one list is usually given to a student, Mel was administered all three word lists to obtain the number of sight words that he could read automatically. On these lists, he scored 8 out of 20, 9 out of 20, and 12 out of 20, for a total of 29 out of 60 words. These scores indicate that he is in the stanine-3 group on a scale of 1 to 9, which implies that his current word recognition is significantly below average.

Spelling

Two tests were administered to measure Mel's spelling ability; a test of written dictation and a test of written vocabulary. These tests are components of the Observation Survey, developed by Marie Clay in New Zealand, and are scored as stanines so that a child's progress may be compared to his or her peers.

The test of written vocabulary is a timed test in which the student is given 10 minutes to write down all of the words he or she can spell correctly. During the 10 minutes, the student is encouraged by the test administrator to write as many works as possible from his or her own memory. Once the administrator observes that the student has written all of the words he or she knows, the administer may prompt the student to write additional words, such as names of people in the student's family or other functional words such as color words, number words, or months of the year. It is not required that the student be able to read all of the words written; however, only words that are spelled correctly are scored. The purpose of this test is to measure a child's existing basic writing vocabulary, so that it can be compared to later tests of written vocabulary to assess the growth and progress that a student has achieved.

During this testing, Mel seemed tentative about writing. He explained, "I don't know how to write any words." In 8-minute segments, using prompts from the administrator, Mel was able to write 21 words: *Mel, I, yes, no, on, a, to, look, of, go* (g reversed), *it, me, Deanna, Mom, cat, we, the, big, dig,* and *my*. He also wrote *bog* for *dog* and *bo* for *do*, which were not counted as correct words because of the reversals of letters. After 8 minutes, Mel said that he did not know any other words and told me that he was finished writing all that he knew. On this test, Mel scored in the stanine-4 group on a scale of stanine 1–9, which indicated that his current writing vocabulary is deficient for a child his age. However, Mel did show improvement in his writing vocabulary as compared to his performance on this task in July of 1997. On this previous test, he only wrote 11 words correctly during the 10-minute test.

Mel also took a test of written dictation. This test assesses a child's ability to record dictated sentences, as read by a test administrator. The test is scored by counting the child's accurate representation of letter sounds of the words. This was the sentence that was dictated to Mel to write:

I have a big dog at home. Today I am going to take him to school.

By repeating the sentence over and over again, Mel was able to hold the sentence in his head so that he could get the words written on paper. After he wrote each word, he would go back and reread what he had written. Upon completion, Mel's sentence looked like this:

I haf a big bog et hom tobay I my goeg to tac hm to so l.

Mel was able to construct the sentences so that the number of words written matched the number of words dictated to him. He was able to spell several words correctly, such as *I, a, big,* and *to*. Mel's reversal of the letter *b* for the *d* in both *dog* and *today* indicates that he continues to have difficulty with writing these letters accurately. His spelling of the words *have* (*haf*), *home* (*hom*), *going* (*goeg*), and *take* (*tac*) indicates that he is paying attention to the sounds he hears in the beginning, middle, and the end of words. Mel's score of 24/37 is a low score for a first grader. As evidenced from this test, Mel would benefit from phonetic instruction and an emphasis on authentic writing tasks to improve his spelling.

Phonics and Phonemic Awareness

Mel was given the Informal Phonics Survey developed by Dr. Steve Stahl at the University of Georgia. This is a criterion-referenced measure intended to assess the child's knowledge of letter sounds in isolation and in words. This measure was used to assess Mel's current understanding of letter sounds in comparison to his scores on this test taken in the summer of 1997. Compared to his July 1997 testing, Mel showed improvement in both consonant sounds and in reading words with a CVC (consonant–vowel–consonant) pattern. Mel was able to identify the sound associated with 19 of the 23 consonant sounds indicating mastery. He had difficulty with the sounds of *x, qu, y,* and the /s/sound of *c*. This outcome is a significant improvement over his 1997 summer performance on this same measure which was 13 out of 23 consonant sounds identified. Furthermore,

Mel exhibited mastery, 10 out of 10, when decoding words with a short vowel sound. His score from last summer on this same measure was 0 out of 10. This improvement in letter–sound correspondence has aided in his reading progress.

Similar to his test results from last summer, Mel continues to have difficulty with consonant digraphs in isolation and in short vowel words, the rule of silent *e*, vowel digraphs, vowel diphthongs, and *r*-controlled vowels and *al*. In all of these subtests, Mel was unable to decode any of the words in isolation with the exception of reading the word *way* as a vowel digraph. However, comparing his 1998 results to those of the summer of 1997, it became apparent that Mel is now attending to the letter sounds more readily. During his 1997 testing, he was unable to read any of the words and did not make any attempts to decode them. In contrast, during this current testing, Mel actively tried to decode the words and often correctly identified the initial and ending sounds of words. For example, when attempting to read consonant blends in short vowel words, Mel read the word *sick* for the word *slick*, *perp* for the word *prop*, *tin* for the word *twin*, and *gin* for the word *grin*, indicating that he was attending to the letter sound correspondence.

The test of phonemic awareness is a test that measures a child's awareness of sounds in spoken words. In this test, the student is not asked to read anything; instead, the student is asked to listen to the examiner and then complete spoken word tasks. There are three sections in this test: blending, isolation, and deletion of sounds. For each subtest, 80% correct is considered a passing score.

Last summer Mel was administered this test, with little success. In July of 1997, he was able complete 50% of the words on the blending component, 50% on the sounds in isolation, and the deletion subtest was too hard to complete any of the questions asked of him. This summer, he has shown progress. He has mastered blending of CVC sounds in isolation, such as hearing *m-a-p* and then pronouncing the word *map*. However, he has difficulty with cluster onsets, such as in sounding out words with initial blends. For example, in the sounds *c-r-a-ck*, Mel said *cack* and for *s-p-a-ce* he said *safe*. Difficulty with consonant blends was also identified in the cluster onset of the deletion subtest for Mel. He did not understand how to separate the initial sounds, so he deleted the entire blend. His answers looked like this:

The word is *flight*. Take off the /f/sound. Mel's response: *ight*
The word is *crash*. Take off the /c/sound. Mel's response: *ash*
The word is *spot*. Take off the /s/sound. Mel's response: *ot*
The word is *plug*. Take off the /p/sound. Mel's response: *ug*
The word is *stone*. Take off the /s/sound. Mel's response: *one* (long *o* sound)

These results indicate that Mel can adequately blend sounds that follow the CVC pattern, such as in words like *set* and *ten*. However, Mel has difficulty with blending two consonant sounds together. Mel continues to need systematic instruction to address this problem and improve his decoding and spelling skills.

READING

Durrell Analysis of Reading Difficulty— Word Recognition and Word Analysis

The Durrell Analysis of Reading Difficulty is a norm-referenced test which measures oral reading, silent reading, listening comprehension, listening vocabulary, word recognition, word analysis, and spelling. It compares the performance of the student to that of other students from a sample taken of students across the United States. Rankings are given for performance that correspond to lowest, middle, and top thirds of respective grade-equivalent levels.

Mel was only given the oral reading, silent reading, and listening comprehension components of the Durrell Analysis of Reading Difficulty because other tests were used to measure his word recognition, word analysis, and spelling.

Oral Reading

The oral reading portion of the Durrell Analysis includes a timed oral reading of the passage, a score for the correctness of the reading (no more than seven errors), and a score for the comprehension questions following the reading. All of these scores figure into the overall ranking. There are eight passages ranging from preprimer to sixth-grade level. Mel was only administered the first preprimer oral reading passage. This passage, entitled "The Cat," describes the life of a house cat. Mel read the passage in 55 seconds and had nine errors in reading. Of the five comprehension questions, he answered two correctly. However, he answered these two questions based on his prior knowledge of cats. For example, to one of the questions asked, "What does the cat drink?" Mel answered "Milk," which was correct. However, he could not read the word milk in the passage. Later, he told me that he knew the answer to the two questions because he had a cat at home. Based on Mel's time and his reading miscues, his oral reading level was low first-grade or preprimer level.

Silent Reading

The Silent Reading portion of the Durrell Analysis includes a timed silent reading of the passage as well as a score for free recall following the reading, both of which are figured into the overall ranking. There are eight passages ranging from the preprimer to sixth-grade level. To assess Mel's silent reading performance, only the first passage was given. Entitled "My Dog," Mel read the passage in 24 seconds, but he was only able to recall one memory of the story he had just read, indicating that he had difficulty reading the text. Mel scored below the preprimer level in silent reading.

Listening Comprehension

The Listening Comprehension portion of the Durrell Analysis was administered to assess Mel's listening comprehension. This test includes an oral reading of a passage by the examiner, followed by comprehension questions. The overall ranking relies only on the students' performance on the comprehension questions. There are six passages ranging from first- to sixth-grade level. Passages through grade 4 were administered.

On the grade 1 passage, Mel only answered three out of seven questions correctly. When asked the questions about the passage, he answered "I don't know" many times. However, Mel scored better on the harder passages that contained more context. On the grade 2 passage, he scored 7 out of 7; on grade 3, he scored 5 out of 7; and on grade 4, he scored 6 out of 8. Listening comprehension broke down for Mel on the fifth-grade level. For this passage, entitled "Heroes of the West," Mel scored 0 out of 7. Therefore, Mel's listening comprehension is on the fourth-grade level and is much higher than his oral reading or silent reading comprehension. This finding suggests that Mel could read much higher-level texts with comprehension if he could recognize words automatically.

SUMMARY AND RECOMMENDATIONS

Mel is 10 years old and currently reading on the preprimer level. Compared to his testing during July of 1997, he has made good progress in letter identification, letter sounds, and writing vocabulary. However, he continues to have difficulty with decoding and retaining newly learned sight words. His reading miscues and lack of decoding frustrate him and often result in defeated responses to text, such as "I don't know what the word is. You read it to me." Although his knowledge of reading and his understanding of text have improved over the past 12 months, he continues to struggle at the preprimer level, which seems to have affected his confidence level.

Mel has a good attitude about reading and often has lengthy discussions with me about books he likes to read and gives descriptions of his favorite stories. Because he can comprehend texts at a much higher level (grade 4) than his independent reading level (preprimer) but needs assistance in reading texts at a preprimer level, we recommend that Mel be immersed in a program that will highlight both of these areas: to address his high interest in harder-to-read texts and to develop reading fluency using books on his instructional level. We recommend the following goals and activities for such a program:

1. *Develop sight-word vocabulary in context and in isolation.* Mel has difficulty remembering sight words in context of books on his instructional level. Therefore, Mel needs to have plenty of opportunities to read texts on his instructional level with the assistance of a proficient reader who will attend to the sight words with which Mel has difficulty. These difficult words may be written on flashcards as pairs, and Mel can play a memory game with them: He must flip the two matching cards and correctly read them in order to win the pair.

Once Mel has practiced a group of words (perhaps six or seven) several times using the memory game, he could play "Three Strikes and You're Out." Taking the stack of cards, one card is flashed for Mel to read. Upon reading the word correctly three times, the card is "out" and is put into a separate pile. These cards can be revisited at a later date to double check that Mel has retained them.

2. *Practice oral reading.* Mel enjoyed reading aloud every day and came to expect that activity at the beginning of the lesson. As a motivating and educational activity, Mel taped most of the books that he had already practiced reading. After he read the book on tape, he would listen to the tape and follow along in the story. This gave him another opportunity to reread the text and check the reading that he had recorded. Often, he would find words that he had misread during the taped reading, or he would comment on the expression he used on the tape.

Encouraging and allowing these kinds of discussions are not only motivating but also allow students opportunities to independently address miscues in their own reading. Furthermore, giving Mel plenty of opportunities to reread familiar stories will help him develop fluency and allow him time to independently practice what he has already read. Having a tape recorder to record Mel's oral readings at home would be beneficial.

3. *Develop decoding skills.* Mel has difficulty decoding words and needs explicit instruction on letter–sound correspondence. To assist in this development, Mel needs to have plenty of opportunities to write authentic stories, with some assistance. Providing opportunities to write about information that interests him will allow him time to think about letter sounds and the sequencing of those sounds. Using sound boxes also helps Mel visualize the number of letters needed in a word. For example, if Mel has difficulty writing the word *with*, he could be assisted by drawing a set of four connected boxes, one box for each letter, and then filling in the letters of the sounds that he knows. For instance, the person assisting him could say the word very slowly, so that he hears *w-i-t-h*. Mel would write in the letters as the person pronounced the word for

him. Sentences and stories that Mel writes also could be used as material for him to reread or even to tape on a tape recorder. Providing him with many opportunities to write and to read to others what he has written will help build Mel's confidence in writing and improve his decoding skills.

In addition, Mel also could practice writing his own creative sentences using the sight words that are printed on the flashcards (see Recommendation #1). This exercise would improve his identification of sight words and develop his written vocabulary of words simultaneously.

4. *Read texts to Mel on his listening comprehension level.* It is important for Mel to be read to by others on his listening comprehension level (grade 4) and to be encouraged to discuss what the text's content. This activity will keep Mel's interest high and engage him in literacy conversations that develop his understanding of story structure, setting, characters, and story sequencing. Furthermore, after having read a story to Mel on his listening comprehension level, he could do some writing in response to the reading. This may take the form of a sentence or a story; either way, it will provide him with another meaningful connection between reading and writing.

5. *Content-area reading.* Going into fourth grade, Mel needs to be exposed to science and social studies content-area reading. With his strong verbal skills and grade-level listening comprehension, Mel needs to be exposed to information in these content areas to develop his knowledge and understanding of the world around him. Using books of interest to him as well as textbooks from school, Mel should be encouraged to learn the information of the curriculum and be supported in his efforts to read the material. Material could be read to him, and Mel could discuss and write about what he heard. Another activity would be to read passages of the text to Mel and have him reread portions of it aloud to a more able reader who could provide reading support. By doing so, Mel could practice reading his familiar sight words and be exposed to the relevant vocabulary.

APPENDIX

Summary of the Tutoring

Mel has been a delightful child to tutor. He came to the tutoring sessions ready to work. He was prompt and prepared for our meetings, which allowed us to maximize our time working on reading activities. Mel always seemed excited and willing to learn new information. He gave his best effort when trying new tasks and was compliant to instructions given. Although Mel exhibited some attentional difficulties, he worked hard and wasted little time during tutoring sessions. Often Mel just needed to know the session agenda before beginning the tutoring session. Once we had made a list of activities for the day, Mel would reference the list, checking off completed assignments, and efficiently moving on to the next task. This list became a successful, functional literacy experience for him as he was able to reread what I had written as the day's agenda and practice rereading familiar words.

During our time together, several goals were targeted to improve Mel's reading and writing. These included activities in oral reading, word recognition, decoding, writing, spelling, and reading strategies. Each of these areas is discussed below.

Oral Reading

Mel spent a significant amount of time engaged in oral reading of texts. Before reading a new text, time was spent preparing to read the book that would be read aloud. These prereading activities included "picture walks," whereby Mel looked at the pictures on each page of the book and predicted what he thought the story would be about. This activity allowed him time to enjoy both an aesthetic part of reading and to prepare him to read the text based on the story's pictures. Picture walks also improved Mel's success at reading the text, because the pictures told a story with which he familiarized himself before attempting to decode and comprehend the accompanying print.

Mel spent the first part of every tutoring session rereading a text that he had read for homework. He enjoyed this part of the lesson and felt successful in this activity, as he often noted, "That book is easy now." Providing opportunities to reread texts allowed Mel time to engage with familiar print so that he could have more experiences sight words and reading fluency. Mel liked to tape the readings of these stories and play them back. After he taped a story, he would replay the tape and reread the book, tracking with his eyes the text he heard from the tape. Such opportunities helped Mel encounter fluent reading, whereby he could practice words by sight without having to sound out everything, and allowed him time to identify reading miscues on his own. On several occasions he noted that he had misread a word on the tape and would correct himself during the playback.

During the tutoring sessions, Mel read aloud several books. These included:

Hedgehog Is Hungry
Baby Lamb's First Drink
The Hungry Kitten
Lizard Loses His Tail
Brave Father Mouse
Hermit Crab
Cars, Cars, Cars
The Lady with the Alligator Purse
My Grandma
The Amazing Popple Seed
Magpie's Baking Day

He also read longer text broken into chapters—*In a Dark, Dark Room* and *Sailor Jack*—as well as selected poetry from Eloise Greenfield and Jack Prelutsky.

Word Recognition

Mel spent a large portion of each tutoring session engaged in sight-word vocabulary activities. Words used for word recognition games were taken from the Ohio Word List and from frequently used words in texts that he had difficulty reading. Two games were used to improve Mel's word recognition. These included Memory and "Three Strikes and You're Out." When playing Memory, Mel received several pairs of matching word cards, which were shuffled and placed facedown in rows. After turning over one card, Mel would have to read the word on the card before turning over a second card in hopes of finding its match. Mel loved this game and could match seven pairs of words without difficulty, each time priding himself on his ability to beat me during every game. After a couple of rounds playing Memory with the words, the cards were reshuffled into a pile to play "Three Strikes and You're Out." Mel would draw the top card and pronounce the word. If he pronounced it correctly, he would get one strike on the back of the card. If he could isolate a chunk of the word and pronounce its sound, he would get an additional strike. For example, if the word was *dark*, he would read the word *dark* and give me the sound made by *ar* in the word, thus earning two strikes on the word. Once the word had three strikes, the word was "out"—retired into a stack of word cards mastered. During Mel's tutoring, he mastered 34 sight words. Some of the words Mel mastered included *them, that, then, who, was, dark, some, spring, looking,* and *baby.* Some of the chunks he correctly identified were *ing, th, er, ar, in, ch, st, spr,* and *spl.*

Another strategy I used with Mel to improve his word recognition was to make word cards for words that he mispronounced when reading, so that he could compare the mispronounced word with the actual printed word after he had finished reading. For example, every time that Mel saw the card with the word *did* on it, he would say *and.* He had the same confusion with *them,* replacing it with the word *they,* and *this* with the word *that.* Making word cards for the mispronounced words along with the correct words forced Mel to look at the entire word and at the word parts before saying the words when he played the game. This strategy made Mel more accountable to the text, as he had to look at all of the parts of the words and not just the beginning letters.

Decoding

Because Mel's initial testing indicated that he had difficulty decoding words, we focused on decoding of words as another tutoring goal. Although Mel could recognize, and give the sound of, letters in isolation, he encountered difficulty deconstructing the letter sounds of words, which caused problems when he tried to read unknown words. To improve his decoding skills, we focused on the consonant digraphs *sh, th,* and *ch;* consonant blends *sl, tr, st, fl,* and *br;* short-vowel words that follow the CVC pattern; *y* at the end of words; the sound of *ar* and *ing;* and long *a.* With identifying these sounds as the area of focus, two activities ("making words and chunking") embedded in direct instruction, were used to improve Mel's decoding. During the making words activities, Mel would have to spell words that I called out, using letter tiles. All of the letters used would eventually spell one big word. For example, in one activity that focused on the sound and spelling of *ing,* Mel had to spell the following words: *in, pin, pig, rig, rip, rips, nips, spin, snip, pins, sing, ring, rings,* and *spring.* Mel began these activities with some apprehension, telling me that he could not spell. I assisted him during the first two lessons by saying the words very slowly and telling him the number of letters in each word that he had to spell with tiles. And I modeled for him how to sort the words by patterns at the end of each lesson. By the third lesson, Mel said "Don't help me. I can do it." He would freely try to spell the words, identifying word sorts according to patterns he saw in the words. For the words mentioned above, for example, Mel sorted the words into categories of *in, ig,* and *ing* and then read the groups of words aloud.

Mel also played a game we called *chunking.* I would write a word on a dry erase board and Mel would practice chunking the word into parts. For example, I would write the word *that* on the board. Mel would underline the chunk *th* and the chunk *at* and then say the word aloud. Some of the words we practiced included chest (*ch* and *est*), bring (*br* and *ing*), drink (*dr* and *ink*), and today (*to* and *day*). Mel enjoyed this game because he had to identify parts of words and then put the sounds together to read the word. When playing this game, Mel sometimes impulsively guessed the word; but, over time, he slowed down and began to look at the word parts and become more accountable to the print in front of him, without guessing.

Writing

Writing also was included in Mel's daily tutoring sessions in order to develop sound recognition and spelling. During the writing time, Mel could write about anything he chose. His writing topics were always interesting and varied. They included personal topics, such as his field trip to Rock Eagle and his ear piercing downtown, as well as topics generated from texts that he had read, such as *The Lady with the Alligator Purse* and *My Grandma.* Mel's writing was usually only one or two sentences in length, but he was always excited about writing. To assist Mel in writing longer words, I would have him practice writing the word in sound boxes so that he could see how all of the letters fit together (see Recommendation #3 on p. 259 for description of sound box activity). Mel liked this because it reminded him of the game Hangman, and he did not have to know every letter to figure out the word. After writing, Mel would reread his writing and illustrate his sentence with a picture.

Strategies

As Mel read during the initial assessment, it was noted that he was not strategic in his reading. Because Mel thought that "sounding out the words" was the only way to read, a daily discussion of strategies was implemented to increase his repertoire of strategies for word identification when reading text. Every day when reading, Mel would be instructed to use strategies other than sounding out the words to assist him in reading words that he could not recognize automatically. These strategies included looking at the pictures, thinking about the story, looking for chunks in unknown words, and rereading the sentence containing the difficult word. Although Mel never initiated these strategies on his own and would have to be prompted to use a strategy when he was stuck on an unknown word, he was able to become a better reader when he did implement a strategy. Mel usually chose to look at the picture to assist him in reading the unknown word. Although this is an appropriate strategy for him to use for now, while he is still reading text with accompanying pictures, it is not a strategy that he will always be able to use. Therefore, I would always recommend that Mel be encouraged to use other strategies such as looking at chunks in the words or rereading the text to assist him in decoding difficult words.

Principal Results

Because Mel was a diligent worker who came on time and read outside of reading clinic time, he was able to make good progress during his tutoring sessions. Mel was initially assessed at reading below a preprimer level, and was assessed at reading at the mid-first-grade level at the end of the session. Furthermore, Mel made significant progress in word recognition, decoding of words, and spelling. Finally, Mel showed improvement in his general understanding of how reading works and how to decode unknown print. (* indicates significant progress on posttesting as compared with initial testing.)

Observational Survey		
Word Recognition	31/60	
Test of written vocabulary	35 words written in 10 minutes	
Test of dictation	34/37	
Informal Phonics Survey		
Consonant digraphs	2/3	
Consonant blends in short-vowel words	9/12	
Rule of silent *e*	0/4	systematic instruction indicated
Vowel digraphs	3/10	systematic instruction indicated
Vowel diphthongs	1/6	systematic instruction indicated
r-controlled vowels and *al*	0/6	systematic instruction indicated
Test of Phonemic Awareness		
Blending	13/15	
Simple rime	5/5	
Cluster onset	3/5	

Cluster rime	5/5
Isolation	20/20
Onset rime	5/5
Cluster onset	5/5
Simple rime	5/5
Cluster rime	5/5
Deletion	14/20
Onset rime	5/5
Cluster onset	0/5
Simple rime	5/5
Cluster rime	4/5

Mel made significant progress with his understanding of phonemic awareness. As noted in his dictation test, Mel improved over the session from an initial score of 24 out of 37 to a score of 34 out of 37. Observations during the written dictation and the written vocabulary revealed that Mel was thinking about letter–sound matching as he wrote the words. During the postdictation test, Mel was asked to write the following sentence:

I can see the red boat that we are going to have a ride in.

He wrote:

I can sse the red but theat we ir going to chas a rid in.

As Mel wrote this sentence, he stopped and asked me if the word *see* was spelled *s-e-e* or *s-s-e*. Telling him that I could not tell him the answer, he wrote out the two words on a scratch piece of paper and decided that *sse* looked right to him. Interestingly, Mel also stopped when he wrote the word *boat* (spelled *but*) to double check how he had formed the letter *b* and told me that he did not want to accidentally make a *d*.

Mel's writing vocabulary improved significantly as well. As the initial test indicated, Mel wrote 22 words correctly during an 8-minute time. (The test lasts for 10 minutes but at 8 minutes, he said he was finished and could not write any more.) During the posttest, Mel wrote 35 words, most of which were dictated to him. He was careful to say the word slowly to himself as he wrote, and he stopped when writing words with *b*'s and *d*'s to check for their correct formation. On this postassessment, he formed all words containing *b* or *d* correctly, in contrast to misspelling three words on his initial assessment due to incorrect formation of *b* or *d*. Furthermore, unlike his 8-minute performance during the initial assessment, I had to stop Mel from writing at the 10-minute mark during the postassessment.

Mel also improved in his phonemic awareness. During the posttesting he was able to identify two of the three consonant digraphs and to blend nine out of 12 consonant sounds, indicating that he is beginning to pay more attention to print and to be more accountable for the letter sounds in words.

Further Recommendations

In the future, Mel should continue many of the same activities he participated in throughout his tutoring sessions. Combining reading and writing experiences to improve Mel's word recognition and his identification of letter–sound associations will greatly help jim develop his literacy abilities. Continuing with a program that includes rereading texts, reading new texts, writing, spelling, word recognition, and decoding will address many of the reading difficulties that Mel continues to experience.

In addition to the recommendations already given, it is important to note three other suggestions that could not be covered in the short tutoring sessions that I had with Mel but would aid in his development as a reader. These include content area reading, journal writing, and confidence-building reading. These are explained below.

Content Area Reading

As Mel enters fourth grade, he will be expected to interact more with expository texts. Therefore, it is important that Mel begin to spend some of his time reading nonfiction texts. In order to read these harder texts, I recommend several activities. First, he could engage in paired reading experiences in which he reads the easier parts of the text and a partner reads that harder words of the text. After reading several paragraphs together, Mel and his partner should stop reading and discuss what they have read and learned. Because Mel enjoys factual information and has excellent listening comprehension, he should be able to discuss any text written on a fourth-grade level. Second, passages from content area texts can be taped so that Mel can listen to them and follow along with the words. Taping should be done slowly so that Mel can follow the taped text he hears with the printed text that he sees. Third, passages from content reading texts can be read aloud to Mel and then Mel can do a rereading of the material with someone's assistance. Mel enjoyed having me read aloud to him because it gave him access to the information so that he could discuss it and write about it. Finally, in conjunction with the content-area text reading, Mel could read shorter and easier nonfiction chapter books that relate to the content-area material being studied in the classroom. This would allow him time to develop his reading fluency on an instructional level that could quickly become an independent reading text after several repeated readings. Reading easier texts also will expose him to the vocabulary relevant to a particular topic of study.

Keeping a Journal

Mel would benefit from a consistent daily period of journal writing. With assistance, he can write several sentences about topics that interest him. A daily writing activity wherein Mel would be expected to write at least two sentences would help him develop his understanding of letter–sound correspondences as well as give him the opportunity to see himself as a writer. Mel enjoyed writing during his tutoring sessions; he just needs lots of practice to build his confidence and abilities.

Confidence-Building Reading

Mel should read to younger children who are not yet reading. This activity will build his confidence and provide him with opportunities for repeated readings of easy texts to improve his sight-word vocabulary. This activity also will place him in the new position of viewing himself as a capable reader who can instruct a younger nonreader.

Mel is now reading at a level where much progress can be made if he continues to receive the assistance that he needs and is expected to succeed and achieve as a reader. Providing Mel with familiar rereads and easier texts to practice reading on his independent level will help build Mel's confidence. However, he also would benefit from intense and direct reading instruction of more challenging texts, whereby he is expected to work at mid-first-grade instructional level in both reading and writing.

References

Adams, M. J. (1990). *Beginning to read: Thinking and learning about print*. Cambridge, MA: MIT Press.

Adams, M. J. (1998). The three-cuing system. In J. Osborn & F. Lehr (Eds.), *Literacy for all: Issues in teaching and learning* (pp. 73–99). New York: Guilford Press.

Allington, R. L. (1983). Fluency: The neglected reading goal. *The Reading Teacher, 37*, 556–561.

Allington, R. L. (1984). Content coverage and contextual reading in reading groups. *Journal of Reading Behavior, 16*, 85–96.

Anderson, R. C., & Pearson, P. D. (1984). A schema–theoretic view of basic processes in reading. In P. D. Pearson (Ed.), *Handbook of reading research* (pp. 255–292). White Plains, NY: Longman.

Beach, S. A. (1992). *Toward a model of the development of reader resources in the emergence and acquisition of literacy skill.* Unpublished PhD dissertation, University of California at Riverside.

Bear, D. R., Invernizzi, M., Templeton, S., & Johnston, F. (2000). *Words their way: Word study for phonics, vocabulary and spelling instruction* (2nd ed.). Upper Saddle River, NJ: Merrill.

Beaver, J. (2001). *Developmental reading assessment*. New York: Pearson Learning.

Betts, E. A. (1946). *Foundations of reading instruction*. New York: American Books.

Biemiller, A. (1970). The development of the use of graphic and contextual information as children learn to read. *Reading Research Quarterly, 6*, 75–96.

Bloom, B. S. (1969). *Taxonomy of educational objectives: The classification of educational goals*. New York: Longman.

Burke, C. L. (1987). Reading interview. In Y. M. Goodman, D. W. Watson, & C. L. Burke (Eds.), *Reading miscue inventory: Alternative procedures*. Katonah, NY: Richard C. Owen.

Byrne, B. (1998). *The foundation of literacy: The child's acquisition of the alphabetic principle (Essays in developmental psychology)*. Brighton, UK: Psychology Press.

Carbo, M., Dunn, R., & Dunn, K. (1986). *Teaching students to read through their individual learning styles*. Englewood Cliffs, NJ: Prentice-Hall.

267

Chall, J. S. (1996). *Stages of reading development* (2nd ed.). Fort Worth, TX: Harcourt-Brace.

Chomsky, C. (1979). Approaching reading through invented spelling. In L. B. Resnick & P. A. Weaver (Eds.), *Theory and practice of early reading* (Vol. 2, pp. 43–65). Hillsdale, NJ: Erlbaum.

Clay, M. M. (1993a). *An observation survey of early literacy achievement.* Portsmouth, NH: Heinemann.

Clay, M. M. (1993b). *Reading Recovery: A guidebook for teachers in training.* Portsmouth, NH: Heinemann.

Clay, M. M. (2000). *Running records for classroom teachers.* Portsmouth, NH: Heinemann.

Cunningham, A. E., & Stanovich, K. E. (1991). Tracking the unique effects of print exposure in children: Associations with vocabulary, general knowledge, and spelling. *Journal of Educational Psychology, 83,* 264–274.

Cunningham, J. W., Erickson, K. A., Spadorcia, S. A., Koppenhaver, D. A., Cunningham, P. M., Yoder, D. E., & McKenna, M. C. (1999). Assessing decoding from an onset-rime perspective. *Journal of Literacy Research, 31,* 391–414.

Cunningham, P. M. (1999). *Phonics they use: Words for reading and writing* (3rd ed.). Boston: Addison-Wesley.

Cunningham, P. M. (2001). *Phonics they use.* New York: HarperCollins.

Cunningham, P. M., & Cunningham, J. W. (1992). Making words: Enhancing the invented spelling-decoding connection. *The Reading Teacher, 46,* 106–115.

Dale, E. (l946).The art of reading. *Ohio State University News Letter, 9,* 1.

Davis, A. P., & McDaniel, T. R. (1998). An essential vocabulary: An update. *The Reading Teacher, 52,* 308–309.

Dolch, E. W. (1936). A basic sight vocabulary. *Elementary School Journal, 36,* 456–460.

Donahue, P. L., Voelkl, K. E., Campbell, J. R., & Mazzeo, J. (1999). *NAEP 1998 Reading Report Card for the Nation* (prepublication ed.). Washington, DC: U.S. Department of Education, Office of Educational Research and Improvement.

Duke, N. (2002, August). *Comprehension.* Paper presented at the Institute for Statewide Literacy Initiatives, Harvard University.

Ehri, L. C. (1998). Grapheme–phoneme knowledge is essential for learning to read words in English. In J. L. Metsala & L. C. Ehri (Eds.), *Word recognition in beginning literacy* (pp. 3–40). Mahwah, NJ: Erlbaum.

Ehri, L. C., & Sweet, J. (1991). Fingerpoint-reading of memorized text: What enables beginners to process the print. *Reading Research Quarterly, 26,* 442–462.

Elkonin, D. B. (1973). U.S.S.R. In J. Downing (Ed.), *Comparative reading* (pp. 551–579). New York: Macmillan.

English, F. W., & Frase, L. B. (1999). *Deciding what to teach and test: Developing, aligning, and auditing the curriculum.* Thousand Oaks, CA: Corwin Press.

Farr, R. (1992). Putting it all together: Solving the reading assessment puzzle. *The Reading Teacher, 46,* 26–37.

Fry, E. (1977). Fry's readability graph: Clarification, validity, and extension to level 17. *Journal of Reading, 21,* 242–252.

Fry, E. (1980). The New Instant Word List. *The Reading Teacher, 34,* 284–289.

Fry, E. B., Fountoukidis, D. L., & Polk, J. K. (1985). *The new reading teacher's book of lists.* Englewood Cliffs, NJ: Prentice-Hall.

Gambrell, L. B., Palmer, B. M., Codling, R. M., & Mazzoni, S. A. (1995). *Assessing motivation to read* (Instructional Resource No. 14). Athens, GA: National Reading Research Center, University of Georgia and University of Maryland.

Ganske, K. (2000). *Word journeys: Assessment-guided phonics, spelling, and vocabulary instruction.* New York: Guilford Press.

Garner, R., & Kraus, C. (1981). Good and poor comprehender differences in knowing and regulating reading behaviors. *Educational Research Quarterly, 6,* 5–12.

Gaskins, I. W., Downer, M. A., Anderson, R. C., Cunningham, P. M., Gaskins, R. W., Schommer, M., & the teachers of Benchmark School. (1988). A metacognitive approach to phonics: Using what you know to decode what you don't know. *Remedial and Special Education, 9,* 36–41.

Gaskins, I. W., Ehri, L. C., Cress, C., O'Hara, C., & Donnelly, K. (1996). Procedures for word learning: Making discoveries about words. *The Reading Teacher, 50,* 312–328.

Gillet, J. W., & Temple, C. (1990). *Understanding reading problems* (3rd ed.). Glenview, IL: Scott-Foresman.

Goodman, K. S. (1993). *Phonics phacts.* Portsmouth, NH: Heinemann.

Goodman, K. S., & Goodman, Y. M. (1977). Learning about psycholinguistic processes by analyzing oral reading. *Harvard Educational Review, 47,* 317–333.

Goodman, Y. M., Watson, D. J., & Burke, C. L. (1987). *Reading miscue inventory: Alternative procedures.* Katonah, NY: Richard C. Owen Publishing.

Gough, P. B., Juel, C., & Griffith, P. L. (1992). Reading, spelling, and the orthographic cipher. In P. B. Gough , L. C. Ehri ,& R. Treiman (Eds.), *Reading acquisition* (pp. 35–48). Hillsdale, NJ: Erlbaum.

Guthrie, J. T., & McCann, A. D. (1996). Idea circles: Peer collaborations for conceptual learning. In L. B. Gambrell & J. F. Almasi (Eds.), *Lively discussions! Fostering engaged reading* (pp. 87–105). Newark, DE: International Reading Association.

Guthrie, J. T., McGough, K., & Wigfield, A. (1994). *Measuring reading activity: An inventory* (Instructional Resource No. 4). Athens, GA: National Reading Research Center, University of Georgia and University of Maryland.

Harste, J. C., Burke, C. L., & Woodward, V. A. (1982). Children's language and world: Initial encounters with print. In J. A. Langer& M. T. Smith-Burke (Eds.), *Reader meets author/ Bridging the gap* (pp. 105–131). Newark; DE: International Reading Association.

Hasbrouck, J. E., & Tindal, G. (1992). Curriculum-based oral reading fluency norms for students in grades 2 through 5. *Teaching Exceptional Children, 24*(3), 41–44.

Hayes, David A. (1989). Helping students grasp the knack of writing summaries. *Journal of Reading, 33,* 96–101.

Henderson, E. H. (1981). *Learning to read and spell: The child's knowledge of words.* De Kalb, IL: Northern Illinois University Press.

Henk, W. A., & Melnick, S. A. (1995). The Reader Self-Perception Scale (RSPS): A new tool for measuring how children feel about themselves as readers. *The Reading Teacher, 48,* 470–482.

Hoffman, J. (1987). Rethinking the role of oral reading. *Elementary School Journal, 87,* 367–373.

Hutchins, P. (1968). *Rosie's walk.* New York: Simon & Schuster.

Jacobs, J. E., & Paris, S. G. (1987). Children's metacognition about reading: Issues in definition, measurement, and instruction. *Educational Psychologist, 22,* 255–278.

Johns, J. L. (1993). *Informal reading inventories.* DeKalb, IL: Communitech International Incorporated.

Johns, J. L. (2001). *Basic Reading Inventory.* Dubuque, IA: Kendall-Hunt.

Johnston, P. H. (2000). *Running records: A self tutoring guide*. Portland, ME: Stenhouse. [Book and audiocassette]

Koskinen, P. S., Wilson, R. M., & Jensema, C. J. (1985). Closed-captioned television: A new tool for reading instruction. *Reading World, 24*(4), 1–7.

Krahn, F. (1979). *Robot-bot-bot*. Boston: E. P. Dutton.

Kuhn, M. R., & Stahl, S. A. (2003). Fluency: A review of developmental and remedial practices. *Journal of Educational Psychology, 95*, 3–21.

LaBerge, D., & Samuels, S. J. (1974). Toward a theory of automatic information processing in reading. *Cognitive Psychology, 6*, 293–323.

Leal, D. J. (1993). The power of literary peer group discussions: How children collaboratively negotiate meaning. *The Reading Teacher, 47*, 114–120.

Leslie, L., & Caldwell, J. (2001). *Qualitative reading inventory–III*. New York: HarperCollins.

Manzo, A. V. (1969). The ReQuest procedure. *Journal of Reading, 2*, 123–126.

Manzo, A. V., & Casale, U. P. (1985). Listen–Read–Discuss: A content reading heuristic. *Journal of Reading, 28*, 732–734.

Martin, B., Jr. (1983). *Brown bear, brown bear, what do you see?* New York: Henry Holt.

McKenna, M. C. (1983). Informal reading inventories: A review of the issues. *The Reading Teacher, 36*, 670–679.

McKenna, M. C. (l986). Reading interests of remedial secondary school students. *Journal of Reading, 29*, 346–351.

McKenna, M. C. (2001). Development of reading attitudes. In L. Verhoeven & C. Snow (Eds.), *Literacy and motivation: Reading engagement in individuals and groups* (pp. 135–158). Mahwah, NJ: Erlbaum.

McKenna, M. C. (2002). *Help for struggling readers: Strategies for grades 3–8*. New   York: Guilford Press.

McKenna, M. C., & Kear, D. J. (1990). Measuring attitude toward reading: A new tool for teachers. *The Reading Teacher, 43*, 626–639.

McKenna, M. C., Kear, D. J., & Ellsworth, R. A. (1995). Children's attitudes toward reading; A national survey. *Reading Research Quarterly, 30*, 934–956.

Morris, D. (1993). The relationship between children's concept of word in text and phoneme awareness in learning to read: A longitudinal study. *Research in the Teaching of English, 27*, 133–154.

Nagy, W. E. (1988). *Teaching vocabulary to improve reading comprehension*. Newark, DE: International Reading Association.

National Reading Panel. (2000). *Report of the subgroups: National reading panel*. Washington, DC: National Institute of Child Health and Development.

Owocki, G., & Goodman, Y. M. (2002). *Kidwatching: Documenting children's literacy development*. Portsmouth, NH ; Heinemann.

Palincsar, A. S., & Brown, A. L. (1984). Reciprocal teaching of comprehension fostering and comprehension monitoring activities. *Cognition and Instruction, 1*(2), 117–175.

Paris, A. H., & Paris, S. G. (2001). *Children's comprehension of narrative picture books. Center for the Improvement of Early Reading Achievement*, Technical Report No. 3-012.

Paris, S. G., & Oka, E. R. (1986). Children's reading strategies, metacognition, and motivation. *Developmental Review, 6*, 25–56.

Paris, S. G., Pearson, P. D., Cervetti, G., Carpenter, R., Paris, A. H., DeGroot, J., Mercer, M., Schnabel, K., Martineau, J., Papanastasiou, E., Flukes, J., Humphrey, K., & Bashore-Berg,

T. {in press). Assessing the effectiveness of summer reading programs. In G. Borman & M.Boulay (Eds.), *Summer learning: Research, policies, and programs*. Mahwah, NJ: Erlbaum.

Perfetti, C. A., Beck, I. L., Bell, L., & Hughes, C. (1987). Phonemic knowledge and learning to read are reciprocal: A longitudinal study of first grade children. *Merrill-Palmer Quarterly, 33*, 283–319.

Peterson, B. (1991). Selecting books for beginning readers. In D. E. DeFord, C. A. Lyons, & G. S. Pinnell (Eds;), *Bridges to literacy: Learning from Reading Recovery* (pp. 119–147). Portsmouth, NH: Heinemann.

Phelan, P. (Ed.). (1996). *High interest-easy reading: An annotated booklist for middle school and senior high school* (7th ed.). Urbana, IL: National Council of Teachers of English.

Pinnell, G. S. (1995). *Listening to children read aloud: Data from NAEP's integrated reading performance record (IRPR) at grade 4.* Washington, DC: National Center for Education Statistics.

Pressley, M., & Woloshyn, V. (1995). *Cognitive strategy instruction that really improves children's academic performance*. Cambridge, MA: Brookline Press.

Pugh, K. R., Mend, W. E., Jenner, A. R., Katz, L., Frost, S. J., Lee, J. R., Shaywitz, S. E., & Shaywitz, B. A. (2001). Neurobiological studies of reading and reading disability. *Journal of Communication Disorders, 34*, 479–492.

Raygor, A. (1977). The Raygor readability estiamte: A quick and easy way to determine difficulty. In P. D. Pearson (Ed.), *Reading: Theory, research, and practice: Twenty-sixth yearbook of the National Reading Conference* (pp. 259–263). Clemson, SC: National Reading Conference.

Read, C. (1971). Pre-school children's knowledge of English phonology. *Harvard Educational Review, 41*, 1–34.

Rhodes, L. (1981). I can read: Predictable books as resources or reading and writing instruction. *The Reading Teacher, 34*, 511–518.

Riccio, C. A., & Hynd, G. A. (1996). Neuroanatornicaland urophysiological aspects of dyslexia. *Topics in Language Disorders, 16*(2), 1–3.

Rigby Education. (2001). *Rigby PM benchmark kit*. Barrington, IL: Author.

Rosner, J. (1975). *Helping children overcome learning difficulties*. New York: Walker.

Schumaker, J. B., Deshler, D. D., Alley, G. R., Warner, M. W., & Denton, T. H. (1982). Multipass: A learning strategy for improving reading comprehension. *Learning Disability Quarterly, 5*, 295–304.

Shankweiler, D., & Liberman, I. Ɏ. (1972). Misreading: A search for causes. In I.F. Kavanaugh & I. G. Mattingly (Eds.), *Language by eye and by ear* (pp. 293–317). Cambridge, MA: MIT Press.

Shaywitz, S. E. (1996). Dyslexia. *Scientific American, 275*(5), 98–104.

Shinn, M. R. (1992). Curriculum-based measurement of oral reading fluency: A confirmatory analysis of its relation to reading. *School Psychology Review, 21*, 459–479.

Shinn, M. R. (Ed.). (1989). *Curriculum-based measurement: Assessing special children*. New York: Guilford Press.

Silvaroli, N. J. (1977, April). *Norm-referenced tests do not diagnose*. Paper presented at the A. Sterl Artley Symposium, University of Missouri–Columbia.

Smith, F. (1988). *Understanding reading* (4th ed.). Mahwah, NJ: Erlbaum.

Spear-Swerling, L., & Sternberg, R. J. (1996). Off track: When poor readers become "learning disabled." Boulder, CO: Westview Press

Stahl, S. A. (1999a). *Vocabulary development*. Cambridge, MA: Brookline Press.

Stahl, S. A. (1999b). Different strokes for different folks? A critique of learning styles. *American Educator*, 27–31.

Stahl, S. A., & McKenna, M. C. (2001). *The concurrent development ofPhonological awareness, word recognition, and spelling*. Center for the Improvement of Early Reading Achievement (CIERA), Technical Report No. O1–O7. Online: *www .ciera.org/libraryl archi ve/2001-07/ 200 lO7.htm*

Stahl, S. A., & Murray, B. A. (1994). Defining phonological awareness and its relationship to early reading. *Journal of Educational Psychology, 86*, 221–234.

Stahl, S. A., & Murray, B. A. (1998). Issues involved in defining phonological awareness and its relation to early reading. In J. Metsala & L. C. Ehri (Eds.), *Word recognition in beginning literacy* (pp. 65–88). Mahwah, NJ: Erlbaum.

Stahl, S. A., Duffy-Hester, A. M., & Stahl, K. A. D. (1998). Everything you wanted to know about phonics (but were afraid to ask}. *Reading Research Quarterly, 33*, 338–355.

Stahl, S. A., Heubach, K., & Cramond, B. (1994). *Fluency-oriented reading instruction*. Washington, DC: U.S. Department of Education Office of Educational Research and Improvement Educational Resources Information Center.

Stanovich, K. E. (1980). Toward an interactive–compensatory model of individual differences in the development of reading fluency. *Reading Research Quarterly, 16*, 32–71.

Stanovich, K. E. (1986). Matthew effects in reading: Some consequences of individual differences in the acquisition of literacy. *Reading Research Quarterly, 21*, 360–407.

Stanovich, K. E. (1991). Word recognition: Changing perspectives. In R. Barr, M. L. Kamil, P. B. Mosenthal, & P. D. Pearson (Eds.), *Handbook of reading research* (Vol. 2, pp. 418–452). New York: Longman.

Sulzby, E. (1985). Children's emergent reading of favorite storybooks: A developmental study. *Reading Research Quarterly, 20*, 458–481.

Taylor, B. M. (1986). Teaching middle grade students to summarize content textbook material. In J. F. Baumann (Ed.), *Teaching main idea comprehension* (pp. 195–209). Newark, DE: International Reading Association.

Topping, K. (1987). Paired reading: A powerful technique for parent use. *The Reading Teacher, 40*, 608–614.

Torgesen, J. K., & Bryant, B. (1994). *Test of Phonological Awareness*. Austin, TX: Pro-Ed.

Torgesen, J., & Wagner, R. (1999) *Comprehensive test of phonological processing*. Austin, TX: Pro-Ed.

Treiman, R. (1993). *Beginning to spell: A study of first grade children*. New York: Oxford University Press.

Tuinman, J. J. (1971). Asking reading-dependent questions. *Journal of Reading, 14*, 289–292.

U.S. Department of Education, National Center for Education Statistics. (1995). *Listening to children read aloud*. Washington, DC: Author.

Uhry, J. K. (1999). Invented spelling in kindergarten: The relationship with finger-point reading. *Reading and Writing: An Interdisciplinary Journal, 11*, 441–464.

Vygotsky, L. (1978). *Mind in society*. Cambridge, MA: Harvard University Press.

Wallach, M. A., & Wallach, L. (1979). Helping disadvantaged children learn to read by teaching them phoneme identification skills. In L. B. Resnick & P. A. Weaver (Eds.), *Theory and practice of early reading* (Vol. 3, pp. 197–216). Hillsdale, NJ: Erlbaum.

Watkins, J. H., McKenna, M. C., Manzo, A. V., & Manzo, U. C. (1994, April). *The effects of the*

Listen–Read–Discuss procedure on the content learning of high school students. Paper presented at the meeting of the American Educational Research Association, New Orleans.

Wylie, R. E., & Durrell, D. D. (1970). Teaching vowels through phonograms. *Elementary English, 47,* 787–791.

Yussen, S. R., & Ozcan, N. M. (1996). The development of knowledge about narratives. *Issues in Education, 2,* 1–68.

Zutell, J., & Rasinkski, T. (1989). Reading and spelling connections in third and fifth grade students. *Reading Psychology, 10,* 137–155.

Index

f indicates a figure, *t* indicates a table.